Franciscans and their Finances:
Economics in a Disenchanted World

David B. Couturier, O.F.M. Cap.

FRANCISCAN
INSTITUTE
PUBLICATIONS

Published in the United States
by Franciscan Institute Publications
St. Bonaventure University, St. Bonaventure, NY 14778

Cover design by Jill M. Smith

ISBN: 978-1-57659-388-2
eISBN: 978-1-57659-389-9

Library of Congress Cataloging-in-Publication Data
    Couturier, David B.
    Franciscans and their finances : economics in a disenchanted world / David B.
Couturier, OFM. Cap.
        pages cm
    ISBN 978-1-57659-388-2 (pb : alk. paper) -- ISBN 978-1-57659-389-9 (eb-
ook) 1. Economics--Religious aspects--Catholic Church. 2. Capitalism--Religious
aspects--Catholic Church. 3. Economics--Religious aspects--Christianity--History of
doctrines. 4. Capitalism--Religious aspects--Christianity--History of doctrines. 5. Fran-
ciscans--Theology. 6. Franciscans--United States. 7. Capuchins--United States. I. Title.
    BX1795.E27C68 2015
    261.8'50882553--dc23
                                    2015015971

Printed and bound in the United States of America
Franciscan Institute Publications makes every effort
to use environmentally responsible suppliers and materials
in the publishing of its books. This book is printed on acid-free, recycled paper that is
FSC (Forest Stewardship Council) certified.

It is printed with soy-based ink.

ACKNOWLEDGMENTS

A Franciscan with a vow of poverty writing a book on riches is an anomaly. A Franciscan with a background in clinical psychology and organizational development doing so is a paradox. Delving deeper and deeper into the complexities of today's economic models and assumptions from a religious perspective could not have been done without the support and encouragement of friars, friends and colleagues. I want to acknowledge a few who were outstanding in their kindness, expertise and patience.

Dr. John Morgan and Dr. Kendra Elizabeth Clayton of *The Graduate Theological Foundation* provided a stimulating and encouraging academic environment early on in which to test and express these ideas. Serving as the Dean R. Hoge Professor of Pastoral Planning and Church Management at the Foundation has been a distinct privilege and honor.

Sr. Margaret Carney, OSF, STD, President of *St. Bonaventure University* provides a model of bold leadership and humble Franciscan communion. Trying to keep pace with her energy, creativity and love of all things Franciscan is inspiring. I thank her for her appointment of me as Dean of the University's School of Franciscan Studies. I also thank the friars and the entire faculty at SBU for their generous welcome. My colleague, Jill M. Smith, is an untiring worker at the University's *Franciscan Institute* and I thank her for the diligence and creativity she brings to her work every day.

The Capuchin friars around the world and, most especially, those in my Province of New York and New England have been my brothers for many years now. We are simple men who love Jesus deeply and are inspired by our brother, Francis of Assisi. I have found in my brothers a simple courage and a powerful compassion for people day after day, year after year. The fact that these humble men are willing to take up a new form of economics in our age goes to the boldness of their faith.

I want to single out two friars who have been especially supportive of my work over these past several years. The first is the
former Minister General of the Capuchin Order, Bishop John
Corriveau, OFM.Cap. This text will indicate how influential his
insights have been in my own scholarly research. I thank him.

The second friar is Cardinal Sean O'Malley, OFM. Cap., the
Archbishop of Boston. Several years ago, he asked me to come
and serve as the Director of Pastoral Planning for the Archdiocese
of Boston. Serving as one of his advisors gave me the opportunity
to see church leadership in difficult times. What I experienced was
Franciscan leadership in its most dedicated form: humble, courageous, imaginative and focused on the poor and suffering. I thank
him for his fraternal witness and immense kindness.

I also thank two Franciscan groups that sharpened my ideas on
economic matters and Franciscan principles of justice. The first is
Franciscans International, the non-governmental organization at the
United Nations. I served as its first President and as a Board member for many years. FI's commitment to justice, peace and the care
of creation around the world has been impressive. Also, I thank
the leadership of the *Franciscan Action Network* in Washington, DC.
They gave me the opportunity and the mandate to think about
economic issues as their research analyst. Some of the chapters
within were first written as "white papers" for FAN. I am grateful
for their Franciscan witness of justice.

There are many Franciscan scholars to whom I owe a debt
of gratitude, all of whom are associated with the *Franciscan Institute* at St. Bonaventure University: Dominic Monti, OFM, David
Flood, OFM, Michael Cusato, OFM, Robert Karris, OFM, Ed
Coughlin, OFM, Bill Short, OFM, Regis Armstrong, OFM Cap.,
and Jean-Francois Godet-Calogeras, among so many others. Their
truly ground-breaking work allows the field of applied Franciscan
studies now to flourish.

Lastly, my family has been amazingly supportive of me
throughout the years. Words cannot express the gratitude I feel
and the debt I owe for their love and kindness.

DEDICATION

Larry Silvestro for a great friendship over many years and to your children, *Lisa and Larry.* (Thanks for letting me be their uncle.)

Maurice Paquette and *Jim Paquette*, nephews who inspire me, I want to put on paper what you already know. I love you very much.

Rev. Edmund Luciano III, thanks for the laughs we have shared enjoying this wonderful world *in modo italiano.*

TABLE OF CONTENTS

INTRODUCTION
ECONOMICS IN A DISENCHANTED WORLD

We now live in a disenchanted world, in which God recedes and is considered but an option in the search for ultimate meaning and value. It is a world where the rule of contemporary economics is so profound and pervasive in our lives that few question its originating principles or test its underlying ontological foundations. As long as the money keeps flowing, even if debts rise dangerously and the stakes against one's own fate are not unreasonably or suspiciously high, we mostly don't want to know what is on the other side of the economic tracks or on the underbelly of our economic arrangements.

For most men and women and, indeed, one could say, for most Christians, there may be a kind of soft resignation that the economic structures we have and the economic principles we hold are, in fact, the only ones available to us. They may be the best we can do, given the sinful condition of humankind and humanity's penchant for avarice, greed and self-interest.[1] At least, we tell and console ourselves, our contemporary models make good use of a sinful state and channel private greed for common good, most of the time and for most everyone who wants them to do so.

But, what if our economic dogma are not true, at least not wholly so? What if our economic arrangements are not inevitable? What if our economic models no longer work? After all, noted economist Thomas Piketty recently suggested that the rising tide of income inequality in the world is not an accident. It is rather part and parcel of capitalism today, a structural deficit that threatens our very democratic order.[2]

In the midst of this, what if we are merely suffering from what Walter Brueggemann calls a "monopoly of imagination" that has

---

[1] Such is the view of Michael Novak, cf. Edward W. Younkis, "Michael Novak's Portrait of Democratic Capitalism," *Journal of Markets and Morality* 2:1 (Spring, 1999), p. 8-34.

[2] Thomas Piketty, *Capital in the Twenty-First Century* (Cambridge, MA: Harvard University Press, 2014).

conditioned us to believe that *competition* is the only lens through which life can be properly viewed or experienced?[3] What if there are other alternatives? And finally, what if the economic challenges and suffering of the world could be analyzed from another vantage point? This book will explore alternatives.

Most Christians and most religious would be shocked to learn that the architects of the economic liberalism on which our social lives are built hold theological positions that are diametrically opposed to our most basic Christian idioms. Machiavelli, Hobbes, Locke and the other artisans of economic liberalism have persuaded the world of the "fecundity of evil," that, in the realm of politics and economics, we should no longer attempt to strive after "the good," and evil should be the primary force and originating source of the political order.[4] Goodness, it is held, is too unstable and unpredictable to be the logic of economics. Nature and grace can no longer found humanity's progress in a world constructed for self-sufficiency and individual determination. The logic of modernity is stark, indeed; it holds that public good can only be achieved through the power of violence, fear and aggressiveness. The best we can do, these philosophers argue, is to use violence, fear and competitive aggression to our advantage. We need to use evil to create a common good. As such, modernity ordains an ontological privacy that now determines the inevitability of the competition, isolation, and indeterminability that illustrate our postmodern situation.

In this new logic of the fecundity of evil, religion is sent to the corner by the artisans of the "new economy." It is sent there to fashion a new faith that is more individual and less critical of the secular-scientific worldview that proposes the self-sufficiency of humankind and the infinity of its desires. And there, religion has stayed for almost three hundred years trying to fight the logic of modernity, often with modernity's own tools of practical reason.

However, a new voice is emerging. It is a self-consciously religious voice. It speaks from the heart of a theological tradition that lifts the veil covering the ontological premises of contemporary politics and economics. It is a voice no longer willing to sit idly by as

---

[3] Walter Brueggemann, "Welcoming the Stranger," *Interpretation and Obedience* (Minneapolis, MN: Fortress Press, 1991), pp. 290-310.

[4] Pierre Manent, *An Intellectual History of Liberalism*, (Princeton, NJ: Princeton University Press, 1995), p. 15.

millions die of hunger or live in crushing poverty each and every day. It is a voice that will no longer be relegated only to the corridors of charity, leaving the halls of justice empty of humanity's benevolent nature. It is a voice willing to speak up as contemporary forms of "democracy dissolve(s) society"[5] and erode the common good of its relational and, indeed Trinitarian, heritage and teleology.

That voice comes from the Capuchin-Franciscan Order, a religious community of men founded in the 16th century as a reform movement of the Order founded by St. Francis of Assisi in the 13th century. In the 1990s and early 2000s, the Capuchin Order began a reform of its economic principles and structures and moved toward a more relational form of economics between its members and provinces. The Capuchin-Franciscan Order's project to re-order itself towards a fraternal economy is yet but a small, still voice in the loud and chaotic turbulence that is modern economic liberalism.[6] It begins with a foundational Franciscan theological principle that God is good, all good, supremely good, all the time and to everyone. That insight may seem naïve to modern ears and best left to the private realm of Sunday devotions. But, this is because we have been trained by the architects of modernity to neutralize our most potent beliefs and to domesticate our most powerful dogma. We hardly see the social relevance and the political power of these grand theological truths.

The Capuchin Order has decided to rethink its economic principles and to reorganize its economic structures. When an international organization with outposts in almost 100 countries makes that determination nowadays, it is usually to maximize its profits and to make itself more efficient. Nothing could be further from the truth for these Franciscans. Their motive and their goal are nothing more and nothing less than communion, a communion of life beyond the borders and boundaries that normally condition social life in the world today. They are reorganizing themselves for no other purpose than to be more faithful to their charism of evangelical brotherhood.

At the 2000 Capuchin General Chapter held in Rome, three brothers from Africa stood before the assembled delegates and chal-

---

[5] Manent, *op.cit.*, p. 106.

[6] The Capuchin-Franciscan Order is a religious community of men, founded in the 16th century as a reform of the fraternity started in the 13th century by St. Francis of Assisi.

lenged them to "hear the cry of the poor" in Africa. The fact that
this needed to be said in a room filled with dedicated religious and
compassionate men from every corner of the earth shocked the delegates. Had not missionaries supplied for the needs of hundreds of
thousands, perhaps even millions of Africans, over the years? Had
not Provinces around the world gathered money and goods to do
what was possible to lift African men and women up from the dregs
of poverty? All these efforts notwithstanding, these three delegates
were asking for something more than just a fairer distribution of the
world's goods. They were asking for love and the justice that flows
from love. And this was a new economic starting point or, at least,
one that had been underground since the ascendancy of economic
liberalism.

Franciscans hold to a simple proposition that God is good and
that men and women are not simply competitors for the scarce resources that flow from a stingy God. They are brothers and sisters
of a good and gracious God. And so, Franciscan economics, if we
can name it as such, is an attempt to flesh out this insight, to create
a model of human relations that does not premise nor preordain
inevitable fear, aggression, and competition as the lot and fate of
humankind. Franciscans understand God as a free communion of
persons without domination or deprivation and so reject any system,
however successful or efficient it may be, founded on ontological
privacy. Sinfulness may be a real and debilitating factor in human
relations, but, it does not hold ontological weight or theological priority over grace and redemption. With that belief in mind, the conviction grows that sinfulness can no longer sit unchallenged on the
pediments of Wall Street.

FRANCISCANS AND THEIR ECONOMICS

This is a book about Franciscans and their economics. It is a
text about how Franciscans are thinking about their finances in
a world that is fascinated, fixated and, in many places, frustrated
by the condition and the structures of modern economics. It is
a manuscript situated within the context of growing income inequality and desperate levels of unemployment and underemployment, especially among the world's young adults. It is a book on

the cusp of ever-widening forms of globalization and an attempt to think about one of the most critical areas of life (i.e., finances) from within the bold assumptions of the Franciscan intellectual tradition. As such, it is a tentative work of dialogue between two narrative forms of discourse today: modern economics and the newly emerging *ressourcement* of Franciscan theology.

It may seem incongruous that Franciscan men and women with vows of poverty would be so bold as to comment on modern economics, even as cautiously as this book will attempt to do. In the public imagination at least, Franciscans seem to occupy (or should occupy) a world apart from the mundane interests of mortgage rates, wage drifts, arbitrage pricing, and the Nash equilibrium. And yet, history shows that it is precisely Franciscans, with their strongly incarnational view of service in and for the world, who have been thinking about, commenting on and reforming economics from their earliest years.

Perhaps it is the very vow of poverty that drives Franciscans to think so intensely and creatively about economic activity. One might suggest that the absence of wealth has driven the economic imagination of Franciscans in much the same way that the absence of food focuses the mind of the person who is hungry. But, it is more than that. The truth is that Franciscans live and work among the most vulnerable people in the world, in some of the most desperate places on earth. It is this solidarity with the poor that brings Franciscans face to face with the real life consequences of economic assumptions with an immediacy that many others can escape.

There are about a million Franciscans around the world and they are religious men and women with vows and they are secular women and men with families and jobs, as well. They are lay and cleric, Protestant and Catholic, all living out their vocation under the inspiration of the Poor Man of Assisi. Whether they serve in hospitals or medical clinics, in soup kitchens or social service agencies, in inner city schools or parishes on the edge of town, they minister with the spirit of peace and joy they have inherited from the two great founders of the Franciscan movement, Francis and Clare of Assisi. And yet, however much they minister in the background, they are not unaware of the backstory that often drives the poor to the vulnerable side of life. It is this backstory that motivates the way Franciscan think about finances.

THIS BOOK'S BACKSTORY

There is a backstory to the development of this book. It begins with a request back in 2011 to address the *Conference on Pastoral Planning and Council Development* at their national convention in Chicago. This group, made up largely of the U.S. Catholic Church's premier strategic planners, had asked me to look out over the horizon and to try and name the challenges emerging and the opportunities cresting for the community of faith. They wanted me to point out some of the most salient and perhaps least acknowledged features of the shifting social and cultural landscape so as to help pastoral leaders and ministers serve the people of God in a more effective way.

They had asked me to do this, not as a sociologist or as an economist (which I am not), but as a psychologically-trained organizational consultant who had worked on the psychological dynamics of church institutions for close to twenty years. My field of research has been the socio-analytic study of organizations, especially religious ones. That is, for more than 20 years I have been studying the psychological dynamics of institutions, especially those that affect institutions collectively. I have been looking at the challenges that make organizations anxious and the opportunities that make them defensive. And I have concentrated my efforts especially on religious organizations. I have put this understanding to bear on the work that I have done as an organizational development specialist and pastoral planner of church institutions, such as parishes, dioceses and religious congregations, among others.

I chose as the title of my talk, "The Catholics we are Becoming," because, after much research, I had come to the conclusion that Catholics were indeed changing and dramatically so. Catholic institutions were experiencing unprecedented levels of challenge in a more and more complex, diverse and globalized world of service and work. And these challenges were making Catholics anxious and, in some places, defensive, not just individually, but more intriguingly, collectively so. That is, anxiety and defensiveness were manifesting themselves in corporate behaviors and communal responses. What was very interesting to me was how "unconscious" these responses were, for the most part.

The field known as the "socio-analytic study of organizations," reminds us that institutions operate as organizational systems at two distinct and inter-related levels: the rational and non-rational. On the one hand, we know that institutions react to risks with intelligent and rational strategies. They meet challenges with mission and vision statements, with operational and strategic plans, and determine their effectiveness with assessment tools. And yet, on the other hand and simultaneous with these rational operations, organizations also run by non-rational, below-the-surface cultural schemes and emotions that oftentimes defy and even sometimes undermine common sense and ordinary logic. Corporations can be quite deliberate, conscious and conscientious in what they do. And, institutions can be unnervingly unconscious with regard to their biases and blind spots. Organizations, just as individuals, can have emotional needs that obscure common sense and the common good. That is, corporations, to use an aviation metaphor, can fly their businesses into terrain, because they don't know how to match their institutional instincts and their corporate data with their emotional needs as an organization. This is true of all organizations. It is true of religious institutions, as well.

Religious institutions operate on these same two levels. They have their canon (church) law and they also have their institutional cultures. They have their mission statements and they have their emotional fears. They have their strategic plans but they also have their social defenses. And, truth be told, religious institutions can be, more often than not, more aware of the former than they are of the latter.

In my talk to the country's pastoral planners, I laid out the new challenges that were making Catholics anxious, focusing especially on the challenge that seemed to be the least one talked about, i.e. that having to do with money, finances and economics. I was intrigued by how little the economic challenges facing religious institutions were being dealt with openly and assertively. My analysis began with a brief review of the changing dynamics of Catholic life, which I now reprise.

The Catholic experience in America began with a generation of founders who came to this country as immigrants with two (religious) goals in mind: to defend the faith in an alien land and to move their generation of Catholics up and out of disadvantage as quickly as possible. These were men and women who arrived on these shores yearning for the freedom and opportunity that this frontier country could provide. They were not always received well. In fact, they faced incredible bias and prejudice. And yet, they worked hard and prospered because they grounded themselves in a communal effort to build the structures and institutions that would protect their faith and provide the jobs and social security they would need to thrive. This generation of founders left a tremendous legacy of institutional development in thousands of colleges, universities, schools, hospitals, orphanages, social service agencies and parish outreach programs.

This founding generation handed off these structures to a new generation of Boomers whose task was a bit different. The challenge of Boomers was not to "defend the faith" but to "sustain it" and share its blessings across all the diversities inherent in the American experience. Freed from their so-called "religious ghettoes," Catholics entered the mainstream and maelstrom of diversity that is the American experience. The founding generation of Catholics left Boomers with a powerful network of supporting institutions (schools, colleges, hospitals, social service agencies, etc.) that allowed Catholics to scale the heights of social and economic prejudice with amazing speed and durability. In the founding generation, Catholics were not divided by class in America, as much as they were separated by language and culture. That is, Catholics segregated themselves from one another by the languages they spoke and the regions from which they came. They did not segregate by economic class. In fact, the cohesive nature of Catholic parishes allowed Catholics who were making it to see, understand and help those who were struggling. They believed together and they worshipped together and they held to the principle that Catholics should help one another defend the faith and advance the American dream.

The founding generation also gave their children a presumption of trust in priests and religious men and women, in a "clergy" (broadly speaking) that had heard the needs of the people and responded with effective and supportive structures. The clergy and religious who accompanied our forebears to this country shared and supported the conviction of ordinary Catholics that the way up and out of disadvantage was through a strong faith and through institutions that helped the poor and protected the vulnerable from the vicissitudes of a volatile economic environment.

One of the most intriguing and salient parts of my research was the recognition of an increasing stratification and separation of the economic classes in traditional parishes of the heavily populated Northeast region of the country. The Boomer generation of Catholics oversaw a migration of Catholics away from language-and-culture based parishes, with various levels of economically-challenged parishioners, to parishes that were different by economics, not culture of origin.

And, while all this was happening, Catholics stopped talking publically about economic challenges, at least they stopped talking about them in and with the church. The conversation among Catholics, at least the talk supported by the bishops, shifted to discussions about ideology and identity, the tinderbox of the developing culture wars. No group was being disenfranchised more by this largely unconscious shift in discourse than the up-and-coming generation of emerging adults, now-known as Millennials and Mosaics, most especially those locked in poverty and served by failing institutions.

What I learned in my research and shared in my talk was that the social landscape of America (and, indeed, around the world) was changing quickly for the new generation of young adults today. While bishops were more and more concentrated on the supposed shifts in ideology and identity among the flock and while they increasingly focused their efforts on the development of catechisms, the young were already experiencing a massive shift in economic conditions that severely threatened their prospects for a secure future. The trauma they were facing seemed to fall on blind eyes and deaf ears. Here is how I wrote my analysis:

> If there is a major difference between the situation of the builder and boomer generations and that of the new generation of emerging adults (ages 22-40), which is 50.7% of the adult population today, it may be this – our strong Catholic institutions of support are out of sync with the developmental needs of this younger generation of Catholic adults.

> We have before us a generation of young adults who are ne-
> gotiating life and faith in a wholly different way…. This is a
> generation that is being forced by the new and untested rules
> of economic engagement to delay their decisions and commit-
> ments about careers, love and family well beyond the time that
> the church is structurally able to engage them.
>
> This generation has a new set of challenges in front of them
> which has to do with two overwhelming realities: the reinven-
> tion of work in America and the rules (and rising fears) govern-
> ing the 'new economy.'[7]

Bishops and young people seemed to be seeing two different
realities and experiencing two different worlds. What I had learned
was that young people were increasingly alienated from the church.
The bishops supposed it was because of secular influences and a
large-scale philosophical shift away from objective values. Young
people, it was imagined, were falling prey to a secular imagination
that bracketed out questions of God and the critical role of objective values.

While there is no doubt that the rise in the secular imagination is real and increasingly influential, what I found curious was
that studies indicated that young Catholic adults still believed the
fundamental dogma of the Church. They believed in God; they
recognized Jesus as Savior. They believed Christ was present in the
Eucharist and held to the belief in the Resurrection of Jesus and
life after death. On all the major scales of the Nicene Creed, young
Catholic adults maintained their faith. What was changing was their
"practice of the faith" and the fit they experienced between daily
life and work and the "practices" that the Church proposed for
managing life's mysteries today. These included questions about
attendance at weekly Mass, going to Confession, the use of artificial contraception, and much of what is prescribed in the area of
"sexual morality." Young adult Catholics were experiencing a less
than satisfying or coherent fit between their concerns in daily life
and work and what the Church was proposing as answers for those

---

[7] David B. Couturier, "The Catholics We are Becoming," *Origins* (June 2, 2011), p.
58.

concerns. And one of the most salient areas of concern among young adults was economics.

I learned that one of the reasons why many young people no longer trusted the church was because they inchoately felt that the church no longer understood or addressed one of the areas of their lives that worried them the most and over which they felt increasingly powerless: economics. While the bishops were hammering away at the culture wars and the supposed loss of Catholic identity among young adults and treating these symptoms with renewed emphasis on dogmas and catechisms, young people were becoming increasingly worried about jobs, unemployment, debt and their shrinking prospects for making it in America. Bishops were talking about one thing and young adults were suffering another.

It is a new generation of Catholics who place economics, debt, and the rise in income inequality[8] at the top of their list of modern ethical problems.

The backstory of this book, then, is the need for a more robust and sustained thinking about the economy, especially among those of who are not trained economists but who live with the consequences of economic decisions every day. And who better to serve as initial dialogue partners for new thinking than Franciscans? They have been reflecting on money and finances from the time when St. Francis first challenged the economic assumptions and behavior of his own family and culture.

FRANCIS AND HIS TIMES

Francis of Assisi (1182-1226) lived in a time of incredible violence and enormous greed. The son of a wealthy cloth merchant, he lived the high-life and fast lane adolescence of an up and coming new generation of financial entrepreneurs. He was a walking advertisement for his father's fashions and he was his father's promise for an economy based on hard work and merit not inheritance. He and his father were devoted to a new social ideal whereby families could work their way into the upper class and actually create status for those not born into privilege. It was a radical

---

[8] Anthony B. Atkinson, *Income Inequality: What Can Be Done* (Cambridge, MA: Harvard University Press, 2015).

ideal that Francis and his father, Pietro, promoted and a dangerous one for the times in which they lived.

The medieval world knew almost nothing of "upward mobility," as we know and suppose it. And the "*majores*" of Francis' day were not about to allow access to wealth that easily. The world, as they knew and wanted it, was designed for a hierarchy of the few above the many

The tensions that developed in the 12th and 13th centuries around these questions of access and merit, privilege and power often turned deadly. It was a contest that Francis was at first willing to take up.

His adolescent dreams were of becoming a knight for the good and glory of Assisi. It was a dream that his father was only too willing to support with the best military gear available. Francis went to war with the blessing and the hopes of his family. But, something happened to Francis at the Battle of Collestrada, something that shook him to the core of his soul. Taken prisoner of war, he languished in prison for the better part of a year until ransomed by his father. He was never the same afterwards.

Like many soldiers before and after him, Francis had seen the bloody and fatal consequences of war. However, Francis went further by questioning the roots of the violence and greed that consumed his time. He understood something that many had missed in their justifications for violence in the name of privilege, namely that God was being implicated and even convicted by association with the greed of the day.

Francis had grown up on the apocalyptic and majestic images of God that were current in the Middle Ages. It was common belief that God looked after the world but with a threatening glance and a thunderous judgment against evil. As a boy, Francis would have shaken with dread as he pondered the character of the Almighty in his time. But, something changed in his view of God after his experience of war. His well-chronicled conversion included not just a sensitivity to the poor and a wondrous appreciation for the lowliest of creatures in nature. He found his way to a dramatic and radical love of the humble God, the naked divinity, the approachable incarnate Christ of the Gospels, one whose fundamental stance turned out to be mercy and compassion, and not angry judgment.

Francis came to the conviction that it was this tender and kind God that was obscured and defaced by the violence and greed of his day. And so, it became Francis' mission to reveal once again the goodness of God, which was to be found in abundance in the lowliest and most vulnerable of creatures. In the paradoxical way of mystics, Francis' "economy of abundance" was created by a poverty of dispossession.

Francis embarked on a new mission – to see and experience the world in the fullness of a God who was good, all good, supremely good, all the time and to everyone. And he discovered the remarkable principle that the way to experience the fullness of God was through a process of emptiness. That is, the way to enter the majesty of God was through experiences of minority. In order to experience the abundance of a good and gracious God, Francis had to open up new spaces emptied out of self-aggrandizement and competitive aggression. He had to find his way to the luxurious nature of God's kindness through the portals of vulnerability.

His contemporaries had proposed that the way towards God was through an imitation of majesty and the accumulation of power, prestige and privilege. Francis had learned just the opposite. The way to fullness was by emptiness. And, as his Franciscan brothers and sisters soon learned, this had enormous impact for their use of money and their activities in the economic world. As we will see in this book, their efforts to develop a fraternal or relational economy were not designed to reject or denigrate the world. They did not embark on poverty to castigate and bypass the natural world in order to "get to heaven" as quickly as possible. Quite the opposite!

Francis' re-thinking of the economics of his time, concentrated on the development of his fraternity's use of goods and money, was aimed at the construction of security, joy and peaceful relations, elements of life sorely lacking in the culture of his time. Francis' rule was anticipating Christ's return to "create a new heavens and a new earth," by living in the simplicity of life that forced the brothers and sisters to live in communion and not in competition with one another. Francis wanted his fraternity to experience the fullness of God, not God's stinginess. And so, he created an economic model and plan of life that re-directed the brothers and sisters away from aggression and power-building.

THE STRUCTURE OF THIS BOOK

There are two ways to approach our argument. One is through historical research and there are fine Franciscan scholars who are laying the groundwork for understanding Francis' (and his immediate followers') plan of action with regard to their economic activity.[9] This book takes another track, one which we might render as "applied Franciscan studies." While depending on the immensely fine work of the scholars of medieval Franciscan history, this text tries to use contemporary issues and concerns as a launching pad for the discussion of fundamental Franciscan values, especially in an area that has received so little attention, which is the experience of Franciscan finances today. We want to use the experience of economics today, as it is undertaken in the world with which we are most familiar, postmodern American life. This is not to suggest that American economic life is the only economy experienced by Franciscans. As this text will discuss, the opposite is the case. Franciscans today live in multiple and, sadly, unequal economies. And it is that fact that is so often hidden from view and so rarely discussed in church circles. And so, I take as my starting point contemporary experiences of the economy in one part of the world. I hope that my use of an "applied Franciscan study" can be considered a type of action research that stimulates thought and furthers deeper study.

This book is, then, a compilation of articles spanning the last several years. They are pieces that were first addressed to various audiences but with a singular intent – to help Franciscans think about their economic world in a new way. Some of these chapters have been published before but as occasional pieces in response to particular events or questions. It is time to bring these pieces together to begin a more coherent dialogue between the Franciscan world and others with greater expertise. In truth, it is fair to say that Franciscans are looking for a way of thinking about economic situations that may be more consistent with their deep intellectual tradition. As we will see, much of modern economics has bypassed that tradition. It built its powerful financial architecture without

---

[9] One thinks of the fine work of M. Cusato, J. Dalarun, D. Flood and S. Piron.

recognition of the discussions and dialogue that preceded the Enlightenment. We presume that prior dialogue in this text.

This book is a challenge to Franciscans and non-Franciscans alike. Like most Americans, ordinary Franciscans rarely take time out to mull over economic assumptions. They are busy working hard, saying their prayers and serving the poor. Like most folk, they tend to presume that the economic models they are using and the paradigms on which these models are based are fundamentally fair and consistent with their core beliefs. And yet, concerns are growing and minds are shifting on these core assumptions.

This work asks Franciscans to step back and think about these presuppositions. This work also asks those who are not Franciscans to listen in as we mull over our financial situation from the point of view of our long Franciscan intellectual tradition.

This book begins with the Great Recession of 2008. In fact, it takes us back to the challenges and concerns we faced then. I had come to Boston just at that time to serve in our formation community. Almost immediately I got involved with leaders of the *Institute for Policy Studies*, a think-tank of social and economic theorists, located a block away from where I lived. I met them just as the economy was tanking.

The neighborhood I lived in and the parish church I was serving in were hurting badly. Already a poor neighborhood with a wonderful diversity of cultures and languages, we found families becoming even more traumatized by severe lay-offs. We encountered elderly, already reticent to talk about money, who were becoming increasingly isolated in their economic pain and financial challenges. We learned the reason why – they blamed themselves for financial mistakes they "must have made," and were ashamed of their situation. They didn't realize nor did they understand that the whole economy (around the world) had turned sour. They didn't understand the structural mistakes and criminal activity that took place many levels above them. They laid the blame on their own shoulders. As the Great Recession rolled on and more and more people found themselves in deeper crisis, I found myself leading discussions on what we could do together to get through this awful time.

What struck me at the time was how little "religious people" knew the basic frame of the problem. So many of us seemed paralyzed by the crisis we were experiencing, because everything seemed so chaotic and unstable. The Great Recession didn't make sense. Even though I was not an economist, people were asking me to try and explain what was happening. I was being asked to interpret difficult trends and abstract concepts in an area of life where most of us are amateurs. I relied on experts and friends from the fields of economics, sociology, and organizational development to tutor me.

This book's first article was my attempt to make sense out of what was happening. It wears the history of that turbulent moment. It takes us back to the time of the Great Recession and explains in a simple way what we knew then. It is, in many ways, a cautionary tale of excess and pride, of biases and blind spots. We restate and rehearse that period so as not to repeat it.

Clearly, we know more today. We know what banks and mortgage companies did by chopping up, bundling, and re-packaging loans. We know how banks had made themselves "too big to fail" and too grandiose to take responsibility. We know how many corporate executives gave themselves a free pass and, in many cases, wonderful "golden parachutes." We know now how many of us wanted the fantasy of unlimited possibilities without financial sacrifice to be true. We know how much the gap between the upper 1% of the economic pyramid and the rest of us has widened over the years, causing unprecedented levels of income inequality. This first article is a reminder. It is also a test case of our applied Franciscan study. We look at these financial conditions and economic concerns from the perspective of fundamental Franciscan values. We step out from behind our ministerial screens to ponder our own economic assumptions. This first article sets the stage, as crises often do, for imaginative new thinking. It begs for some new economic conversations among Franciscans and those interested in the Franciscan imagination.

Soon after sharing that first article, *Franciscan Action Network* (FAN), an advocacy group of Franciscans located in Washington, DC, asked me to continue writing on "economic themes." As the country worked its way through the Great Recession, *FAN* realized how important it was to provide some language and conceptual tools that Franciscans could use to make sense of the economic turmoil we were in. The next two articles ("I Still Desire to Work" and "Franciscans as Consumers") provide those further insights.

They focus Franciscans on two areas of their life that are changing dramatically. The first is the world of work and the second is their life as consumers. I have written previously about the "reinvention of work" in religious communities of men.[10] In that previous article, I explained how dramatically the world of ministry and pastoral service was changing and how it is part of a great "reinvention" in the whole sphere of labor all across the world. Globalization is a phenomenon that continues to impact work in both the secular and religious worlds. The second article, then, looks at the issue of work today and tries to ferret out Franciscan principles that will help us respond more effectively to the problems of unemployment and underemployment. As I write this introduction, a few years after "I Desire to Work" was first published, I need to point out that the problem of unemployment and underemployment has not eased. Internationally, we face a looming global crisis of widespread unemployment and mal-employment, especially among young adults.

In the last several years, we have watched as the unemployment rates among young adults in Spain and Greece have spiked over 55%. The long term consequences of a generation of young adults unable to marry or start a family or who do so under unbearable conditions of economic instability are significant. We note that the rise in youth discontentment and violence in the Middle East is due in large part to the failure of many countries to provide employment, even for young adults with laudable post-secondary educations. The situation of rampant youth unemployment is not a passing problem, but a global structural weakness that Franciscans cannot ignore.

Using a Franciscan lens, we focus on the problem of work as it developed at the time of the Great Recession. Although rates of unemployment have dropped since that time, the conditions of underemployment and mal-employment have not ameliorated. Many who have gone back to work after a desperately long period of unemployment have had to settle for jobs significantly below their levels of education and expertise. Wages have remained stag-

---

[10] David B. Couturier, "The Re-Invention of Work in Religious Communities of Men," New Theology Review 11:3 (August 1998), pp. 22-35.

nant. The gap between the upper class and the middle and lower classes has widened significantly. And the conditions for youth employment around the world seem as dangerous and unsteady as they have ever been. The article on work is an attempt to invite Franciscans back into a conversation about the reinvention of their work and the work of their brothers and sisters here and around the world, especially those who are young.

Franciscan finances are tied to the larger context of unemployment and under-employment. A generation of young adults who cannot find adequate employment destabilizes the peace of the world and jeopardizes future stability. It is in our interest to understand and address the dynamics of employment in our ministerial sites.

The third article focuses on Franciscans as consumers. Honestly Franciscans don't often think of themselves as consumers. They profess vows of poverty and live rather simple and unadorned lifestyles. It is easy to see why they would not tag themselves as consumers. And yet, they are and significantly so. Like everyone else in the West, Franciscans live in a consumptive society. This article demonstrates why it is critical that Franciscans now take that identity on in a serious, reflective and ethical way. It posits that Franciscans, even with their vows of poverty, are significant players in the world of modern consumption. We must admit the part we play in the great economic drama of our time and learn how to respond to it ever more ethically. Clearly I am not calling on Franciscans to mimic the identity of the modern day consumer, not by any means. What I am asking is that Franciscans inspect a part of their life that they often fail to acknowledge forthrightly, precisely because they are religious under vows. Franciscans are consumers and the challenge is not to become unconscious about what modern consumption entails and invites. It is to take up the work of being ethical consumers.

There are many Franciscans who already challenge the impact that a mindless consumptive mentality is having on the planet. There are also many others who have yet to see how their own Franciscan heritage requires an inspection of economic behaviors, both personally and corporately. The article on "Franciscans as Consumers," sets out the reasons why that scrutiny is so religiously and ethically important.

The last article in this first section turns to consumerism once again and how it is affects young people today. We will develop a Franciscan "theology of stuff" and provide thoughts on how we can declutter our souls of their dependence on a materialized identity.

THE DEVELOPMENT OF A FRATERNAL ECONOMY

These first articles give Franciscans an opportunity to think about their financial actions in a more serious way. The presumption of this book, as readers will learn, is that the world of economics is not a world unto itself, with unassailable doctrines and untouchable assumptions. Modern economics is a practical science based on first principles and fundamental assumptions. Our goal is to provide Franciscans with some rudimentary tools with which to test out these principles, assumptions, policies and practices.

The first articles of this text lay out some of the troubling conditions emerging in our society: job insecurity, unemployment and under-employment, the reinvention of work, income inequality, wage stagnation, and a growing distrust in family life itself (*"postfamilialism"*). They are accompanied by a rise in global terrorism fed by massive rates of youth unemployment. But, are there threads that connect these trends? The second part of this book attempts to lay bare those connections.

The second part of this book is dedicated to the development of the concept of "fraternal economy" in one Franciscan community. We turn to the Capuchin-Franciscan Order, a 16th century reform group of the Franciscan Order, which has been trying to develop a more relational or "fraternal" way of exercising its economic activities, one less tied to the individualistic, aggressively-competitive models we have inherited. To begin this experiment has required them to look at the economic conditions under which they serve the poor around the world and ask themselves hard questions about their own economic structures and the assumptions they hold about them. They have had to ask themselves about their own economic arrangements and how these procedures and practices align with their fundamental Franciscan beliefs. These conversations have not been simple or easy.

Capuchins have had to address the income inequalities within their own ranks and the philosophical assumptions and theological explanations they have given to justify them. They have had to review the reinvention of their work and the choices they have made to keep pace with the postmodern world in which they seek to serve with passion and hope. Sensitive to their founding Franciscan principles of communion and brotherhood and facing a rising tide of economic inequality and privacy from within (largely unconsciously and inchoately), the Capuchins recognized they had to pivot toward a more fraternal form of economics than the one modern models afforded them.

The experiment of Capuchin friars in building a more relational form of economics in the approximately 100 countries in which they can be found is suggestive and challenging. It is also in its initial stages. It starts from the foundational Franciscan concept of "gospel brotherhood" and wonders how an Order based on a fundamental principle of communion could live in conscience with divergent and unequal economies within the fraternity itself. That is, it asks how friars could live in the Northern Hemisphere with secure incomes, world-class educations and health care, and tolerate a situation whereby the men they call their brothers in the Southern Hemisphere are structurally deprived of sufficient income, solid education and adequate health care. How, they asked themselves, is this structural inequality commensurate with a theology of "gospel brotherhood?" The final articles of this book take on that subject and develop what we might call a "pastoral psychology of Franciscan economics." These articles on "the fraternal economy" are taken from research done for *The Graduate Theological Foundation*, a research foundation for ministry professionals, and published in a text entitled, *The Fraternal Economy: A Pastoral Psychology of Franciscan Economics.*[11] They have been revised for a new audience.

This section of the book asks a jarring question: how does a religious community of men dedicated by vows to a Franciscan vision of communion and Gospel brotherhood tolerate embedded economic inequalities within their global fraternity even as the culture around them justifies these structures of indifference? How

---

[11] David B. Couturier, *The Fraternal Economy: A Pastoral Psychology of Franciscan Economics* (South Bend, IN: Cloverdale Books, 2007).

do they maneuver in a way that is more consistent with their Gospel mission as brothers in an economy designed for privacy and competition?

In the end, we cannot and have not written anything approaching a comprehensive text on "Franciscan economics." Instead, we are providing only initial thoughts, provocative themes, and suggestive avenues by which Franciscans (and those intrigued by the Franciscan imagination) can discuss one of the most powerful engines of opportunity and anxiety in today's world.

This book will require the indulgence of experts in the field of economics. That field is elegant in its complexity and we cannot match its profound architectural features. We can, however, ask fundamental questions that arise from Franciscanism's essential elements: the inherent dignity of each and every person (regardless of station of life), the goodness of God and God's creation, the interdependence and solidarity of all creation, and the positive destiny and call of the human family toward peace and communion. We will look at our Franciscan economics through those lenses.

It is my wish that these elements will illuminate a new pathway of hope in a time that the philosopher Charles Taylor argues has become increasingly disenchanted.[12] Taylor has described a world increasingly shorn of meaning, objective value, transcendence and relationship, one provoked and replaced by an ideology of aggressive and isolating consumption. If this text provokes conversation and new partnerships across generations and class boundaries in and out of Franciscan communities, it will have achieved some good. And so, I hope.

---

[12] Charles Taylor, *A Secular Age* (Cambridge, MA: The Belknap Press, 2007).

SECTION ONE

FRANCISCANS AND FINANCES

Chapter One
Franciscans and the Great Recession

In 2008 America was facing an unprecedented financial crisis. Credit was tightening, unemployment was rising and the cost of living was going up. Increasingly, Americans were afraid that they were going to lose their jobs and the vital medical benefits that went along with them. The recession of 2008 was forecasted to be longer, deeper and harder than anything we had seen since the Great Depression. Franciscans were not immune to these global dynamics. Their institutions would feel the crunch. This article was written at the beginning stages of the Great Recession and asked key questions: What can we do to weather this "perfect storm?" What can we do to help our brothers and sisters get through and make sense of this economic crisis? What in the Franciscan tradition can help us rebuild a legitimate economic security? This paper looked at the history of this crisis and outlined some principles and tools Franciscans could use to make sure that their next steps in the economic world were sure and just.

The Great Recession that (actually) began in 2007 hit Franciscans, as it did most Americans, with unparalleled force. The economic situation of many Franciscan communities was already structurally weak due to the disproportionate rise in the number of elderly members, the ballooning costs of health care, a decades-long vocation shortage that meant fewer young wage earners, unfunded liability on ministerial properties and friaries, the high cost of insurance and the rising costs for energy, food and education, along with a dramatic drop in the number of Catholics going to church and contributing to its mission. Because Franciscans, on the whole, receive stipends rather than salaries for the ministries they do, they depend on donations to supplement for the work they do in hospitals, schools, clinics, parishes and social service agencies among the poor and in the missions. They work with and among the poor.

And it was the poor who were most vulnerable to the ravages of the Great Recession. Savings were wiped out; access to higher education was closed off; state funding for supplemental services were dramatically cut, unemployment became a tragic reality and wages were cut even for the working poor. Franciscans found themselves once again among the poor struggling to make do in an economy that had turned against the poor and minority communities with a vengeance.

Now, some years later, the recovery has begun. It is a slow recovery and, for poor and minority communities, it is a very, very slow recovery. Unemployment rates have dropped, but many of the so-called new jobs created in the recovery period are part-time and, on the whole, do not match the experience and expertise of American workers. The stock market has rebounded but the benefits of that rebound continue to flow upward, to those few at the top of the economic pyramid who could weather the turbulence of our economic times. It was the Great Recession that revealed just how uneven the lanes of opportunity truly are in America today. It revealed the two "economies" emerging in America: the one that serves the interests of the privileged few and the one that burdens the shrinking middle and the burgeoning lower class.

The Great Recession hit Franciscans with such force because it crashed as religious life was already reeling from a "perfect storm" of crises: an unparalleled vocation shortage that shows no signs of ameliorating, scandals reaching back decades for which priests and bishops continue to bear responsibility, responsibility for foreign missions that are growing but depend on shrinking American religious community support for their survival, and the vast reinvention of work in religious communities, forcing religious men and women to serve in new and unchartered ways.

The rest of this chapter is a look back in time to the origins of the Great Recession. It was written during the early days of the recession to explain what was happening and to find ways that Franciscans could help their communities weather the economic turbulence of the time. For many Franciscans, it was the first time in a long time that they engaged in direct talk about economics with those they served.

A BIT OF HISTORY

In December, 2008, the Bush administration admitted what most Americans already knew. We were in a recession and had been for some time, in fact for at least a year. Recession is technically difficult to define. Most economists describe it as a decrease of less than 10% in a country's GDP (Gross Domestic Product) over two consecutive quarters. The National Bureau of Economic Research defines it as a 'significant decline in economic activity lasting more than a few months.' Difficult to classify, a recession is not hard to feel, however. In a recession, living costs go up, as incomes get squeezed. It is a sustained period of economic stagnation as spending falls, business investment shrinks, and companies begin laying people off as sales across multiple sectors dry up. It is a time when financial fears go up and economic trust goes down.

We pretty well know the origins of this particular financial crisis. They're found in what are called subprime loans! Simply put, because of deregulation in the banking industry and a whole lot of greed, banks made housing loans available to a whole class of people whose credit worthiness and ability to pay back the loan were always shaky, at best. Unusually low introductory mortgage rates teased people into the real estate market who would never have qualified under ordinary circumstances and in normal times. With these low introductory rates in place, people bought homes they couldn't afford, over the long haul. Often without so much as a down payment, people secured 100% adjustable (versus) fixed rate mortgages. With these adjustable rate mortgages, people bought new homes or remortgaged existing homes with fervor or, better, on a wing and a prayer. Everything was fine, at least at the beginning, because on the front end of an adjustable mortgage, payments are low, unusually so. It's when the adjustable rates kicked in, as they must, that large numbers of families found themselves in severe financial trouble. They could afford the teaser introductory rates, just not the larger adjustable ones which followed.

When the mortgage rates finally adjusted (upwards, of course), the amount people were required to pay for their mortgages on a monthly basis jumped dramatically; in some cases, doubling or tripling. Unfortunately for these sub-prime borrowers, their incomes were only calibrated to the initial teaser rates, not to the final adjustable ones. It wasn't long before these borrowers found themselves behind the proverbial eight ball. Some tried to stay afloat and make their monthly mortgage payments by borrowing from their credit cards. With interest rates running between 18 and 22% and a whole host of late payment fees, sub-prime families found themselves in a quicksand of debt, unable to pay their mortgages or their credit cards. For many, bankruptcy became the only option. The numbers of people across the country unable to make their mortgage and credit card payments skyrocketed. Banks found themselves with empty loans and dozens of foreclosed properties on their hands. They started to hemorrhage money uncontrollably. Some well-known and highly esteemed banks started to fail. The government needed to step in to forestall rolling bank failures and a nationwide loss of confidence in banks. Because financing is no longer local and many of these loans had been parceled out across the world in our new globalized economic network, the trauma that once could have been cauterized at the local level quickly became an international disaster.

This whole venture sounds so irresponsible. Why would any reputable company engage in a loan sharking-type enterprise of giving mortgages to people who obviously did not have the means to sustain the life of the loan? The simple and most truthful answer is Greed. Consumers got greedy, bankers got greedy and the government, because of its deregulation policies, stopped watching out for and stopped protecting us from these greedy behaviors. No one was minding the store as these loans were sliced up and re-packaged ("bundled") and then sold to other banking partners (around the world) who ostensibly took legal and financial responsibility for their ever-smaller pieces of the loan. Unfortunately, many of these end-of-the-line owners didn't know what they actually had or what was implied by having them. Their focus, like everyone else's, was on making (quick) cash and not on being the responsible agent of other people's money.

Why was all this attractive? Again, the simple truth is the best. People were making money every step along the way. Every time these loans were divvied up, sold off or handed on to some other party, someone was making money, quick money, easy money. At the end of the day, no one really knew who owned the loans and who was responsible for making good on their promises. It was at this point that banks finally closed their spigots and stopped lending money or making promises to one another. The banking system began to shut down. The economic system's most prized possession—trust—was in very short supply and, without it, the economy started to become paralyzed. Without trust, banks don't lend money to one another. Businesses can't get credit for supplies and companies start pulling back on production. When factories can't crank out products, people get laid off or start worrying about their jobs. In this climate, consumers stop spending money and the whole cycle of supply and demand grinds down to a point of deep stagnation. A recession can easily turn into a depression, since a depression is simply a longer, deeper, and more aggravated form of a recession.

Most Americans know things are bad. What they don't know or find hard to admit is that things have been bad for quite some time, at least for the middle and lower class in America. Before we turn our attention on what we can do, let's trace how life has been economically for the middle and lower-middle class in America.

LIFE INSIDE THE BUBBLE

If you asked most Americans to describe the economic climate of the 1990s and the early years of the 21st century, you would probably get a very positive assessment. The end of the twentieth century is remembered as "good times." The Cold War was over. Unemployment was low and productivity was high. Americans went to college in record numbers. Gas prices were down and so were food prices, relatively so, due to low energy and transportation costs rippling through the system. Americans spent like there was no tomorrow – literally. The personal savings rate dipped below 0 percent for the first time since the Great Depression, hitting a negative .5% in 2005. (This was down from a personal savings rate of 9% in 1985.) Even though Americans were spending more than they were earning, credit was plentiful and Americans became accustomed, for the first time in their history, to living their lives in debt and without shame. In 2004, the credit card industry took in $43 billion in late-payment, over-limit and balance transfer fees.

The average household credit card debt increased 167% between 1990 and 2004.

Just below the surface of these good times, trouble was brewing. Americans were accumulating huge debts, well beyond their means to repay in any systematic or coherent fashion. The average household consumer debt in 2004 is estimated to have been between $9,000 and $13,000. Between 1990 and 2004, America's total credit card debt increased from $243 billion to $735 billion. It is clear that more and more people began using their credit cards to buy groceries, fill prescriptions and pay for their medical care.

Something more than personal lapses and individual moral failures is at work here. It is clear that Americans have been living beyond their means and on borrowed money and lots of it. But a closer look reveals that there are structural factors at play that make it necessary for families to go into debt. Below the radar of ordinary American spending are some very troubling social forces that make it difficult for more and more Americans to get by. A list helps us contextualize and understand this financial crisis better. Here's what's been happening while ordinary Americans have been trying to make a living.

- The average American worker is worker longer and harder and for less money. The average worker now spends 200 more hours a year on the job than he or she did in the 1970s, an extra five weeks per year. The average middle income family experienced an increase of ten additional weeks per year in annual paid household workload. You would think that more work would translate into more money and spending power. Just the opposite happened. Americans have been working harder but falling further behind.
- Why are Americans working so hard? It's not because they want to work longer hours and with less vacation time and fewer benefits than any of the other industrialized countries of the world. They have to do so. Driving the cycle of overwork is not the greed to have more, but simply the desire to maintain what families now have. The fact is that wages, adjusted for inflation, have remained distressingly stagnant, while the costs for food, housing, energy, college, day care and health care have soared well beyond the rate of inflation. The modern

economy is not an escalator that carries people up and out of disadvantage. Today it is more like a treadmill whose settings are gradually increased. People have to run faster just to stay in place.

- Most people are afraid to complain about the increased demands for time at work because they are terrified of losing their health benefits. The rate of U.S. health care spending as a percentage of GDP (Gross Domestic Product) rose from 5% in 1960 to 16% in 2004. In 2005, 46.6 million people in America had no health care insurance at all; 15 million more people than just 10 years before. Although 80% of those who are uninsured actually work, full or part-time, the cost for securing and maintaining health insurance today remains largely out of reach for a good portion of our American workers. Without universal health care protection, they are forced to cobble together their out of pocket solution to higher fees and prescription costs, or simply go without health care.
- A popular saying is that "the poor are getting poorer and the rich are getting richer." It is not only popular, it is also true. The number of families and individuals in poverty and economic hardship has risen. The poverty rate for 2005 was 12.6 percent, up from 11.7 percent in 2001. There are 36 million Americans in poverty and the bulk of these (13 million) are children. One third of all African-American children in America lives in poverty; 23.9% of all African-American seniors live in poverty, compared to a national average of 9.8% of all elderly, 65 and over.
- What is emerging is a frightening picture of growing economic inequality and financial disparity in America. Money made in the 1990s and early part of the 21st century flowed upward; it didn't trickle down as promised. More and more Americans are working harder and harder so that a smaller and smaller group of people at the top can do well, enormously well. (In the 1970s, the wealthiest 1% of the population owned 20% of all private wealth. Today, the top 1% owns over 34% of all private wealth.)

This inequality shows itself in stark and subtle ways. An Oil Price Information Service study indicated that lower income

Americans spend 8 times more of their disposable income on gasoline than their wealthier neighbors do. Fewer and fewer well-off Americans are relying on the public services, civic organizations, and community structures that everyone else must depend on. Living in gated communities, playing at private clubs, designing their own recreational venues, the well-off in America have simply "privatized" their family's educational and security needs. Instead of relying on and sharing the burden of public education, community libraries, and public transportation, they have simply left the "public square," withdrawn from community action, and become more and more isolated from the public parks, public works, and common wealth we all depend on to make American democracy work well for all of us. No wonder they want further tax cuts! Power is shifting in America and ordinary voters, unionized workers and wage earners are losing ground to big money investors and campaign contributors who are more interested in corporate interests than in our common tasks and responsibilities.

The crisis we face is deeper than any quick bailout can fix. Andree Zaleska of the Boston office of the Institute for Policy Studies said it succinctly – "We are not going back to some golden age of economic growth based on empire, unfettered capitalism, and cheap energy – nor do we want to! We have to prepare ourselves and our communities for transformation."

A shift is what is demanded of us as Franciscans. Old Testament scholar, Walter Brueggemann, writing on the moral-theological foundations of the current economic crisis, says that we have to change from "autonomy to covenantal existence, from anxiety to divine abundance, and from acquisitive greed to neighborly generosity."[1]

A FRANCISCAN PERSPECTIVE

In 2007 I published a text on a Franciscan approach to economics.[2] The book originated in a challenge posed to the Ca-

---

[1]Walter Brueggemann, "From Anxiety and Greed to Milk and Honey," Sojourners (February, 2009), p. 20

[2] David B. Couturier, *The Fraternal Economy: A Pastoral Psychology of Franciscan Economics* (South Bend, IN: Cloverdale Books, 2007).

puchin Order by three African Capuchins at the Order's General Chapter of 2000. The three friars were reviewing the state of the Order in Africa, trying to contextualize the political and ecclesial challenges facing Africans, when they humbly and pointedly accused the worldwide fraternity of "not hearing the cry of the poor in Africa." The charge stung and confused the delegates listening to them. Hadn't the Order sent legions of missionaries and developed hundreds of parishes, schools and clinics? Hadn't the Order supplied financial resources for the establishment of the Order, along with churches and schools, in both Eastern and Western Africa? Hadn't hundreds of European and North American priests and brothers labored intensively and for decades to make a positive difference in the lives of Africans? What had we not heard? What had we not seen? The three friars were clear. We had not understood the poverty of the poor of Africa. We did not understand its roots and its causes, its origins in a Western economic system and worldview that valued competition over compassion, individualism over the community, and materialism over the spirit. The friars asked us to listen more closely to their concerns and to work with them to develop solutions that would heal and mutually benefit both sides of the growing global economic divide.

This challenge accelerated the Capuchin Order's analysis of its own economic models, already in progress and led by then Minister General, now Bishop, John Corriveau, OFM. Cap. In a series of 20 circular letters to the Order, Corriveau had enunciated a vision for a new way of living our common life and sharing our resources in a more globalized world. Rejecting the underlying aggression and competition of late 20th century market fundamentalism, Corriveau called on Capuchins to rebuild our local, provincial and international economies on more solid and more secure principles of communion and compassion. Calling on friars to develop a "fraternal" economy, Corriveau suggested that we could build stronger economic ties and a more stable network of international relationships, if we were willing to forego the spasms of fear that classical capitalism's "scarcity thinking" (as opposed to classical Bonaventurian 'abundance thinking') promotes. My book traces the history of this line of thought and provides formators with some tools on how to begin training the next generation for this new economic paradigm.

The first thing we have to learn is that Franciscans have something vital to say about contemporary economics. This is not new. Franciscans have always been involved in the economic questions of the day. The early friars were intimately involved in the debates about currency and the proper use of resources and power in the 12th and 13th centuries. Francis' teaching on poverty was never meant to reject the world and jettison the friars into some parallel, disembodied universe without commerce or common good. Quite the contrary! Francis' intent was to have friars understand the troubled roots of the economy of his day and to have them face the violence and the greed that fueled the development of the rising feudal economy. Francis' penitential humanism was to be a stimulus to a new economic security among the brothers and in society, fueled not by greed but by a humble recognition of a common heritage as sisters and brothers under one good and loving God.

Capuchins believe it is time to take another look at the Franciscan tradition for help in developing a more relational economic paradigm for the 21st century. In my book, I outline five principles that we believe can help us construct a more relational experience of economic activity than is presently displayed in the "pick yourself up by your own bootstrap" idiom of aggressive capitalism. The five principles are:

- *Transparency* – mutuality in all things. All the goods, economic activities, and ministerial decisions are at the service of the whole. There are no hidden schemes by leadership or membership.
- *Equity* – Individuals and communities get what they need and contribute what they have for the common good and the building up of communion. Service replaces entitlement.
- *Participation* – Build mechanisms of cooperation and communion of persons without domination or deprivation.
- *Solidarity* – Those who have more give more to those deprived. All work to undo structures of sin that serve as obstacles to communion.
- *Austerity* – The minimum necessary, not the maximum allowed. Live and work simply, so that others can simply live and work.

Think about the present financial crisis. Had any of these five principles been working in the financial system, we would not have gotten into the traumatic global situation we are in. These principles are derived from the wellspring of Franciscan theology, specifically meditations on the Trinity and our participation in God's inner life of communion. Franciscans are asked to use these five principles when working through their economic decisions, both privately and communally.

COMMON SECURITY CLUBS

One of the greatest dangers of this current economic crisis is that people will try to face its challenges alone. Most Americans are too ashamed or embarrassed to share their economic troubles with others, so used are they to the paradigm of privacy that surrounds our most cherished economic myths. The fact is that more and more Americans feel isolated. A recent Duke University study found that 25% of Americans say they have no one with whom to share their personal troubles – more than double the number who felt this isolated in 1985.[3] What Franciscans can do is to bring our strong communal instincts to bear on a dangerously isolating experience and do so in specific ways.

The Boston-based *Institute for Policy Studies* is developing a model and methodology for small groups of people to come together to talk about the current economic crisis and how it is impacting them. Participants spend time in what are being called "Common Security Clubs," discussing the root causes of the economic crisis, using reading materials provided by the IPS for this purpose. Most of the group's discussion time is spent talking to one another about what they can do together to increase their own economic security and to work for policy changes that will benefit the common good.

The IPS is providing participants with a simple 3 stage model for coming together. The recommended size of a group is between 10 and 20 adults who commit to an initial five meetings with a facilitator. The first step is to learn and reflect. Using videos,

---

3   Miller McPherson, Lynn Smith-Lovin, Matthew E. Brashears. "Social Isolation in America: Changes in Core Discussion Networks over Two Decades," *American Sociological Review* 71:3 (June 2006), p. 353-375.

Bible study, and shared readings, participants are asked to focus on the larger economic forces that are shaping our lives. The group's goal is to come to a common understanding of why the economy is in distress, what are its historical factors, and what is a vision of a healthier, more sustainable economy? The bottom line question here is – why are we so economically insecure now and what can we do together to develop a more secure foundation for our economic lives in the future?

The second step for these "common security clubs" is to provide mutual aid and local action. The question the group is asked is a direct one – what can we do together to increase our economic security, right here and right now? Here is where questions become personal and call out for action. For one person, it may be – how can I get out of debt? For another, it might be – How can I keep my home and forestall foreclosure? And for yet another person, it may be – how can I exit the rat race of consumerism, downscale my consumption and live a more ecologically-friendly existence? The group focuses its attention on making concrete alternatives possible in one another's lives, at the point of one's deepest economic insecurity.

The third step is for these small groups to decide whether to engage in further social action, based on their experiences and mutual needs. Different groups will respond differently to the economic insecurity issues that are emerging. Some will begin to lobby members of Congress to reform the health care system; others will call on Congress to stop foreclosures or to press for living wage legislation. Each group decides for itself how it will engage the economy in a more relational, or fraternal, way.

One member of a Common Security Club summed up the goal of this practical, hands-on initiative, when she said, "Let us pray together that our private pain now becomes our shared concern, that together we find ways to overcome our fear and anxiety, and be present to one another. Let us not be afraid, but take action together."

FRANCISCANS AND THE FINANCIAL CRISIS

Franciscans have a long history of accompanying the poor through the most difficult of economic times. We have tended the leper, sheltered the homeless and given food to the hungry time and time again. And we are doing so today in our hospitals, clinics, soup kitchens and food pantries all across America and, indeed, around the world. But, this crisis demands something more from us. It calls on us to address the origins of this global financial meltdown. It begs us to name the spasms of fear that an ideology of scarcity requires and replace them with a theological vision of a God-given abundance, as St. Bonaventure reminds us (*bonum diffusivum sui*). As Franciscans we believe in a God who is good, all good, supremely good, all the time and to everyone. We believe this God of ours is different from the stingy and distant God of Wall Street. Our God calls us into a relational economy that places a premium on compassion, not aggression, as the driving force of economic relations. As Franciscans we can use our tradition to develop a more reliable and common security that will build peace, eradicate the most severe forms of poverty and protect the environment. It's time for Franciscans to gather their friends and neighbors to talk about economic challenges and concerns and to find a faithful pathway out of anxiety and greed to a more relational economy.

CHAPTER TWO
I STILL DESIRE TO WORK:
FRANCISCANS AND THE PROBLEM OF
UNDEREMPLOYMENT IN AMERICA

Research into the life of St. Francis of Assisi indicates that he struggled mightily with the issues of work throughout his life. Work needs to be on the minds of Franciscans again. In this article written at the time of the Great Recession (2009), we learn how the plight of Americans worsened. While the rates of unemployment have dropped since then, the problems of under employment and mal-employment continue. Workers who have returned to the labor force after an unprecedented recovery time have found jobs well below their experience and expertise. Many are employed only on a part-time basis. The fear that unemployment or under-employment will equate to a catastrophic loss in family health insurance has been ameliorated somewhat by the passage of the Affordable Care Act. But, the inability of young people to break into the work force to the degree that their expensive educations warrant remains a deep concern both here and around the world. This paper provides an historical review and presents some Franciscan principles to guide our thinking and practice, as we continue to work together for a job reform that truly promotes justice.

> *"And I used to work with my hands, and I still desire to work. I firmly wish that all my brothers give themselves to honest work. Let those who do not know how to work learn, not from the desire to earn wages for their work, but as an example and in order to avoid idleness. When we are not paid for our work, let us have recourse to the table of the Lord, seeking alms from door to door. The Lord revealed to me a greeting, as we used to say, "May the Lord give you Peace."*
> *(St. Francis, in Francis and Clare: The Complete Works, I.Brady and R. Armstrong, 1982, p. 155.)*

Research into the life of St. Francis of Assisi indicates that he struggled mightily with the issues of work throughout his life.[1] He fought his father's business practices, nearly lost his life in the economic wars between Assisi and Perugia, and, in the ever expanding economy of his day, had to challenge his brothers to a new and radical work ethic, one that emphasized trust, not only in God but in the bonds of brotherhood, as well.

Amid the greed and violence that regularly accompanied the turbulent intellectual, economic, demographic and commercial polarizations of the 12th and 13th century Christian Europe, Francis promoted a new experience of social peace by the paradoxical embrace of austere poverty and extravagant generosity. His "fraternal economy" was meant to be an antidote to the aggressive competition and violent revenge emerging in his post-feudal world. Francis' scandalous refusal even to touch a coin unleashed a cultural re-imagining of human dignity and economic life that reverberates through economics to this day.[2]

Long before the likes of David Hume and Adam Smith, Franciscans were writing creative new rules about the circulation of money, price determination, contracts and market forces. And the Franciscan distinction between ownership, temporary possession and the use of economic goods gave theological credence to the potential of wealth or, better, the "work of wealth" to create real social opportunity and the common good. It would not be until the pontificate of John Paul II, some eight centuries later, that a "theology of work" would be put into such a positive light again. For it was John Paul's lasting legacy to lift work from its inherited pall as a "punishment for sin" and recast it as each individual's participation in a Trinitarian mission in and for the world – to co-create with the Father, to co-redeem with the Son, and to co-sanctify with the Spirit.[3]

Work needs to be on the minds of Franciscans again. The plight of workers in America is worsening by the day and the con-

---

[1] Giacomo Todeschini, *Franciscan Wealth: From Religious Poverty to Market Society* (St. Bonaventure, NY: Franciscan Institute Publications, 2009); Dominic Monti, "Franciscan Life and Urban Life: A Tense Relationship," in Roberta McKelvie, ed. *Franciscans in Urban Ministry* (St. Bonaventure, NY: Franciscan Institute Publications, 2002), p. 5-15.

[2] Todeschini, *op.cit.*

[3] Laborem Exercens (1981), n. 25-27.

sequences for peace both here and abroad are as enormous as they are worrisome. This paper will outline the challenges to employment in this time of the Great Recession and offer some Franciscan principles to guide our thinking and practice, as we work together for a job reform that truly promotes justice.

WORK SINCE THE GREAT RECESSION

Since the near total collapse of the world's economic systems in September, 2008, Americans have gotten used to bad economic news. At the end of October, 2009, the U.S. economy completed its 23rd straight month in a recession that began in December of 2007.[4] This current stretch has surpassed the recession of 1981-1982 as the longest lasting recession in seventy years. It is estimated that the economic meltdown we've just experienced has washed away more than $20 trillion in wealth and we are likely to face trillion dollar deficits for years to come.

But, these grim figures don't tell the whole tragic story. That narrative belongs to the lives of ordinary Americans working harder for less money, if they have jobs. It belongs to the tens of millions of American workers, newly unemployed, who want to work but cannot. It is the story of families spiraling into severe economic distress because of a growing new trend in America – adult workers who are underemployed. These are millions of Americans who have watched their hours shortened and wages slashed. They hang onto jobs with hours reduced and benefits cut, because they are afraid they will find nothing else in this employment-starved economy. The long-term impact of this growing rate of underemployment on health care and Social Security has yet to be fully determined.[5]

Alongside the unemployed and underemployed is a new group of malemployed. These are the skilled and educated workers and newly-minted college graduates who are unable to use their occupational skills and formal education at work, despite their substan-

---

[4] Andrew Sum, et al., *The Economic Recession of 2007-2009. A Comparative Assessment of Its Duration and Labor Market Severity.* Center for Labor Market Studies, Northeastern University, March 2009.

[5] *Ibid.*

tial investment of time, effort and debt. A recent report indicates that 28% of all employed bachelor-degree holders between the ages of 21-29 years are working in jobs that typically did not require a college degree.[6] The malemployed include the increasing numbers of teachers, engineers and scientists who find themselves stocking shelves at local department stores, just to survive. The loss in American productivity, creativity and ingenuity is staggering and may be long term.[7]

A LOOK AT UNEMPLOYMENT AND UNDEREMPLOYMENT

Let us take a snapshot of employment across America today and discuss some next steps for Franciscan action.[8]

- The number of unemployed in America has risen by 8.2 million people, since the start of the Great Recession at the end of 2007, and the general unemployment rate has jumped by 5.3 percentage points. Unemployment now stands at 10.2% and is likely to go higher.
- It is now clear that the stimulus package approved last year did not go far enough. It is estimated that the *American Recovery and Reinvestment Act* (ARRA) created or saved approximately 170,000 to 235,000 jobs per month and that, without ARRA, losses in the month of October, 2009, would have topped 400,000. However, those numbers do not account for the jobs needed to match population growth. That is, just to keep pace

---

[6] Andrew Sum et al., "The Great Recession of 2007-2009: Its Post-World War II Record Impacts on Rising Unemployment and Underutilization Problems among U.S. Workers," (Center for Labor Market Studies, Northeastern University, June 2009), p. 16-17.

[7] It is estimated that these higher levels of unemployed and underemployed are costing the economy about $1 trillion per year in gross domestic product, according to James Glassman, senior economist at JP Morgan and Co., cf. *The Statesman* (April 12, 2009), http://www.statesman.com/business/content_business/stories/other/04/12/0412underemployed.html.

[8] For the statistics below, I rely on the works of Andrew Sum et al., "The Great Recession of 2007-2009: A Comparative Analysis," *op.cit.,* and of economist, Heidi Shierholtz at the Economic Policy Institute, http://www.epi.org/analysis_and_opinion/entry/at_10.2_octobers_unemployment_is_a_wake-up_call. I refer readers to their excellent analysis.

with population growth in the country, the economy would need to add about 127,000 jobs each month, which means the economy would have had to create 2.8 million jobs over the time of this recession (i.e., 22 months). Instead, we find ourselves about 10.9 million jobs shy of what would be needed to return to pre-recession employment levels.

- It is harder finding a job, once unemployed, than ever before. Those who have lost jobs are experiencing record-high lengths of time securing a new one. Currently, the time an individual can expect to be out of work is just over six months (26.9 weeks), which is the longest stretch on record. In this job-starved economy, Americans are running out of savings and patience. Higher numbers of Americans are simply walking away from the job market altogether.[9]
- More and more elderly are going back to work and this is putting new pressure on the ability of new workers to enter the job market for the first time.
- All told, October 2009 job figures show that a record 17.5% of Americans are either unemployed or underemployed and, of these, 5.6 million Americans have been jobless for over six months, the highest number in history.
- The job picture is worse among minorities, so much so that some researchers have determined that the recession has already turned into a *depression* in minority communities.[10] Research indicates that unemployment for black workers was 15.7% in October, 2009, 13.1% among Hispanic workers, and 9.5% among white workers. Before the recession, those unemployment rates were 6.8%, 6.9% and 5.1%, respectively.[11]
- The growth in federal jobs, as a result of recovery efforts, has not been as effective as it could have been. That growth has been totally offset by the job loss at the state level. While the

---

[9] Robert Reich, former Clinton Cabinet Secretary and now an economist at the University of California at Berkeley said recently: "We're seeing many more people who are losing their connectedness to the labor force... There is a profound weakening of ties to the labor market among a large portion of our working-age population." *The Statesman* (April 12, 2009) at http://www.statesman.com/business/content/business/stories/other/04/12/0412underemployed.html.

[10] Barbara Ehrenreich and Dedrick Muhammad, "The Recessions Racial Divide," *The New York Times* (September 12, 2009).

[11] Cf. Shierholtz, *op. cit.*

federal government added 16,000 jobs during the time of the recession, state governments lost 16,000 jobs.[12]

The media has recently focused our attention on the outrageous packages being given to the executives of institutions that American taxpayers had to bail out. And rightly so! But, these reports are out of focus when they distract us from the real story of our economic situation – the ever-widening and deepening pain sweeping across middle-class America. Franciscans need to focus attention on job loss and wage reduction and their long-term consequence on the health and stability of this country.

We turn our attention to the emerging structural issues to which we must pay attention.

STRUCTURAL ISSUES

The hurt facing our families is real and it is growing at an alarming rate. Truth be told, Americans have been hurting for a long time. It is just that the hurt has been hidden from view by the enormous credit card debt that Americans have been amassing to pay for the rising cost of their health care, food, energy and education.

We are facing three structural problems that need ethical analysis and Franciscan response.

The first is **chronic wage stagnation.** The average American worker is working longer and harder and for less money. The average worker now spends 200 more hours a year on the job than he or she did in the 1970s, an extra 5 weeks per year. But, more work has not yet translated into more money and spending power. Just the opposite is true. Americans are working harder but have fallen further behind.

The fact is that wages, adjusted for inflation, have remained distressingly stagnant, while the costs for food, housing, energy, college, day care and health care have risen well beyond the "expected" rate of inflation. I repeat the commonly used analogy – the modern economy is not an escalator that carries people up and

---

[12] *Ibid.*

out of disadvantage. It is more like a treadmill whose settings are gradually increased. People have to run faster just to stay in place.

The second structural problem is the **growing gap between rich and poor.** What is morally troubling is the emergence of a growing economic inequality and financial disparity across America. Money made in the 1990s flowed upward; it didn't trickle down as promised. More and more Americans are working harder and harder, so that a smaller and smaller group of people at the top can do well, enormously well. In the 1970s, the wealthiest 1% of the population owned 20% of private wealth. Today, the top 1% owns over 34% of all private wealth. Even parishes that were once distinguished by ethnicity and the languages spoken now seem divided into parishes that have the resources to meet their ministerial needs and those that do not.

The third structural problem is **wage reduction.** Companies used to shrink labor costs and maintain profits by layoffs. Now companies are turning to severe pay cuts, downgrades in rank, furloughs and shortened workweeks to maintain their profit margins. Some Americans are working 20% more for 50% less.

Now, we will look at a Franciscan approach to job reform.

FRANCISCANS AND WORK REFORM

The first of these is a commitment to the inviolable dignity of the human person. As noted above, Francis refused to touch the coinage of his day. This strange phobic reaction served a larger theological position – that money cannot symbolize and will never contain the value that Francis found in even the lowliest of God's creatures.

In the extreme violence and greed of his day, Francis needed a symbolic action that would testify to his lived sense that all men and women shared a transcendent desire for the infinite God, one that could not be contained within the commercial desires of his world. This is a good lesson for us. Too often today, work is seen only within the political ambit of profit maximization. The human person is easily reduced to his/her economic benefit as a consumer. Franciscans will argue for the fullest determination of human potential that includes much more than what an individual can consume or produce in and for the marketplace. Legislation, therefore, that tips too heavily on the side of the guarantees afforded employers or shareholders misreads the anthropological foundations of the common good.

Franciscans, for their part, see work under another rubric, that of vocation and call. Work connects us to the living God and bonds us to the common good of all creation. In this light, unemployment and underemployment obstruct the communion that exists between the individual and God. Franciscans believe in a strategy of full employment that provides a living wage to all Americans who have a desire and capacity to work and protects the rights and needs of those that cannot.

Our Franciscan moral attitude requires the recognition of an inherent right to work and the means that protect and advance every individual's status as the subject of work. Profit can never be the bottom-line of economics; the human person is. Systems that foster the disposability of workers in the pursuit of higher profit margins for the few are both economically short-sighted and morally wrong.

Beyond this, Francis believed in the abundance and generosity of God. As St. Bonaventure noted. Francis experienced God as a fountain fullness *(fons plenitudo)* of grace, goodness and creativity, spilling out into a diverse world configured to God's good purposes.[13] Modern economics, on the other hand, begins with a theology of scarcity, positioning God as irrelevant or unaware of the stark realities of our commercial world, substituting the infinity of goods for the infinity of God. Modern economics maintains that economic security derives from an ontological privacy that determines the inevitability of competition and isolation in social interactions and the innumerability of goods in a free market.

Paradoxically, the early Franciscan commitment to austerity and simplicity was their insurance against insecurity and the engine to creativity. Dependence on one's neighbor, the construction of a cosmic solidarity, fraternity and the forgiveness of sins would be their fortress against the inevitable anxieties of an uncertain and sometimes malevolent world. In Franciscan thought, there is an in-

---

[13] Ewert Cousins, *Bonaventure and the Coincidence of Opposites* (Chicago: Franciscan Herald Press, 1978).

timate connection between labor, community, ecology and peace. The common good of all creation is indivisible.

We need a new practice of work in America that is less aggressive and more relational, a task made more difficult by our world's prevailing philosophies of work.[14] We need an ethic of work that supports families, connects neighbors and builds a "civilization of love." In a Franciscan approach, work is not just another platform for privacy, self-interest and aggressive competition. Work is the proving ground of solidarity and solidarity is the engine of entrepreneurship in a truly relational economy.

---

[14] See Chapter Five in this work on "The Development of the Fraternal Economy."

CHAPTER THREE
FRANCISCANS AS CONSUMERS:
ETHICAL RESPONSIBILITIES

It is estimated that the average American spends about $370.06 of
their consumer dollars per week on food, housing, transportation,
apparel, health care, entertainment, personal insurance, and other miscellaneous expenses. That comes to about $52.86 per day.
(Other estimates put the consumer spending of the average American in the range of $90-100 per day.)[15]

While there is no comparable consumer expenditure index
for Franciscans, a survey of a major province of Franciscans indicates significant consumer influence. Franciscans spend money
on the development of their ministries and fraternities. Because
Franciscans generate economic activity to support their religious
lifestyle (i.e. food, housing, health care, and insurance, etc.) *and*
to bolster and improve their ministries, we can estimate that the
average Franciscan's total consumer spending could be as high as
$190.69 per day. This means that some Franciscan Provinces could
be generating total consumer activity in the tens of millions of
dollars every year.

Franciscans don't often think of themselves as consumers.
Our Franciscan vow of poverty often keeps us from identifying
with the streams and currents of modern economic life. Our stress
on a life "sine proprio" ("without anything of our own") height-
ens our sense that we should be exempt from the turbulence of
the market and the troubles of Wall Street. But, the fact is, we are
consumers and we spend.

We go to the local pharmacy for our medicine and to the corner *bodega* for our milk. We shop at *Macy's* and *Wal-Mart, Target*

---

[15] Consumer Expenditure Survey, US Bureau of Labor Statistics, 2010, http://ww-
w.bls.gov/opub/focus
/volume2_number12/ cex_2_12.htm

and *Piggy-Wiggly's*. We buy from *Amazon. Com* and *QVC*. Whether as Provincials or Guardians, local ministers or directors, ordinary brothers or sisters, we are constantly making choices about what to buy and wear, what to purchase and use, what comes into our convents and friaries, and what ends up on our dinner table.

But, how do we think of ourselves as "consumers" and what drives our economic choices? What role does our Catholic faith and our Franciscan commitment play in the choices we make as consumers? What impact might our economic choices have on the lives of people around the world?

In this chapter, I explore the great issue of "consumerism" and how it impacts our religious and spiritual lives. I want to highlight why we as Franciscans need to develop a new language of desire and a more assertive spirit and practice of *ethical consumerism*. I will treat one area where Franciscans can use their new found ethical consumerism for a moral good today, i.e. to stop the spread of human slavery in the global marketplace.

The Religious Challenge to Consumerism

A look at any Franciscan house or province budget signals immediately that Franciscans are consumers. Our line items are filled with diverse economic categories – electricity, heat-oil-gas, new equipment, health insurance premiums, dental, food, telephone, internet, books, liturgy supplies, etc. We share with other Americans the daily tension of making ends meet as prices go up and we find ourselves as religious caught living off "stipends" and not salaries ('stipends' being the equivalent compensation that is ½ or 2/3 of what 'salaries' might be worth for the same job.)

Beyond this, we also struggle as do other Americans with the philosophy of life that is said to fuel the economic engine of progress, *consumerism*. Long before we ever think of entering religious life, we are children immersed in a culture of consumption, such that every aspect of our lives is touched by the "need and greed" mentality of modern aggressive consumerism.[16] Studies show that children as young as four are now seriously and continuously

---

[16] Juliet B. Schor, *Born to Buy: The Commercialized Child and the New Consumer Culture* (New York: Scribner, 2004).

targeted by marketers for their ability to influence their parents' economic decisions, what is called their "consumer potential."[17] Children receive a ceaseless barrage of TV messages about the connection between self-image, identity and product. Experts tell us that this "consumption mentality" is eroding childhood and evidence is mounting that children are suffering the physical, social, emotional and cognitive deficits that arise from consumerism's assault on childhood.[18] It should come as no surprise then that Franciscans today, especially younger Franciscans, face the same cultural temptation that their secular cohorts face, seeing and judging themselves by the tenuous tenets of *having* rather than *being*.

No religious figure in modern history has written or spoken more loudly or clearly about the growing dangers of consumerism than Pope John Paul II. In his encyclical, *Sollicitudo Rei Socialis*, he defined consumerism as the condition of an "excessive availability of every kind of material goods," which makes us "slaves of 'possession' and of immediate gratification."[19]

According to John Paul II, consumerism is one of the most pronounced moral and ethical dangers facing the modern world. He taught that consumerism erupts when economic life trumps every other value in the social order of things, when "the production and consumption of good become the center of social life and society's only value – not subject to any other value."[20] It emerges when every other good is made subordinate and subservient to it.

John Paul was not criticizing our desire to have good things in life. He was not against technological advancements that would improve the quality of human life. Far from it! For John Paul II, the Gospel was the sign and sacrament of human progress and it was the role of Christianity to serve that advancement. However, he also warned that what was at stake in today's business-mentality was the very definition of human progress itself. What was wrong, he suggested, "is a style of life that is presumed to be better when it is directed toward 'having' rather than 'being,' and which wants

---

[17] Jennifer Ann Hill, "Endangered Childhoods: How Consumerism is Impacting Child and Youth Identity," *Media Culture Society* 33:3 (April 2011), p. 347-362.

[18] *Ibid.*

[19] John Paul II, *Sollicitudo Rei Socialis* (1987), no. 28.

[20] *Ibid*, no. 41.

to have more, not in order to be more but in order to spend life in enjoyment (of things) as an end in itself."[21]

What is troubling about consumerism, he and others have noted, is that it proceeds from a reductionist philosophy of the human person, one that narrowly defines men and women by their economic potential and the satisfaction of their material wants alone.[22] Consumerism reduces us to what we can earn, what we can spend, and what we can purchase. Consumerism turns our values upside down and inside out. Truth, beauty and goodness are no longer the human person's terminal, theocentrically-ordered self-transcendent values. Consumerism turns them into emotional tools and slogans to serve commercial interests. In this way, Beabout and Echeverria remind us, wisdom, virtue, community, intimacy, happiness and the common good are inverted and made to serve the economic aspirations and financial greed of the marketplace.[23]

Fr. John Kavanaugh, in his book *Following Christ in a Consumer Society,* defines consumerism as a system of life, a "religion," and a total worldview that "disposes us to view everything – ourselves, others, nature, and religion – as a commodity, as replaceable and marketable commodities."[24] Fr. Kavanaugh goes further in his hard description of consumerism or what he calls the "commodity form of life":

> What this means, in effect, is that there is no intrinsic human uniqueness or irreplaceable value. The person is only insofar as he or she is marketable or productive. Human products, which should be valued only insofar as they enhance and express human worth, become the very standards against which human worth itself is measured. If our life's meaning is dictated by mercantilism and production, then our purpose and value are defined essentially in relation to what we can buy, what we can sell, or – at the very least - what we can hold on to.

---

[21] John Paul II, *Centessimus Annus,* no. 36.

[22] Gregory R. Beabout and Eduardo J. Echeverria, "The Culture of Consumerism: A Catholic and Personalist Critique," *Journal of Markets and Morality* 5:2 (Fall 2002), p. 342.

[23] *Ibid.*

[24] John Francis Kavanaugh, SJ, *Following Christ in a Consumer Society: The Spirituality of Cultural Resistance* (Maryknoll: Orbis Books, 1986; revised edition, 1991), 22, 10.

The uniqueness of an individual's way of being, of the unrepeatable personal qualities in knowing and loving, of relating to life in such a way that can never be duplicated by another person, much less by a thing – these human qualities inevitably disappear in a universe whose ultimates are productivity and marketing… The Commodity Form touches our experiences through the style of life we are expected to assume: consumerism, competition, hoarding, planned obsolescence, and unnecessary waste.[25]

David F. Wells, in his book *Losing our Virtue*, summarizes the anthropological inversion that consumerism creates when he describes its modern psychological dogma, "I shop, therefore I am."[26] We are prone to consumerism, he says, because "our self-understanding as human beings created, fallen, and redeemed by God, has vanished, leaving us with a sense of emptiness, or depletion."[27] What contemporary culture has created is an "empty self" set up for demographic definition, commercial construction, marketable options, and profitable identities. As Wells notes,

As the self emptied out, it became a receptacle to be filled with the impressions of others. Thus, the freedom to "be one's self" was soon held hostage by the views of others, the world of fashion, and the pressure of social trends.[28]

In the first edition of *The Fraternal Economy*, I described the dangerous impact that consumerism has on our ability both personally and corporately to make good decisions.[29] I came away with the conclusion that an unrestrained and un-reflected attachment to consumption, the kind of attitude that consumerism promotes today, has a devastating impact on a Franciscan's ability to desire what God desires for the world and for humankind. Consumerism atrophies our transcendental desire for God and our efforts to seek the good, especially for those who are most vulnerable in our society.

---

[25] *Ibid.*

[26] David F. Wells, *Losing our Virtue: Why the Church Must Recover its Moral Vision* (Grand Rapids, MI: Eerdmans, 1998), p. 221.

[27] *Ibid.*, p. 99.

[28] *Ibid.*, p. 99.

[29] David B. Couturier, *The Fraternal Economy: A Pastoral Psychology of Franciscan Economics* (South Bend, IN: Cloverdale Books, 2007).

How Consumerism Atrophies Desire

There are various ways that Franciscan desire is atrophied in the new global consumerist economy.

First, there is the limitless *proliferation of desire*. In a consumer-based society, we simply want more and more and more. Focused on people as objects of desire or competition and nature itself as a commodity, we no longer want to *be* or become more; we simply want to *have* more. Thus to accomplish this for a consumption-based economy, marketing and advertising must overtime collapse the distinction between need and want and between necessity and superfluity. We never know when enough is enough. We don't know where to draw the line of excess. The reach of our need and want simply run to infinity. Consumers are trained to exceed their satisfaction and to desire above all else a steady, indeed an infinite, array of goods, products and services.[30] St. Francis once noted that the only thing a Franciscan owns is his/her sin. Everything else truly belongs to God. That ontology provides Franciscans with their proper life orientation: we belong to God and we find our way to God through the virtues we develop, with the help of God's grace. But, consumerism corrodes the incentives toward character development. The proliferation of (commercial) desire requires only the acquisition and consumption of material things. It subordinates all else to its commercial interests

Second, there is the *materialization and commodification of desire*. In classical Christianity, the end or purpose of desire was the divine, since as Scripture reminds us, "We have no true and lasting city here." (Hebrews 13:14). St Augustine would give this desire its classical enunciation in his phrase, "Our hearts are restless until they rest in Thee, O God."[31] In classical Christian thought, our deepest desire was God, because, after all, we are creatures dependent on a good and gracious God and only God can satisfy the longings of the human heart.

---

[30] Couturier, *op.cit.*, p. 81-84.
[31] Augustine, *The Confessions* (Lib 1,1-2,2.5,5: CESL 33, 1-5).

However, in early 21st century economic thought, God is privatized and desire becomes first and foremost a material reality.[32] Our deepest desires are reduced and refocused on things and products. The desire for the infinity of God is translated into the desire for an endless array of goods and products, which have little meaning or substance, except in their surplus. While our desire remains infinite in its expectations and demands, it remains forever unrealizable and unfulfilled. By a slight of hand, consumerism turns even the desire for God into a commodity, swapping the infinity of God with the infinity of goods. It may be said that consumerism conditions us to accept the eternal exchange and redundant replacement of what we desire. In a consumptive world, there is no substance, only substitution. Franciscan life is oriented around the key value and experience of "Gospel brother/sisterhood." Consumerism weakens those bonds, as things encroach and substitute for fraternity.

And, finally, desire undergoes *segmentation and isolation*. What I mean by that is that consumerism destroys the possibility for communion, because, devoid of truth, beauty and goodness, it has no power to unite us or bring us together in any substantial way. (Think of the faux camaraderie and then the fatal stampedes created when stores open early on Thanksgiving for Christmas holiday shopping!)

Consumerism can only polarize and divide. Marita Wesley-Clough is a trend expert for the Hallmark Card Company, the one responsible for projecting the wants and desires of Hallmark's customers. In detailing retail trends on customers in the 21st century, she describes two powerful effects of consumerism – emotional overload and the inability to discern what's right and good. Here is how she phrases it:

Trend cycles seem to be emerging more rapidly as a result of technology, accelerated social diffusion, instantaneous commu-

---

[32] For an exploration of this privatization of God, cf. Ross Douthat, *Bad Religion: How we Became a Nation of Heretics* (New York: Free Press, 2012), p. 211-240. This is the fundamental confusion that attends the rise of the "prosperity Gospel" in some evangelical churches today. David W. Jones and Russell S. Woodbridge, *Health, Wealth and Happiness: Has the Prosperity Gospel Overshadowed the Gospel of Christ* (Grand Rapids, MI: Kregel Publishers, 2010.)

nication and more willingness to accept – or inability to escape new ideas... When everything is accessible instantaneously, the ability to assimilate, to differentiate and to choose becomes more difficult.[33]

Wesley-Clough describes the cultural and emotional damage of today's globalization on consumers, when she says –

Under those circumstances, a culture can suffer from a feeling of mental and emotional paralysis, a kind of frozen frame – like kids in the candy store of the world. It becomes increasingly difficult to discern the truth – to sort out what's best.[34]

A sad consequence of consumerism ensues – isolation and division. In her catalogue of 12 retail trends in the early years of the twenty-first century, Wesley-Clough predicts increased polarization, not only in politics but also in our stores, in our businesses, and in our malls:

Look for increased polarization – whether political, economic, religious or philosophical. Regardless of age, ethnicity or affiliation, individuals long for the security of alignment with those 'like us'. Ethnic 'tribes' within countries and cities; elite social clubs; gatherings of loyal brand devotees, as well as group identities created via fashion, language or symbols. Increased gravitation toward communities of like minds – people whose interests, worldviews or values reinforce our own.[35]

Franciscans under the sway of a consumer culture live by taste and inclination, by palate and preference. Desire loses the moral dimension of dedication and perseverance, as Franciscans make their choices on principles of partiality and temperament. Franciscan desire follows the tenets of commercial desire.

---

[33] Marita Wesley-Clough, "Twelve Consumer Trends and Counter Trends for 2004 and Beyond," www. retailindustry,about.com/cs/retailtrends/a/bl_trends2004.htm.
[34] *Ibid.*
[35] *Ibid.*

Desire in the consumerist culture dissects the world into market shares where the unprofitable are increasingly and swiftly replaced, marginalized or ignored, as the definition of common good collapses into only that of common wealth, whatever can be exchanged, made transparent or proliferated for profit.

CONSUMERISM'S DARK SIDE: CORPORATE HUMAN TRAFFICKING

One may have assumed to this point that consumerism was simply a minor ethical annoyance, a sad but unavoidable byproduct of today's engine of human progress. A few good homilies and some sturdy penances during Confession should set Franciscan attitudes straight. But, there is an even darker side to consumerism today, a very dark side that should trouble the conscience of every Franciscan. And that is the reality of corporate human trafficking, a resurgence of human slavery in the marketplace.

Amid the barrage of goods and products flowing across our air and seas are men and women, girls and boys, being exploited and enslaved as commodities in the global market place. Not only is human slavery making a comeback, it is more pronounced and stronger than at any other period in human history.[36] Human traffickers today are using some of our most respected businesses, the products and services we use regularly, to cover their criminal acts of human exploitation. They use forced and child labor in the long and sometimes intricate supply chain that leads from the production to the distribution of the goods and services we rely on every day. It is up to us as Franciscans to identify those illegal chains of human exploitation in our transactions and try to dismantle them.

It is hard to imagine that human slavery continues to exist. And yet, it does and it is growing. We know that there are more than 30 million slaves suffering in our world today.[37] And it is estimated that there are about 17,000 to 20,000 foreign nationals trafficked into the United States each and every year, with

---

[36] For the reasons for this resurgence and proliferation, cf. htpps://www.free-theslaves.net/SSLPage.aspx?pid=301.

[37] David Batstone, *Not for Sale: The Return of the Global Slave Trade* (New York: Harper One Publishers, 2010), p.1.

upwards of 200,000 "domestic slaves" living and working in America. Human trafficking is the second most profitable form of transnational crime in the world after the sale of drugs, more profitable even than the sale of arms.[38]

Human trafficking is not simply the work of individual criminals in back alleys, on side streets, in foreign countries. It is big business, a diversified corporate enterprise that exists in almost every trade imaginable and it uses many of our most cherished and respected industries to advance ever more desperate forms of exploitation. All across the world, tens of thousands of men and women, girls and boys are forced every day to destroy their bodies in the sweatshops of Europe and Asia and to sell their bodies in the massage parlors and escort services of major American cities, like Boston, Baltimore, New York and Los Angeles.[39]

To accomplish this, human traffickers are using many of the American companies we admire the most as a cover for their criminal deeds. They use our hotel chains, our car rental agencies, and our airlines as part of the supply chain that provides and serves up modern human slavery to the cities and suburbs of America. Not long ago, a story crossed the wires of a Chinese runner in Quincy, MA, who was convicted of being part of a trafficking ring that would pick up young women from Logan Airport and South Station and deliver them to customers in Stoneham, Wellesley, Malden, Burlington and Newton. The local traffickers were running their ads on *Craigslist,* providing the cover of corporate legitimacy to a form of human cruelty that is ever ancient and sadly ever new.

Trafficking victims are the disposable and easily expendable labor pool deceived into accepting job offers that promise them a better life. They come to the capitals of Europe and to the suburbs of America hoping for an education, longing for a better future, ready to build that possibility with hard work at a decent wage. But, they find themselves in short order trapped in a terrifying cycle of isolation, intimidation and threat, forced to work without

---

[38] Louise Shelley, *Human Trafficking: A Global Perspective* (New York: Cambridge University Press, 2010), p. 7.

[39] Shelley, *ibid.,* p. 201-228.

relief or compensation, treated as commodities and held captive through constant forms of physical and psychological abuse.

Human trafficking is a hugely profitable business. At the end of 2010, it was estimated that the 4% of the world's 30 million people who were used as trafficked sex slaves generated $38.7 billion dollars in profits for those managing the human slave industry.[40] Human trafficking is both a global and a local problem, one that exists all around us. It is a neighborhood industry with long supply chains, a *commercial* network that uses legitimate businesses that we have come to rely on and respect as a cover and shield for criminal activities.

And the fact is that, without knowing it, we are all implicated. Each and every day, before we ever get to work, we are, as Kevin Bales indicates, *"eating, wearing, walking and talking slavery"*—getting out of bed and walking on a rug hand-woven by slaves from the carpet belt of Pakistan, India and Nepal, wearing a tee shirt made of cotton harvested by slave labor in West Africa and Uzbekistan. We sip coffee cultivated by slave labor in Africa or Latin America, with sugar harvested by enslaved Haitian workers in the Dominican Republic. We step out the door with our cell phones and laptops at the ready, unaware that the mineral used in these devices, tantalum, was dug out of the ground by poor farmers indentured to armed gangs in the Democratic Republic of Congo. Again, Kevin Bales reminds us with chilling directness-- "Every one of us, every day, touches, wears, and eats products tainted with slavery. Slave-made goods and commodities are everywhere in our lives…"[41]

How can this be? If human slavery is illegal on every inch of the planet Earth, how does the post-modern world tolerate and even accommodate its proliferation?

[40] Siddharth Kara, "Designing More Effective Laws Against Human Trafficking," *Northwestern Journal of Human Rights* 9:2 (Spring, 2011), p. 127.

[41] Kevin Bales and Ron Soodalter, *The Slave Next Door, op. cit.,* p. 137.

CONSUMERISM AND THE CHALLENGE OF CORPORATE HUMAN TRAFFICKING

What is human trafficking? An official definition helps. Article Three of the *United Nations Protocol to Prevent, Suppress and Punish Trafficking in Persons* defines the 'Trafficking in Persons" as the -

> ... recruitment, transportation, transfer, harbouring or receipt of persons, by means of the threat or use of force or other forms of coercion, of abduction, of fraud, of deception, of the abuse of power or of a position of vulnerability or of the giving or receiving of payments or benefits to achieve the consent of a person having control over another person, for the purpose of exploitation. Exploitation shall include, at a minimum, the exploitation of the prostitution of others or other forms of sexual exploitation, forced labour or services, slavery or practices similar to slavery, servitude or the removal of organs...[42]

On the basis of this definition, we see that there are three constitutive elements to the situation of human trafficking.

First, there is the act (what is done) and that is the *recruitment, transportation, transfer, harboring or receipt of a person.*

Second, there are the means (how it is done) *through the use of force, coercion, abduction, fraud, deception, abuse of power or vulnerability, or giving payments or benefits to a person who is in control of the victim.*

And third, there is the purpose (why this is done) – *for the purpose of exploitation, the forms of possible exploitation to include the prostitution of others, forced labor, slavery or similar practices and the removal of organs for profit.*

While sexual trafficking is a well-known form of human slavery, today we must also consider human labor trafficking. Specifically, we are looking at companies and individuals who use sub-contracted employees, businesses whose supply chain includes trafficked labor. One of the most concrete examples involves *Wal-Mart.*

---

[42] For this definition, see – www.unodc.org/unodc/en/human-trafficking/what-is-human-traffciking.html.

Wal-Mart, the biggest private employer in the world (with 2 million employees) and the largest retail company on the planet, sub-contracted with janitorial companies to clean their stores across the United States. For their part, these janitorial companies hired undocumented workers and forced them to work long hours without overtime pay, in unsafe conditions, handling toxic chemicals without protection. The US government brought a case against *Wal-Mart* that involved 345 illegal immigrants at 60 *Wal-Mart* stores in 21 states. In the end, twelve of the sub- contractors pled guilty to hiring the illegal workers and paid $4 million in fines. *Wal-Mart*, for its part, denied any wrongdoing, except for failing to provide proper supervision. It settled with the US government in a judgment that came to $11 million.[43]

Can we as Franciscans really influence the way our companies do business? Can we put pressure on the corporations with which we do business to engage in more ethical practices? Can we do away with human slavery in the supply chains that produce, market and distribute the goods we eat and the products we wear? I believe we can, if we understand the power we have as ethical consumers and recognize the moral and spiritual hazards of today's aggressive consumerism.

OUR FRANCISCAN "POWER" AS ETHICAL CONSUMERS

What does all this mean for corporate human trafficking and the supply chains that feed them? I think it means that we will never be truly successful in dismantling the supply chains that feed corporate human trafficking as long as we ourselves are aligned with or beholden to a consumerist mentality that puts economic aspirations above all other values and refuses to acknowledge the primacy of human dignity over and above all other economic interests or "necessities." To break the supply chains that lead to slavery we must look at our own desires and what has happened to our desire for the infinity of God and how

---

[43] This example is recounted in Ruth Rosenberg, "Tackling the Demand that Fosters Human Trafficking: Final Report," USAID, August 2011, Doc ID: EDH-I00-05-00004, p. 34.

often we have allowed that desire to be replaced with the primacy of goods.

Catholic social teaching would remind us that consumerism will not be solved or even ameliorated by government action alone.[44] Fundamentally, but not totally, consumerism is, as Richard John Neuhaus described it, "a cultural and moral problem requiring a cultural and moral remedy."[45] Therefore, each of us must become more conscious of our moral responsibilities as consumers and do all we can to promote ways of living where the search for truth, beauty, goodness and communion with others is not sacrificed to expedient consumer choices and unfettered profit generation.[46]

We must undertake an *examination of consciousness* when it comes to corporate human trafficking:

Do I care whether the products I buy or use are tainted with human slavery?

Are the price, convenience and availability of goods more important to me than the possibility that those goods might be the result of slave labor?

How much time and effort am I willing to invest in determining whether a product is the result of trafficked labor?

How willing am I to make this problem of human trafficking personal?

How willing am I to work with others to eradicate slave labor from my home and dinner table?

The issue of corporate human trafficking, though arguably complex, must become personal, because, when all is said and done, it is not about market shares, profitability, and government policies. It is about people, human beings bought and sold, tortured and exploited by fraud and for greed.

---

[44] John Paul II, *Centessimus Annus* (1991), p. 36.

[45] Richard John Neuhaus, *Doing Well and Doing Good* (New York: Doubleday, 1992), p. 52.

[46] For an analysis of the debate between culture and government regulation in the control of consumerism in secular and Catholic literature, cf. Andrew V. Abela, "The Price of Freedom: Consumerism and Liberty in Secular Research and Catholic Teaching," *Journal of Markets and Morality* 10:1 (Spring, 2007), p. 7-25.

This is what Pope John Paul II meant when he continually proclaimed that the human person must always and everywhere be the *"subject of the economy"* and never its object.[47] What allows corporate human trafficking to flourish is the subtle erosion of the social and cultural primacy of each and every individual's human dignity and the inviolability of their human rights.

Consumerism is corrosive of those rights by fomenting, as John Paul II told us, a *"radical dissatisfaction"* with life and then creating the commodities that serve as a synthetic palliative against the alienation that consumerism and its marketing have created.[48] We must understand and then resist this deadly game.

And the deadly game is this -- those who are trafficked have tragically become the collateral damage of an affluent consumerist society that reduces the human person to an object of material things (*Centesimus Annus*, n. 19). And not only those trafficked, every one of us, whether on the supply or demand side of human trafficking, we are all damaged by the "radical dissatisfaction" that attends consumerism. As John Paul II, reminded us – the more we possess, the more we want, while our deeper aspirations remain unfulfilled or even stifled.[49]

In lieu of this, we must build an alternative economy. We must create a fraternal or relational economy that places a new primacy on compassion and relationship and not on aggression and competition, one that recognizes our fundamental vocation to give ourselves freely to others and to God, at church, in the home and in the marketplace.

Beyond this, as Franciscans we must use our most forceful language to describe with accuracy what corporate human trafficking and the supply chains that feed them truly are – they are sin, social sin, and they require from the Churches the most comprehensive response to sin we can muster.

---

[47] John Paul II, *Laborem Exercens* (1981); cf. Eileen Kelly, "Papal Economics: John Paul II on Questions of Labor and Capital," *Catholic Social Science Review* (1999), p. 11-20, accessed: www.cssronline.org/CSSR/Archival/1999/1999_011.pdf; Edward J. O'Boyle, "John Paul II's Vision of the Social Economy," in the *International Journal of Social Economics* 32:6 (2005), p. 520-540.

[48] John Paul II, *Sollicitudo Rei Socialis*, no. 28.

[49] *Ibid.*

SUPPLY CHAINS AND SOCIAL SIN

In his social encyclicals John Paul II began to teach that there was a list of social evils that could no longer be properly understood within the framework of "personal sin" alone. Social evils would never be fully addressed or redeemed if seen only under the rubric of personal responsibility. Those social evils included terrorism, religious, cultural and racial discrimination, the diminution of human rights, the stockpiling of nuclear weapons, and the "unfair distribution of the world's resources and of the assets of civilization" that widens the gap that exists between the rich and the poor."[50]

John Paul II put the world on notice that viewing these evils (and many more like them) simply through the traditional prism of personal sin not only misunderstood the dynamics of these social tragedies but also paralyzed us in our ability to redress them, with grace, in any significant way. Therefore and thereafter, John Paul called all of us to a meditation on the dynamics of "social sin."

In my book, *The Four Conversions,* I define "social sin" in the following way:

> Social sin is the refusal of communion that is embedded in the conventions, customs, policies, procedures and practices of our institutions. It is the denial of free communion to certain persons or groups of people, which is structured into the way we bring our communities together. It is the attempt to achieve a type of social harmony by means of domination or deprivation.[51]

What this definition does is invite us into a deeper inspection of all our institutions, for profit and not for profit alike, to see the traces of alienation that hide in the embedded customs, policies, procedures and practices of all businesses.

One of the great lessons of John Paul's moral teaching is that social sins cannot be solved by personal deeds alone. Evil

---

[50] John Paul II, *Reconciliatio et Paenitentia* (1984), no. 2.

[51] David B. Couturier, *The Four Conversions: A Spirituality of Transformation* (South Bend, IN: The Victoria Press, 2008), p. 189.

that has become embedded as normal within the customs and conventions of the way we do business will not be eradicated even by the heroic but isolated acts of individuals. Structural in nature, social sins like consumerism and corporate human trafficking require cooperation, collaboration and united actions, in a word, *solidarity*, to redress them.

And they require our solidarity on several fronts. They certainly require new legislation that will target the demand side of human trafficking, going after companies that profit, even unwittingly, from trafficked labor. The supply chains that support human trafficking must be exposed and the mechanisms that promote trafficking must be dismantled. We must send the clear and convincing message that we do not want slave-tainted goods and products in our homes or on our dinner tables.

I believe that California has given us a model with the passage of its *Transparency in Supply Chains Act*. Beginning on January 1, 2012, the law required retail sellers and manufacturers doing business in the state of California to disclose their efforts to eradicate slavery and human trafficking from their direct supply chains.

Specifically, the law requires those companies doing business in California with annual worldwide gross receipts exceeding $100 million, with sales in California in excess of $500,000 to do five things:

First, they must verify their product supply chains and evaluate the risks of human trafficking and slavery at every step. They have to disclose whether or not this verification was conducted by an outside, third-party, agent or not.

Then, they have to conduct audits of all their suppliers to evaluate their suppliers' compliance with the company's standards for trafficking and slavery in their supply chains. The disclosure to the state (and on their company website) has to specify whether the audit was done independently and whether it was conducted unannounced. (A good model of this effort, by the way, can be found on the Hewlett-Packard website.)

The law requires direct suppliers to certify that the materials incorporated into the product comply with the laws regarding slavery and human trafficking of the country or countries in which they are doing business.

The companies must maintain internal accountability standards and procedures for employees or contractors failing to meet company standards regarding slavery and human trafficking.

The companies must provide training to company employees and to management, who have direct responsibility for supply chain management, particularly with respect to mitigating the risks within their supply chains of products.

California leads the way here. But, it is only a first step and one reserved to a select and restricted class of companies. We need to double our efforts to extend this kind of legislative approach across the country, so that we can be protected from coast to coast against the dangers of slave- tainted goods reaching our churches, friaries, homes and dinner tables.

FRANCISCANS AS CONSUMERS – REDEFINING THE FRANCISCAN SUBJECT TODAY

In his paper, "So What is a Franciscan? Constituting the Franciscan Subject," David Flood, OFM, demonstrates how the early friars fashioned a new common language about who they were, what they did, how they worked, and to whom they belonged in order to break society's control over them:

> They just had to remember who they were, agents of the Spirit, subverting the world to a new way of life, a life on the further side of the destructive way societies are organized, and Assisi first of all. The remnants of society whom the brothers served in the almshouses did not just happen to be there. They were put there. They were put there just as our societies today select out all sorts of people who do not fit in.[52]

The friars were no longer accepting the commonly-held definition of their place as citizens and communicants in the town and churches of Assisi. The early friars were engaging in a

---

[52] David Flood, OFM, "So What is a Franciscan? Constituting the Franciscan Subject," *Franciscan Studies* 63 (2005), p. 35; Patricia Ranft builds on Flood's Franciscan work in her text, "Franciscan Work Theology in Historical Perspective," in *Franciscan Studies* 67 (2009), p. 41-90.

social reconstitution of their experience as citizens and workers in Assisi, rejecting a world divided into the *majores* and *minores*, an enterprise that existed for the exclusive benefit of Assisi's ruling clans. Becoming the "servants of all" indicated a commitment to include the leper and the poor in the enterprise of citizen and church, at a time when they were excluded and shunned as "permissible victims" of church and society. Francis' declaration that the friars would live "spiritually," as agents of the Spirit's holy operation, contrasted with the socially accepted and ecclesiastically expected forms of "living carnally," i.e., according to the divisions and wars that contributed to the wealth of Assisi's prominent families at the expense of the lepers and the poor.[53]

"Living spiritually" today means understanding and respecting the ethical responsibilities we have as consumers. It is our task as Franciscans today to inspect the matrix of meaning that shapes and surrounds our own social, cultural and religious identity as consumers. It is time for Franciscans, at the very least, to accept their responsibility to become *ethical consumers,* proclaiming and living the Gospel's insistence on the immeasurable dignity of each and every person even in (especially in) the marketplace.

But, there is more. The modern and postmodern world has constructed our agency primarily in terms of consumption and the overwhelming anxieties that evolve from it. We now satisfy the social rituals of our inclusion in this consumer world, at least in part, by *"eating, wearing, walking and talking slavery."*[54] We have seen how consumerism impacts and atrophies our desire. Franciscan life, by contrast, creates a new lexicon of desire and thus invites us to a form of life on the other side of the aggressive and destructive ways that society is organized today.[55] Franciscanism subverts the world as we know it, a consumptive world that would have us believe in the God of the Enlightenment who is stingy and distant and a world where we must be in a continuous "war of all against all." Alternatively, Franciscanism invites us to trust and to live as brothers and sisters in the graced world

---

[53] Flood, *op.cit.,* p. 35-47.

[54] Bales, *op.cit.*

[55] Louis Joseph Rouleau, *Desire, Eros and Fulfillment: St. Bonaventure's Anthropology and Mysticism of Desire* (Catholic University of America, Ph.D. Dissertation, 2012).

of an abundant God who is good, all good, supremely good, all
the time and to everyone.

CHAPTER FOUR

THE SEVEN SORROWFUL MYSTERIES OF STUFF: YOUNG ADULTS, CONSUMERISM AND THE UNCLUTTERED SOUL

This chapter is about stuff and young adults.[1] First, it's about stuff - what we buy and sell, what we collect and store, what we pitch and toss away. It's about what piles up in our closets, what pokes out from under our beds and hides in our basements, what gets stored in our garages and what gets buried and made invisible in our landfills. Something is changing dramatically in our relationship to stuff and in our image of ourselves because of the stuff we use and throw away. Our obsession with stuff makes it easy to treat people like stuff and to traffic people like stuff.[2] So, I want to talk theologically about stuff.

This chapter is also about young adults and how stuff affects them. I am referring to the so-called Mosaic generation, between the ages of 18 and 29. They are an amazing group of adults who are not only different from the generations that preceded them but are, as one author noted, "discontinuously different."[3] This is the generation that is developing dramatically new attitudes and different practices in almost every area of life, including religion.

Mosaics are the first generation to live with the volume and velocity of unprecedented technological, social, cultural, religious,

---

[1] This presentation was given as the Seventh Annual John Paul II Social Justice Lecture at Felician College in Lodi, NJ. on April 24, 2014.

[2] Cf. David B. Couturier, "A Franciscan Theology of Stuff: Consumerism, Human Trafficking and Franciscan Action," at http://franciscanaction.org/article/francis-can-theology-stuff-consumerism-human-trafficking-and-franciscan-action/

[3] Attributed to Bob Buford in David Kinnaman, *You Lost Me: Why Young Christians are Leaving the Church* (Grand Rapids, MI: Baker Books, 2011), p. 37.

economic and psychological change.[4] They are not like Boomers and even Gen X'ers who are always catching up to change. This is the generation that has seismic change in its DNA. Because of this, they have perspectives, attitudes and concerns that are distinct to them.

And for that reason, they have a discrete attitude towards social justice that is often underappreciated. It is my thesis that they are developing a prophetic imagination with filters that allow them to see what is happening in politics and what is affecting our relationships to one another and to the planet in a powerfully new way. But, their prophetic imagination is not impacting the Church as fully as it could and should. And that is the case for several reasons.

To begin with, this is the first generation of young people that is decidedly "unreligious."[5] While they often see themselves as "spiritual" and still desire a relationship with God, when it comes to church they are "missing in action." This is a generation with "unbounded commitments" and religion, by definition, is a binding phenomenon. There is a lot of research coming out recently about young people in the mosaic generation and their attitudes toward Christianity and Catholicism. They have hard things to say about the positions and behavior of Christians who go to Church. The research indicates that they often find us hypocritical, shallow, overprotective, defensive and deaf to their real doubts about what those of us "in religion" simply take for granted.[6] The fact that between 60 and 80% of those young adults who went to church regularly as teens will be gone from church for good by the time they are 25 has only driven a deeper wedge between the generations when it comes to church and its teachings on social justice.[7] Unlike the controlling paradigm and prophetic imagination of Boomers that is shaped by the twin (and sometimes odd) correlates of biblical imagery and modernist aspirations, the prophetic imagination of young adults doesn't easily tap into registered eccle-

---

[4] David Kinnaman and Gabe Lyons, *UnChristian: What a New Generation Really Thinks about Christianity* (Grand Rapids, MI: Baker Books, 2007).

[5] David Sawler, *Goodbye Generation: A Conversation about why Youth and Young Adults Leave the Church* (Hamilton, ON: Ponder Publishing, 2008).

[6] Gabe and Lyons, *op. cit.*

[7] Kinnaman, *op.cit.,*

sial formats. Thus, they are hardly recognized as prophetic by the very churches that formed them.

And that's a shame. Young adults have a lot of passion and concern about social justice and I believe they have a prophetic imagination that is different from that of previous generations. One of their concerns is about stuff and how stuff is changing us, making us and our planet sick.

YOUNG ADULTS AND THE CONSUMER CULTURE

Dr. Charles Derber, professor of sociology at Boston College, speaks about a quiet revolution going on among young adults over the issue of stuff. He writes:

> A quiet revolutionary struggle is brewing in the minds of the U.S. "millennial" generation, those 80 million Americans between the ages of 16 and 34. They are wrestling with the fundamental edict of capitalism: Buy and you shall be happy. The millennials have not rejected consumerism, but they have also not embraced it fully. They experience its very real downsides – that also afflict millions of older Americans and go to heart of capitalist sustainability and morality.[8]

The mosaic or millennial generation has been especially hard hit by the effects of the Great Recession of 2008. Their prospects for the so-called American dream have gotten slimmer, as jobs disappeared and income inequality grew. They have seen their debt levels balloon and the inevitable and sure bond between a good education and solid employment broken. They are the first generation displaced by the realities of the reinvention of work and the radically new rules of the new economy.[9]

Along the way, as the economy has slowed and institutions have failed them, young adults are less sure about modernity's foundational dogma of "inevitable human progress." As one mo-

---

[8] Charles Derber, "Consumerism and its Discontents," *TruthOut* (May 27, 2013) accessed at: http://truth-out.org/opinion/item/16582-consumerism-and-its-discontents.

[9] Thomas Piketty, *Capital in the 21ª Century* (Cambridge: Belknap Press of Harvard University Press, 2014).

saic young adult put it, America's economic ladder to success (college→good job→marriage→house→family→cushy retirement) is in splinters.[10] No rung on that ladder is secure anymore and mosaics know it. Therefore, mosaics have become more suspicious of our "consumer" culture. Again, Dr. Derber recounts the shape of that suspicion.

In a recent study of Boston-area college students on their views of America's "consumer culture," he found young adults worried about the following seven aspects of today's form of consumption:

1. It creates fierce competitive pressure to have more and newer stuff.
2. It complicates their lives, always worrying about how to maintain, pay for and use all the things they buy.
3. It distracts from a quality of life with their family and friends.
4. It creates a "dirty" lifestyle that makes them and the planet sick.
5. It leads to more inequality, with people seeking more at the expense of others.
6. It detracts from political engagement, as America subordinates its social relationships to economic advantages.
7. It imprisons them in a life full of products and empty of meaning.[11]

THE SEVEN SORROWFUL MYSTERIES OF STUFF

Haltingly young adults are beginning to demonstrate misgivings with a consumer culture that another time and generation would have accepted as undeniable evidence of social progress. Stuff and lots of it were once the sure sign that one had "made it" in America. So, what's the problem with stuff? Let me name seven things. Let's call them the "seven sorrowful mysteries of stuff."

1. Sustainability.

---

[10] Lisa Collins, "Happiness Is The New Success: Why Millennials Are Reprioritizing," (January 23, 2012) found at: https://joinmosaic.com/blog/happiness/.
[11] Derber, *op.cit.*

2. Stress.
3. Self-Image.
4. Insecurity.
5. Violence/ Human Trafficking.
6. Cluttering of the Soul.
7. False Picture of God.

Perhaps the first and most obvious problem with the accumulation of stuff has to be in the sheer volume of its production and waste. Today, while Americans represent 5% of the world's population, we generate about 30% of the world's garbage.[12] In a lifetime, the average American will throw away about 600 times his or her body weight, leaving behind a trail of 90,000 pounds of trash by the end of one's life.

The sheer size and scope of the stuff we are hatching and trashing are unsustainable. As the Hard Rain Project Group discusses:

> In the past fifty years, humans have consumed more resources- or stuff- than in all previous history. At the beginning of the 1900s, some 40% of the stuff used in the wealthier parts of the world was renewable – farm, fishery or forestry products- but by the end of that century the figure was below 10%, with the majority of materials now made from metals and minerals or derived from fossil fuels.[13]

We know that, if everybody consumed the way we do, we would need three to five planets to supply for our needs. Every year we toss into our landfills, just by way of example, four million eye glasses, 1.3 billion pounds of tires, 135 million cell phones, and 10 million bicycles.[14]

The first problem with stuff, as we conceive of and treat it today, is that it doesn't go away. We may box it in our garages, cram

---

[12] Robert Malone, "World's Worst Waste," Forbes (May 5, 2006   ) accessed at: http://www.forbes.com/2006 /05/23/ waste-worlds-worst-cx_rm_0524waste.html.

[13] See more at: www.hardrainproject.comstuff#sthash.KRC8UXIV.dpuf.

[14] Katie Arnold-Ratliff, "Trash Facts" Huffington Post (June 3, 2013) accessed: http://www.huffingtonpost.com/2013/06/03/trash-facts-garbage-statistics_n_3361201.html.

it into our closets, haul it away to foreign landfills, but it doesn't go away. Stuff has a way of complicating and dominating our lives. In a sense, in a consumer culture we are the ones who become consumed and overwhelmed by the stuff we accumulate. The Rev. Rick Warren, the author of *The Purpose-Driven Life*, says it cogently:

> Life keeps getting more complicated. And, on top of that, we keep adding more and more stuff to our lives. The problem with stuff is, the more you have, the more it takes to take care of it all – the more you have to clean it, the more you have to protect it, the more you have to insure it, and the more you have to repair it.

> It isn't too long before stuff dominates your life. My guess is you probably have more stuff than your parents did. In fact, today we have an entire industry that we didn't even have 50 years ago. It's called the personal storage units. It's like you don't even have enough room in your house anymore, so you have to put it in a storage unit and pay rent to hold all your stuff.[15]

The extent of clutter's domination of our lives comes through a recent ethno-archaeological study of U.S. family homes. A team of cultural anthropologists at the *UCLA Center on the Everyday Lives of Families* (CFEL) recently published the results of a four year study of how everyday Americans live their lives at home, how they inter-relate, what they use, accumulate and store.[16] They wanted to know how Americans interact with what they have, what impact stuff has on how they function, and what stuff reveals about our social identities. What they found was intriguing.

One of the first things they discovered was that the majority of those middle-class families studied no longer have enough room in their homes for all their stuff. Their stuff was now spilling out into their yards and into their garages. They found that 75% of garages in the study had no room to store a car in it. The typical

---

[15] Rev. Rick Warren, "The Problem with Stuff," (July 26, 2013) accessed at: https://groups.google.com/forum/#!topic/komselgbik/qG8UVOMn36I.

[16] Jeanne E. Arnold, et al. *Life at Home in the Twenty-First Century* (Los Angeles, CA: Cotsen Institute of Archaeology Press, 2012).

garage had about 300 to 650 boxes and storage bins that could no longer fit in the house.

We seem to be developing an America where we have more shoes than we can wear, more toys and electronics than we can use, more cups than we can drink from and more furniture than we can sit on and a culture that is loath to sort and purge. It causes new and elevated levels of stress, especially in women, the UCLA study found. But, we continue this mad pursuit of stuff, nonetheless.

Stuff is bulging out of our closets, poking out from under our beds, hauled away and made invisible in expensive storage units, demonstrating a strange new ambivalence over stuff. We don't use it and we won't share it. Because of this, we need larger and larger places to stack our things. And, as one author puts it, our garages have become the new junk drawer all across America.

What is this ambivalent and paradoxical fascination we have with stuff? It has to do with our self-image and our identity as Americans and it starts early.

IDENTITY AND THE PROBLEM OF CLUTTER

Many factors go into the construction of a healthy self-image, but it is clear that cultural and social influences are increasingly critical in the development of a strong and stable identity. Today's children construct their self-concepts within the strong social context of a culture of consumption, such that every aspect of their lives is touched by the "need and greed" mentality of modern aggressive consumerism. Studies show that children as young as four are now seriously and continuously targeted by marketers for their ability to influence their parents' economic decisions.

By the time a child is three, he or she already recognizes more than 100 brand logos. Not surprisingly, Disney is one of the most ubiquitously recognized-by-child brands in the country. Second in the running is McDonald's. Child brand recognition is very big business. Advertisers spend $12 billion dollars per year to reach the youth market, dipping ever deeper into childhood, even into the toddler years, for their "consumer potential." And it has impact.

In a 2010 study of "Children's Understanding of Brand Symbolism," Dr. Anna McAlister of the University of Wisconsin-Madison noted that – "Children as young as three are feeling social pressure and understand that consumption of certain brands can help them through life."[17] Hooked at three!

Children receive an endless barrage of TV messages about the connection between self-image, identity and product. Experts tell us that this "consumption mentality" is eroding childhood and evidence is mounting that children are suffering the physical, social, emotional and cognitive deficits that arise from consumerism's assault on childhood.[18]

But, after all is said and done, what is so troubling about an identity shaped by stuff? Philosophers tell us that consumerism proceeds from a reductionist philosophy of the human person, one that too narrowly defines men and women only by their economic potential and the satisfaction of their material wants. Consumerism reduces us to what we can earn, spend and purchase. Consumerism turns our values upside down and inside out. Truth, beauty and goodness are no longer ordered to and measured by the divine. These values are reduced to emotional tools and slogans meant to serve largely commercial interests. In this way, Beabout and Echeverria remind us, wisdom, virtue, community, intimacy, happiness and the common good are inverted and made to serve the economic aspirations and financial greed of the marketplace.[19]

Starting very early in life, we are made to define ourselves by what we have and not by what we are. We learn to gauge ourselves by the changing tides of style and the shifting weight of public taste so that our identity is always in flux and ever vulnerable to the mood and tempers of the time.

There is not only a personal toll exacted by our culture of clutter; there is also a deeply social one, as well.

---

[17] Anna McAllister, "Children's Understanding and Brand Symbolism," *Psychology and Marketing* 27:3 (March, 2010), pp. 203-228.

[18] Judith Schor, *Born to Buy: The Commercialized Child in the New Consumer Culture* (New York: Scribner, 2004).

[19] Gregory R. Beabout & Eduardo J. Eccheverria, "The Culture of Consumerism: A Catholic and Personalist Critique," *Journal of Markets and Morality* 5:2 (Fall 2002), p. 342.

CLUTTER AND THE PROBLEM OF SECURITY

A few years ago, Marquette University professor and moral theologian, Fr. Bryan Massingale did an intriguing study of our notion of "national security," as it was developing after the terrorist attacks of 9/11. He explored the evolving understanding of security as it was being devised in the various "national security" documents of the Bush administration and compared it to the biblical understanding of security as found in both testaments of Scripture.[20] His conclusion is instructive.

He found that consumerism had become the engine behind our understanding of freedom and security. A detailed analysis of our national security documents indicated that our very notion of American freedom was migrating from some fundamental correspondence to a broad set of inalienable human rights and the laws of what the Founders' called "Nature's God" to a somewhat mechanical equation with economic freedom. American freedom was beginning to mean nothing more and nothing less than economic freedom, the freedom to buy and sell, to shop and have stuff.

And, with this as a foundational principle, American security was also being recalibrated to mean economic security. We were no longer defending an expansive and broad American "way of life." We were defending the right to shop. In fact, these national security documents ratified that American security was based not just on economic security (the freedom to buy, sell and shop); it was premised on an exceptional notion of America's economic *primacy*. That is, we are free when we shop and consume as we will, but we consider ourselves only truly free when we are on top of the economic pile. And, because of this, we reserve the right to defend ourselves by any means necessary against any nation or group that threatens our economic primacy. America's clutter culture has become not just a generic or harmless form of consumerism. It has become a military consumerism. Here is how Fr. Massingale puts this issue:

---

[20] Bryan Massingale, "The Security We Seek," *Pax Christi USA* (June 2010), p. 4. accessed at: http://paxchristiusa1.files.wordpress.com/2011/01/june2010newsletterweb. pdf.

Underlying the American pursuit and understanding of "security" is a deep sense of fear and vulnerability felt in the aftermath of the homeland attacks of 9-11. Our policy documents constantly play upon and remind us of the threats we face and our vulnerability to cold-blooded evil. Our way of life, a life of undisputed military dominance and unfettered economic prosperity, is under attack from nefarious enemies, both known and unknown, seen and unseen. Our fear and vulnerability demand that we maintain and bolster our military preeminence, in order to insure our continued economic prosperity and consumer lifestyle. Indeed, our national security strategy makes clear the connection between military might and consumerism in ways that we seldom articulate.[21]

What Fr. Massingale reveals is a troubling dimension of our clutter culture, the "underside," if you will, of consumerism today – "the belief that having a disproportion of goods is appropriate, and that using force or violence to get or keep these goods is both necessary and legitimate" and that a "consumer society- the American way of life- depends upon violence, or the threat of violence, to maintain itself."[22]

What we are dealing with here is not only a personal sense of vulnerability but a social one, as well. In the inevitable clash of private interests that is at the heart of the Enlightenment project, there is, as the philosopher Thomas Hobbes declared, an inevitable "war of all against all" being devised that can only be resolved by what Nietzsche called "the will to power." The underside of the modernity that young adults find so suspicious is the "problem of violence."[23]

---

[21] *ibid.*

[22] *Ibid.*

[23] John Milbank speaks of an "ontology of violence" that sublates all modern social theories in J. Milbank, *Theology and Social Theory: Beyond Secular Reason* (Cambridge, MA: Blackwell, 1993).

STUFF AND HUMAN TRAFFICKING

For the past several years, I have been speaking, writing and working on the issue of human trafficking, a multi-billion dollar global industry that continues to enslave men, women and children in all parts of the world, including the suburbs of America, in sexual and commercial industries of every sort.[24] What we now know is that there are long corporate supply chains that allow human traffickers to use our hotels, car rental agencies, big box chain stores and our most cherished companies to enslave vulnerable men, women and children to make our tee-shirts, harvest our chocolate and produce our cell phones in a deadly race for profit at any and all human cost. Unfortunately, each one of us participates on an almost daily basis in the whole cycle of human slavery today. We each have a slavery and human trafficking footprint.

We have developed such an automatic and entitled expectation around stuff that we rarely ask ourselves where it comes from, who makes it, and whose lives are sacrificed for the gross ubiquity of stuff in our homes.

The point I want to make is this. There is a connection between our blithe attitude towards stuff and the proliferation of human trafficking around the world.

We refuse to acknowledge that the stuff bulging out of our closets, poking out from under our beds, rotting away in our landfills outside of town, was once creation, a divine endowment and a promissory note on future glory. Instead, our consumerist mindset has transformed creation into matter and we have made it into stuff. We once believed that we lived in a world enchanted by the divine.[25] But, no more! Enchantment has become waste management. We have stripped the world of its glory and divine import. What we have done to nature, we are now doing to humankind. People have become stuff!

---

[24] David B. Couturier, "A Franciscan Theology of Stuff: Consumerism, Human Trafficking and Franciscan Action," (Franciscan Action Network, 2013) accessed at: http://franciscanaction.org/article/franciscan-theology-stuff-consumerism-human-trafficking-and-franciscan-action.

[25] Cf. Charles Taylor, *A Secular Age* (The Belknap Press of Harvard University Press, 2007).

CLUTTER AND THE FRANCISCAN IMAGINATION

Thus far I have given you some troubling thoughts about the negative consequences of today's growing aggressive consumerism and the clutter it delivers. But, there is good news and there is a hopeful way out. There's a prophetic imagination that can guide us. Not surprisingly, I find it in a Franciscan imagination, a way of seeing oneself, the world and God that has been counter-cultural and counter-intuitive since it was first developed by a young adult at the age of 25, Francis of Assisi, in the 13th century.

When he was an adolescent, Francis wanted nothing more than to be a soldier. The son of a wealthy cloth merchant, Francis lived in a time of incredible violence and amazing greed. Although well-known for his fashion, excesses and party-ways, his adolescence was framed within the backdrop of the fierce economic skirmishes and violent revenges that raged between Assisi and the neighboring town of Perugia. The fantasies of this fashion-conscious young adult revolved around becoming a knight for the good and glory of Assisi.

It was a dream that was encouraged by his father, an up and coming new merchant, who supported his son's youthful fantasies and dramatic excesses. Francis' father wanted nothing more than to break the stranglehold that the traditional patronage system of inherited money had on the ordinary people of Assisi. His father wanted to get money the "new-fashioned" way, by "making it". And so, Pietro Bernadone enticed his son, Francis, with images of glory and outfitted him in the best military gear available. He proudly sent him off to war.

But, Francis' dream of a military career came crashing down quickly, as he was taken prisoner at the Battle of Collestrada. He learned the brutal lesson that the reality of war was unlike the fantasy of war. The sight of hundreds of young men dismembered and strewn along the bloody floor of the Umbrian Valley put an end to all romantic visions of glory and began a restless and relentless search for religious meaning.

When finally released from the prisoner of war camp, Francis returned an unsettled young adult. He had lost his adolescent dream. He scoured the hills and chapels surrounding Assisi looking for an alternative with which to replace it. The God of his youth, the imperial God of the Crusades, the God of the extravagantly dressed soldier bishops of Europe, no longer made sense to him. And so, he roamed the back alleys and poorer haunts of Assisi searching for meaning and struggling for a new and more immediate access to the divine. He found it first in the embrace of a leper.

In a dramatic encounter that would shape the rest of his life, Francis confronted his natural revulsions and embraced a leper he met on the road. In that embrace, God wrapped Francis in a consolation he had been searching for. God enlivened his social and religious imagination with a profound revelation of who God really was and what God really wanted.

In the time of Francis, the leper was the foremost casualty of a society obsessed with violence and money. The leper was the first to fall through the cracks of society, as clerics and rulers lined their pockets and their consciences with the spoils of their never-ending wars. As a result of their meeting on the road, however, Francis now saw something different about life and faith. What Francis saw was the goodness of God, expressed not in puffing oneself up but in emptying oneself out in love. He experienced this in a God who reached down with mercy, always mercy, and revealed Himself as a God who is good, all good, supremely good, all the time and to everyone.[26]

It was for mercy's sake that Francis determined to pull back, far back, from the social obsessions of his greedy and violent world. He would question the inevitability of violence and aggression, starting with simple gestures.

First, he would greet everyone he met with a simple wish of *"pax et bonum"* (peace and all good things). It was not just a slogan or clever moniker for Francis. He was building a new social imagination. He was committed to seeing everyone in his field of vision, not as competitor or a consumer of his father's goods and not as an enemy and threat, as he had been taught from his youth. As a prophetic young adult, he wanted a new social imagination, one that was secured by a bond with the divine. Thus, he resolved that as a friar he would start every encounter in the new ethical space of "peace and all good." And, more than that, Francis would enact his life as a choreography of brothers and sisters. Francis would flat-

---

[26] Giacomo Todeschini, *Franciscan Wealth: From Voluntary Poverty to Market Society* (St. Bonaventure, NY: The Franciscan Institute, 2009).

ten the hierarchies of his day and build congregations and communities not stacked with superiors and subjects. The universe Francis wanted to live in and the one that he saw was a dance of brothers and sisters, Brother Sun and Sister Moon, with everything interconnected and bonded to him because of their original connection to the good and gracious God who created and sustained everything in a harmony of goodness.[27]

Francis didn't see stuff. He saw creation. He didn't hear the one note of profit being played in the background of every transaction. He heard a symphony of created things in what Sr. Ilia Delio calls "the unbearable wholeness of being" radiating out truth, beauty and goodness in every nook and cranny of this amazingly diversified and interwoven canopy of incarnated grace.[28]

For Francis, matter mattered. Nature wasn't an escape into the woods for him, a reward "in the wild" that he took only occasionally for having endured the rat race of a cluttered culture. No. Nature was so much more than that. Nature was life and it was breath and spirit, pulsating a divine energy within and all around him. His fraternity with creation, his brotherhood and sisterhood with nature, was his antidote to the greed and violence of his day. This is Francis' first lesson for uncluttering the soul. We need to develop a new attitude toward nature, toward the things of this earth.

We must learn how to respect our forests, our seas and rivers, our mountain trails and our underwater caverns. We must turn away from modernity's reductionism that sees the earth as just "matter." We need to re-inscribe our souls with the awe and wonder that receives the earth and everything in it as "creation."

Francis refused to pile up things or clutter his soul. Nature was not an enemy and it didn't need to be treated with violence. And so, he lived what others called a "poor" life. But, Francis never saw it that way, because his refusal to own and dominate anything was for him a free and rich life. His bonds of fraternity, even with creation, didn't make him insecure in the least. In fact, he felt amazingly secure in the harmony of goodness that he experienced.

---

[27] Mary Beth Ingham, CSJ, *The Harmony of Goodness* (St. Bonaventure, NY: Franciscan Institute, 2012).

[28] Ilia Delio, *The Unbearable Wholeness of Being* (Maryknoll: Orbis Books, 2013).

UNCLUTTERING THE SOUL

Let me spend just a few more moments talking about the ways we can unclutter our souls using a Franciscan imagination. Young adults may not be going to Church but they are decidedly interested in their spirit. A meditation on clutter could be a crucial connecting point between the young adults of today and the young adult- Francis- of the 13th century. But, let me briefly stray a bit further back to Augustine.

When I was writing my first book, *The Fraternal Economy: A Pastoral Psychology of Franciscan Economics*, I studied how consumerism affects our transcendent desires.[29] We learn something profound about our hearts and our spirit from St. Augustine when he reminds us that our "hearts are restless until they rest" in God. He teaches us that we are constantly yearning for and hungering after the fullness of truth, beauty and goodness. And we scour the world, as he did, to find it. But, as he powerfully reminds us, we will never find it, we will never hold it, and we will never enjoy it until we secure this triad of truth, beauty and goodness in the divine. When all is said and done, what we are searching for is nothing other than God. And what amazed Augustine was that he didn't need to go "out there" to find God. He didn't need to get lost in stuff, trying everything, tasting everything, buying everything to find the beauty, truth and goodness he was yearning for. They were always and already within him. As he says famously,

Late have I loved you, O Beauty ever ancient, ever new, late have I loved you! You were within me, but I was outside, and it was there that I searched for you. In my unloveliness I plunged into the lovely things which you created. You were with me, but I was not with you. Created things kept me from you; yet if they had not been in you they would have not been at all. You called, you shouted, and you broke through my deafness. You flashed, you shone, and you dispelled my blindness. You breathed your fragrance on me; I drew in breath and now I pant for you. I have tasted you, now I hunger and thirst for more. You touched me, and I burned for your peace. (*Confessions*, Bk 10, 27, 38).

---

[29] David B. Couturier, *The Fraternal Economy: A Pastoral Psychology of Franciscan Economics* (South Bend, IN: Cloverdale Books, 2007).

Thus, Augustine reminds us that de-cluttering the soul begins with a re-prioritizing of one's goals and perspectives. It involves a fundamental shift from busy-ness to happiness by way of a simple focus on creative blessedness.

But, there is a problem. Clutter and consumerism are not neutral forces in the soul. The problem with clutter and a culture of consumerism is that they begin to erode the very desire we have for the divine. They eat away at this transcendent desire in three ways. The first way is by proliferating our commercial desires to the point of overwhelming and overshadowing our transcendent desires. Here is what I have previously written about the proliferation of desire:

> Marketing and advertising collapse the distinction between necessity and superfluity. The reach of need and want run to infinity. The consumer is trained to exceed his or her satisfaction and to desire an infinite array of goods, products and services.[30]

So, what marketers and advertisers do is to train us from the time we are very young to want more, infinitely more and more, so that over time we have no idea what it is that we need and how what we need may be different from what we want. The two aspects of commercial desire (want and need) begin to leak into one another and conflate the infinity implicit in transcendence with the innumerability involved in commercial desire.

The second thing that happens to our transcendent desires in an aggressive consumer culture is that they become materialized and commodified. By that I mean that the desires that once were meant to be oriented to the world of the divine are deflated into simply a desire for some marketable product. I have said it this way —

> Secularization collapses or cancels out the incarnate view of the world, which once held that the divine and the material abide in a hypostatic union and commercium.[31]

---

[30] Couturier, *op. cit.*, p. 81.
[31] Ibid.

The human desire for the infinite God relocates to stuff. In an aggressive consumer culture, we trade the infinity of God for the infinity of goods. And when we trade in God, we don't give up our need for the infinite. Infinity, as the great theologian Karl Rahner once held, is the horizon of every thought we think and every act we will.[32] When we trade in God, we simply transfer that need for the realm of the infinite to the realm of stuff. And advertisers and corporations are loving it!

The third thing that happens to our desires is that they inevitably become polarizing. Marita Wesley-Clough is a retail trend expert for Hallmark Cards. She forecasts where things are going in the business world. A few years ago, she predicted increased levels of isolation, tribalization and polarization in the American marketplace. She wrote:

> Look for increased polarization – whether political, economic, religious or philosophical. Regardless of age, ethnicity or affiliation, individuals long for the security of alignment with those "like us." Ethnic 'tribes' within countries and cities; elite social clubs; gathering of loyal brand devotees, as well as group identities created via fashion, language or symbols. Increasing gravitation toward communities of like minds- people whose interests, worldviews or values reinforce our own.[33]

And so, as our desires expand and induce polarization in our interactions, we find that our transcendent desires for that which is true, beautiful and good, now unhooked from their moorings to the divine, become threatened and vulnerable, reduced as they are to the shifting and unstable wants, needs and desires of the marketplace.

---

[32] Theologian, Karl Rahner, speaks of this as *Vorgriff*, the pre-apprehension of being by which the human spirit "reaches out toward what is nameless and by its very nature is infinite." In Karl Rahner, *Foundations of Catholic Faith: An Introduction to the Idea of Christianity* (New York: Seabury Press, 1978), p. 62; also see: Bulcsu Kal Hoppal, "Karl Rahner's Notion of Vorgriff," *Verbum* 6:2 (November, 2004), p. 451-459.

[33] Marita Wesley-Clough, "Twelve Consumer Trends and Counter Trends for 2004 and Beyond," accessed: 11/15/04, www.retailindustry.about.com/cs/retailtrends/a/bl_trends2004.htm.

SINE PROPRIO AND THE NEW NARRATIVE OF RELATIONALITY

Francis of Assisi saw the dead-end of a culture and an economy based on the twin dynamics of violence and greed. He once said that he didn't want stuff because he didn't want to have to defend that stuff at the end of a sword. He had seen and experienced too much of the violent underside of his own father's greed and his society's craving for revenge. And so, Francis decided to live a life of *"sine proprio,"* with "nothing of his own," where he would simply use, not own, the goods of this earth. By not owning things, he would not be tempted to dominate, deprive or domesticate his brothers and sisters by any trick of hierarchy or superiority.

In developing a new fraternity built on the grounds of *"sine proprio,"* Francis took himself and his brothers out of the dynamic of inevitable violence that trapped Assisi and its surrounding cities. Because Francis and his brothers owned nothing, they had nothing to protect and they had no reason to go to war. Francis used to say often that the only thing we really own are our own sins.

Francis invites us to de-clutter our souls in four ways:

- Return to your deeper and truer desires. Get behind and beyond the fabricated and insecure desires of the marketplace. Find the truth, beauty and goodness you're looking for.
- Divest yourself of all that obscures your clear view and ready access to God, yourself, your world and everything in it. Release yourself from the fog and frenzy of consumerism. Learn to live with what you need and re-learn what it means to share.
- Treat the world and everything in it gently. We have been so trained to enter spaces with suspicion, competition and aggression. We need re-think our initial encounter with the world and with ourselves, the one person with whom we can be harshest of all. We should greet everyone with a merciful social imagination of *"pax et bonum"* (peace and all good).
- We should stop playing the part of victim and victimizer that we have been assigned in the commercial liturgy of the consumer-based society.[34] Let me explain.

---

[34] A mosaic-age Capuchin friar, Erik Lenhart, finds correspondence between the first three steps and St. Bonaventure's three levels of the spiritual life: purgation, illumination and union. I thank him for this insight.

The theological and psychological logic of "*sine proprio*" is profound. Francis arrived at this theory of "*sine proprio*" by meditating on the coming of Christ and the poverty of His Incarnation. The Word of God, through whom and for whom all things are created, came to this world with nothing and died on the Cross with nothing. And bringing the realization of this (and his own) poverty to prayer and to liturgy taught Francis another profound lesson, i.e., that ultimately we are not the victims in this world.

Using the insights of theologian, James Allison, we learn how the liturgy revolves around one truth and that is that *we* are not the victims of the universe. Because of our sins, however great or small they may be, we are always victimizers and perpetrators; we are always sinful. Christ, on the other hand, is the only true Victim and the One Sacrifice, poured out and given out once and for all.[35]

Clutter exists to fill in the spaces, to cover the cracks, to disguise the holes in our armored security and armed surety that we have been done wrong and need a never ending supply of consolations. Advertisers and marketers are banking on every insecurity they can uncover so as to hawk a product that will serve as a palliative and somehow demonstrate that we have gotten over our fears and conquered our insecurities, after we have sprayed "Eternity," worn J Brand's "Refuge" or carried Judith Leiber's "New Long Kiss" clutch bag from Nordstrom's.

Knowing how violence and greed were connected to stuff, how this dynamic obscured the experience of a good and gracious God and how it endangered the peace of his world, St. Francis refused to play the part of the victim or victimizer in a greedy world. He would no longer be the victimizer who had to have more to prove himself and he would no longer be the victim who needed more to find himself.

In this way, he created a group of brothers and sisters in fraternities of mutual donation not competition. He created a new economy, a fraternal economy, where stuff is limited to the "minimum necessary not the maximum allowed."

Francis went so far as to refuse his brothers permission even to touch a coin. He did so because in his day coins were the means by which men and women were judged in society and before God.

---

[35] James Alison, *Undergoing God: Dispatches from the Scene of a Break-In* (London: Darton, Longman and Todd, 2006), pp. 33-49.

A person was only as worthy as the stack of coins he/she carried. Francis refused to allow his brothers and sisters to be put on such an insecure and imprecise scale. No coin, he believed, could capture the ineffable mystery and awesome dignity of each and every individual, however limited or financially poor they might be. Francis would not allow coins or clutter to obscure, invalidate or minimize the goodness of God he saw in people.

Conclusion

Our young adults are onto something in their discomfort and suspicion of our growing culture of clutter. Their prophetic imagination leads them to a more relational and less polarized stance in the world. Increasingly, they want more than success. They want happiness.

For all of us to get a sustainable happiness, we will have to engage our ever deeper desires, those transcendent desires that are being compromised by a consumerism we have tragically equated with "the good life." To secure the love, intimacy, closeness and compassion we so desire, we will have to reach beyond the immediate and refuse to settle for the infinity of goods and our presumptive culture of clutter.

And we in the Church must stand with young adults in the perfect storm of unprecedented and seismic social, cultural, technological, economic and religious changes. By listening attentively to their doubts, we can accompany them in their discoveries of a new prophetic imagination that serves this world, re-bonds us as brothers and sisters, and re-connects us with the God who is good, all good, supremely good, all the time and to everyone. It is the God that Francis came to know and love, in Jesus Christ who is the Lord, forever and ever. Amen.

Section Two
The Fraternal Economy

Introducing the Fraternal Economy

In the last several articles, we have been introduced to many of the challenging aspects of the modern economy, those that affect Franciscans and those they minister: unemployment and underemployment, wage stagnation, income inequality, and the re-invention of work all across the globe. We situated Franciscans within the turbulence of a time that has shifted dramatically from a basically relational-culture, founded on family and group cohesion, to a largely global work-culture, oriented to business and career identities. We argued that Franciscans have a part to play in the ongoing discussions about the kind of economics we develop.

Franciscans have been speaking and commenting on finances from the very beginning. Turning away from a monastic model of religious commitment and pivoting toward a more urban and involved-in-the-world service brought Franciscans face to face with the ways that bad economics hurt the poor. And so, the early Franciscans studied contracts and accounting and they commented on the fundamental shape of economic activity.

We suggested that the rise of economic liberalism bypassed much of this Franciscan conversation, in such a way that the architects of the modern economy sidelined religion as a worthy partner in the construction of a more just and secure world. As we have already seen, security would eventually be framed largely in commercial terms. Freedom itself would be wrenched from its prior convergence with objective theo-centric values and be reduced simply to a matter of choice, the ability to buy and sell, acquire and accumulate at will. Economics and religion would exist in separate universes, with hardly a point of reference between them.

We turn now to thoughts about the Franciscan attempt to develop a more "relational" and less "competitive" form of economics among them. Franciscans have always been suspicious of models that require privacy, isolation and aggressive as foundational elements. They are looking for forms of economic activity

69

that build communion rather than competition. They have come to realize that many of the current economic models actually increase insecurity and justify exclusion and inequality as simply the collateral damage of the "invisible hand" of the Market.

It is time that we go behind the screen of all the issues we have located in the first section. Franciscans are still having conversations about finances, but those conversations are not simply about the effects of tough economic times (i.e. unemployment, wage stagnation and greed). They are about first principles and assumptions of economics today. They are re-thinking what others are taking for granted – that the economics we have are the only form or shape that can bring us security, stability, happiness and progress.

Friars are thinking first about their own economic activity and trying to create a more "fraternal economy" among themselves. These thoughts come from a hard realization: that, despite their vowed commitment to serve the world in a spirit of communion and as "gospel brothers," they are living out their vows in a structure of inequality that borders on indifference. That is, they recognize that the world's economic patterns are very much their own, even if our theological foundations are wildly different.

Friars in the Northern Hemisphere (the so-called "developed" world) have realized that their Franciscan brothers and sisters in the Southern Hemisphere (the so-called "developing" world) live in a world of structured exclusion and embedded inequalities. And it is not simply the world's models that carry this inequality, so do our own internal economic models. Our own Franciscan structures participate in this injustice. In many places, our own economic activity feeds the inequality that our theological sentiments deny and hope to transcend.

This second section focuses on how one community of Franciscans, the Capuchins, is trying to re-organize their economic activity by making it more relational and fair across the cultural and class boundaries of our religious world. We expose this experiment by going back to the documents that first introduced it as a worldwide effort. It is still an experiment.

We introduce the fraternal economy in a specific way – as an educational or formational task. After laying out what the Capuchin-Franciscans mean by a "fraternal economy" and what such a turn might mean in our individual and corporate behaviors, we turn our attention to the forms of education that would make it real. We build what may be called a "pastoral psychology" of our Franciscan economics. It is a heady section of new assumptions and principles, based on the Franciscan intellectual tradition.

It is time to put the Franciscan conversation about economics "out there" where others can read and comment on it. Franciscans have been "on the street" since their first founding moments. We make no claim to perfection about what we are thinking and pondering. We are, in many ways, amateurs in our own economic world. But, we are committed amateurs, *jongleurs de Dieu*, committed to making the world better, safer and more secure, especially for the poor that we try to serve day after day.

CHAPTER FIVE
THE DEVELOPMENT OF 'THE FRATERNAL ECONOMY'

It is not from the benevolence of the butcher, the brewer, or the baker, that
we expect our dinner but from their regard to their own interest. We address
ourselves, not to their humanity but to their self love.[1]

Thus does Adam Smith (1723-1790), the father of modern economics, describe the social motivations and economic interests of
individuals, families and businesses in the modern world. Aggressive individual self-concern and business profit-maximizing are
what shape and condition the social good, the common interest
and the shared welfare of nations. He argues that men and women
are constituted of "natural selfishness and rapacity" and are driven
by "vain and insatiable desires."[2] He is not alone in this belief. In a
similar vein, David Hume (1711-1776), the father of empiricism,
argued earlier that "every man [sic] ought to be supposed a knave
and to have no other end, in all his actions than private interest."[3]

It is not particularly surprising or enlightening to hear (moral)
philosophers maintain the depravity of the struggling masses. The
genius of the early defenders of economic liberalism, however,
was the argument that private vice could be channeled for public
virtue and individual greed could be harnessed for common good
as the naturally selfish are, as Smith declared, "led by an invisible
hand to promote an end that was no part of their motivation."[4]

---

[1] Adam Smith, *An Inquiry into the Nature and Causes of the Wealth of Nations*, 1776.
Reprint. (Indianapolis: Liberty Classic, 1976), p. 26-27.

[2] Adam Smith, *The Theory of Moral Sentiments*, 1759. Reprint. (Indianapolis: Liberty
Classics, 1976), p. 184.

[3] This passage is quoted from G. Brennan and J. Buchanan, *The Reason of Rules: The
Collected Works of James M. Buchanan.* Vol. 10. (Indianapolis: Liberty Fund, 2000), p. 68.

[4] Smith [1776] (1976), p. 453-471.

To begin a conversation about the social relations, mutual exchanges and communal expectations of a religious organization, one must acknowledge from the start the pervasive economic forces that condition it. One must understand the prevailing paradigm that shapes the context around it.[5] In the West, for more than two hundred years, that dominant picture has been that of *homo economicus,* an economic theory and horizon of expectations and assumptions founded on the belief that social development is driven by the inevitable propensity of individuals to maximize their self-interests. It is a model of human behavior that identifies only the intelligent pursuit of private gain with rationality.[6]

Economics is thus defined as an activity aimed at reducing scarcity and maximizing advantage through the division of labor and material exchanges.[7] In this way, human beings are in inevitable competition for the scarce resources of the earth. The logical goal of their social activity is the maximization of personal interests and the pursuit of individual happiness with the minimum (i.e. efficient) level of social interference or intrusion. In this model, social relations in the market square are little more than an intelligent compromise and an efficient calculation. Individuals are perceived as "sovereign islands" with scant interdependence and just enough social interaction to pursue individual "happiness." Thus, Francis Woerhling claims that the individualistic economic agent of this (classical) *homo economicus solipsisticus theory* "grudgingly accepts the need to subject his maximization to rules and restraints to earn a reputation. He will tolerate interference with his objectives as long as he has to and with a certain amount of frustration" so as to achieve one's personal ends and meet one's individual needs.[8]

The failure to consider a truly communal life in the economic order shapes the critique of economic theory developed by Richard E. Mulcahey:

---

[5] For an understanding of economic paradigms, cf. Lester Thurow, *Dangerous Currents* (New York: Random House, 1983) and Richard J. Bernstein, *The Restructuring of Economic and Political Theory* (New York: Harcourt, Brace, Jovanovitch, 1976).

[6] Herman E. Daly and John B. Cobb, Jr., *For the Common Good: Redirecting the Economy Toward Community, the Environment, and a Sustainable Future* (Boston: Beacon Press, 1989), p. 5-21.

[7] Francis Woerhling, "'Christian' Economics," in <u>Markets and Morality</u> 4:2 (Fall 2001).

[8] *Ibid.*

Individualism sees in society no real unity. What it calls "society" is a mere mechanism, the interplay of the actions of individuals seeking their own ends, or it is a mere sum of economic relations. It postulates a natural order based on unrestrained freedom, on whose unhindered effect the welfare of all depends. The national economy is viewed as a sum of isolated units, which are bound together only by mere exchange relationships… In socialism the concept of the unity of society is distorted. The collective society which it requires presents the unity of "oneness" rather than a union of the many. The individual is only an "associate," not an autonomous personality.[9]

Daly and Cobb claim that modern economic theory originated and developed in the same stream as Calvinism. They go on to claim that "both were bids for personal freedom against the interference of earthly authority" and rooted in the conviction that "beyond a very narrow sphere, motives of self-interest are overwhelmingly dominant."[10] They make the point that economic theory differed from Calvinism "only in celebrating as rational what Calvinism confessed as sinful."[11]

Although still the dominant economic model in the world, the classical economic theory of *homo economicus* is not without its critics. George Soros, in a entitled *The Crisis of Global Capitalism: Open Society Endangered,* laments that "the ascendancy of the profit motive and the decline in the effectiveness of the collective decision-making process have reinforced each other in a reflexive manner."[12] He goes on to state that "market fundamentalism seeks to abolish collective decision making and to impose the supremacy of market values over all political and social values."[13] What we have today, he says, is a "global economy without a global society."[14]

---

[9] Richard E. Mulcahey, *The Economics of Henreich Pesch,* (New York: Holt, 1952), p. 161.

[10] Daly and Cobb, *op. cit.,* p.6.

[11] *Ibid.*

[12] George Soros, *The Crisis of Global Capitalism: Open Society Endangered* (New York: Public Affairs, 1998), p.xxvi.

[13] *Ibid.,* p. xxvii-xxviii.

[14] *Ibid.,* p. xxix.

In a paper entitled, "Is Economic Theory Wrong About Human Nature?" Pauline Vaillancourt Rosenau claims that serious challenges to traditional, mainstream economic models are emerging from new approaches to economics in the fields of biology, neuroscience, anthropology, psychology, and sociology.[15] In fact, she suggests that major revisions of those theories are needed because traditional economic models are poor predictors of economic behavior. She cites recent experiments in neuroscience that indicate that the non-cooperative pursuit of self-interest actually makes both parties in several experiments worse off. Self-interest does not promote, as traditional economic theory might suggest, simultaneous benefit. In animal experiments, capuchin and tamarin monkeys will discriminate between altruistic and selfish actions, rewarding reciprocity and punishing anti-social behavior.[16]

In traditional economic theory, she maintains, concepts like trust, bonding, and empathy are systematically ignored since it is held *a priori* that individuals cannot but act exclusively on the basis of personal preferences. However, new research in the field of neuro-economics indicates that communities that are consistently low on trust will likely be caught in a poverty trap whereas "high trust societies have higher rates of investment and growth."[17] Whereas traditional economic theories assume that most people are selfish (not altruistic and cooperative), [18]neuro-economists are finding, using MRI imaging, that the human brain is "hard wired" to cooperate rather than compete[19] and "people will tend to behave pro-socially and punish anti-social behavior, at a cost

---

[15] Pauline Vaillancourt Roseneau, Ph.D., "Is Economic Theory Wrong about Human Nature?" (University of Houston School of Public Health: Management and Policy Sciences, 2004).

[16] F.B.M. de Waal and M. Berger, "Payment for Labour in Monkeys: Capuchins Will Voluntarily Share Treats with Other Monkeys that Helped Secure Them," *Nature* 404 (2000) p. 563 and M. D. Hauser, M.K. Chen, et al., "Give Unto Others: Genetically Unrelated Cotton-Top Tamarin Monkeys Preferentially Give Food to Those Who Altruistically Give Food Back," *Proceedings of the Royal Society of London, Series B* 270 (2003), pp. 2363-2370.

[17] P.J. Zak and S. Knack, "Trust and Growth," *The Economic Journal* 111 (2001), pp. 295-321.

[18] R.H. Frank, "Cooperation Through Emotional Commitment," in R.M. Nesse, *Evolution and the Capacity for Commitment* (New York: Russell Sage Foundation, 2001) pp. 57-76.

[19] J.K. Rilling and D.A. Gutman, et al., "A Neural Basis for Social Cooperation," *Neuron* 35:2 (2002), pp. 395-405 and A.J. Sanfrey and J.K. Rilling et al., "The Neural

to themselves, even when the probability of future interactions is extremely low, or zero."[20]

It is not unusual that economic theorists would question their field's fundamental assumptions and appraise, from time to time, its tried and true axioms. It is *indeed* unusual, however, when the critique emerges in the documents of a particular religious congregation of men and one intent on reviewing its own economic practices and social relations, in the light of the Gospel and in fidelity to the spirit of its founder. Such is the project undertaken by the Capuchin-Franciscan Order beginning in the early 1990s. We turn to the documents that emerged from that community's exploration of its economic assumptions and organization. We will trace the theological and spiritual dynamics that gave rise to this community's new call for personal conversion and structural renewal.

'THIS RELIGIOUS ORDER CONSTITUTES A FRATERNITY': THE FRATERNAL IDENTITY AND STRUCTURE OF THE CAPUCHIN-FRANCISCAN ORDER

On September 18, 1996, the General Minister of the Capuchin Order, John Corriveau, OFM Cap. received a letter from John Paul II in which the Pope made an important declaration and clarification about the nature and mission of the Capuchin Order. He wrote,

> This Religious Order constitutes a fraternity, made up of clerics and lay people who share the same religious vocation according to the Capuchin and Franciscan charism, described in its essential characteristics in its own legislation approved by the Church (see Constitutions 4).[21]

Basis of Economic Decision-Making in the Ultimatum Game," *Science* 300:13 (2003) pp. 1755-1758.

[20] G.H. Gintis, "Strong Reciprocity and Human Sociality," *Journal of Theoretical Biology* 206:2 (2000), pp. 169-179.

[21] This quote is found in John Corriveau, *Circular Letter* 11 (February 2, 1997), no.1.1. All references to Circular Letters in this Chapter will be from the book, *To All the Brothers and Sisters of the Order: Circular Letters 1994-2000* (Rome: Cimpcap, 2000).

It was a watershed moment in the history of this religious congregation, in that it clearly defined the charism and plainly identified the mission of Capuchins as that of *fraternal evangelical witness*.
It was, in one sense, the capstone of years of research, reflection
and renewal on the founding charism of Capuchin-Franciscan life,
a project initiated at the Second Vatican Council and sustained by
numerous General Chapters, Plenary Councils and Circular Letters
in the Capuchin Order.[22]

It was as recently as just prior to the Second Vatican Council
that the Capuchin Order considered itself a clerical, not a fraternal,
institute. Although historically always composed of priests and lay
brothers, the Capuchin Order was known primarily for its clerical
ministries and the lay brothers' service that supported them. Within the theological ambit and canonical perspective of a Church
that defined itself (before the Council) as a "perfect society," hierarchically ordered and called by Christ to lead souls back to God,[23]
the Capuchin Order was seen and acted largely as a clerical institute. Understandably, it dedicated itself to the salvation of souls
primarily through its clerical ministries and the auxiliary services
that supported them.[24] Therefore, the contemporary designation
and recognition of the Capuchin Order as a fraternity must give
rise to a radical re-visioning of the Order's mission in the world.

The letter of September 18, 1996, makes it clear that brotherhood, not primarily clerical ministries, defines the character and
spirit of the Capuchin-Franciscan presence in the world. It rep-
resents a powerful mandate of the Church that the international
fraternity re-order pastoral service and evaluate the structures of
the community so that they remain faithful to the integrity of the

---

[22] For clarity's sake, a "General Chapter" is the governing assembly of ex officio
and elected delegates of the Order that meets every six years. A "Plenary Council of the
Order" (or "CPO" or "PCO") is an official assembly of the Order called by the Minister
General and his Council to address important matters of the international fraternity.
"Circular Letters" are occasional epistolaries/letters addressed (primarily) to the brothers
of the Order by the General Minister on matters of fraternal life and service.

[23] Cf. Pius XI, *Mortalium Animos,* January 6, 1928, in which he states, "Christ our
Lord instituted his Church as a perfect society,... which should carry on... the work of
the salvation of the human race."

[24] Cf. John Corriveau, "Gospel Brotherhood in a Changing World," *Circular Letter
20* (March 31, 2002), no. 1.1.

charism of the Capuchin's evangelical fraternal witness.[25] More than that, it returns the Capuchin Order to an original insight, the one that St. Francis of Assisi had when he founded his community to be an order of lesser brothers.

"AND THE LORD GAVE ME BROTHERS"

As an adolescent, Francis of Assisi wanted nothing more than to be a soldier. The son of a wealthy cloth merchant, Pietro Bernadone, Francis lived in a time of incredible violence and amazing greed.[26] His whole childhood and adolescence were framed in the bloody battles and fierce economic skirmishes that raged between Assisi and the neighboring town of Perugia. His adolescent fantasies revolved around the prospect of becoming a knight for the good and glory of Assisi. [27]

It was a dream that was encouraged by his father, an up and coming new merchant who supported his son's youthful fantasies for his own economic purposes. He wanted nothing more than to break the stranglehold that the traditional patronage system of inherited money had on the ordinary people of Assisi. And so, Pietro enticed his son with images of glory and outfitted him in the best military gear available. He proudly sent him off to war.

But, as Armstrong notes, Francis' dream of a military career came crashing down quickly, as he was taken prisoner at the Battle of Collestrada.[28] He learned the brutal lesson that the reality of war was not the fantasy of war. The sight of hundreds of young men dismembered and strewn on the bloody floor of the Umbrian

---

[25] For an understanding of the distinctions between monastic, apostolic and evangelical charisms in religious life, cf. Regis Armstrong, "If My Words Remain in You: Foundations of the Evangelical Life," in Jay M. Hammond, (ed.), *Francis of Assisi: History, Hagiography and Hermeneutics in the Early Documents* (Hyde Park, NY: New City Press, 2004), pp. 64-89.

[26] Cf. Regis J. Armstrong, *St. Francis of Assisi: Writings for a Gospel Life* (New York: Crossroad Publishing Co., 1994), pp. 18-28.

[27] The military imagery is a significant part of his conversion scene before Guido, the Bishop of Assisi, and throughout his life, cf. Lawrence S. Cunningham, "Francis Naked and Clothed: A Theological Meditation," in Jay M. Hammond, *op. cit.,* p. 169, especially n.9.

[28] Armstrong, *St. Francis of Assisi, op. cit.,* p. 20.

Valley put an end to all his romantic visions of glory and began a restless and relentless search for religious meaning.[29]

Francis was taken prisoner and languished sick and in moral torment for months. He left the prisoner of war camp a changed, if not fully settled, young man. He had lost his adolescent dream. He scoured the hills and chapels surrounding Assisi looking for an alternative with which to replace it. The God of his youth, the imperial God of the Crusades, the God of the extravagantly dressed soldier bishops of Europe, no longer made sense to him.[30] And so, he roamed the back alleys and poorer haunts of Assisi searching for meaning and struggling for a physical access to the divine.[31] He would find it first in the embrace of a leper and then in the gift of brothers.

In a dramatic encounter that would shape the rest of his life, Francis confronted his natural revulsion and embraced a leper he met on the road.[32] In that embrace, God revealed to Francis the core of Christianity and the consolation of his tired spirit. God enlivened his social and religious imagination with a profound revelation of who God was and what God wanted of him.

In the time of Francis, the leper was the foremost casualty of a society obsessed with violence and money. The leper was the first to fall through the cracks of society, as clerics and rulers lined their pockets and their consciences with the spoils of their never-ending wars.[33] As a result of his meeting on the road, Francis now

---

[29] John Rathschmidt treats the scenes of war in Francis' youth in his work, "The Embrace of Radical Poverty: Roots of Franciscan Mission," in Regina M. Bechtle, SC. and John J. Rathschmidt, OFM Cap., *Mission and Mysticism: Evangelization and the Experience of God* (Maryknoll, NY: Maryknoll School of Theology, 1987), pp. 97-115.

[30] For an understanding of the importance of clothing and the sumptuary codes of medieval dress, cf. Cunningham, *op.cit.*, pp. 165-178.

[31] For an understanding of the "dilemma" posed by Francis' understanding of the body and the physical aspects of his mystical experiences and conversion, cf. Marilyn Hammond, "Saint Francis as Struggling Hermeneut," in Hammond, *op.cit.*, pp. 210-228.

[32] The encounter is told in Bonaventure of Bagnoregio, *The Major Legend of St. Francis*, in *The Founder: Francis of Assisi – Early Documents*, Vol. II. Regis J. Armstrong, et.al., (eds.) (New York: New City Press, 2000), Chapter I:5, p. 533-535.

[33] Arnaldo Fortini, *Francis of Assisi*. Translated by Helen Moak. (New York: Crossroad, 1981).

saw something different about life and faith. What Francis saw was the goodness of God, expressed in the self-emptying love and (kenotic) mercy of a God who is good, all good, supremely good, all the time and to everyone.[34] When remembering that decisive moment in his life, Francis would quote Luke's Gospel 10:37 to interpret the significance of it. It was *misericordia*, the heart's gracious experience and the God-given expression of mercy that he found as the motivation of his action. And it is mercy that thus became the foundational virtue of Francis' experiment with fraternal life. Armstrong points to a passage from *The Letter to a Minister*, one that he says, "alone would be sufficient to reveal the saint's gospel vision of fraternal life."[35] There he connects the kind of love and mercy that flowed from the original encounter with the leper and the later experience of fraternity:

> ... I wish to know in this way that you love the Lord and me, His servant and yours: that there is not a brother in the world who has sinned — however much he could have sinned — who, after he has looked in your eyes, would ever depart without your mercy, if he is looking for mercy. And if he would sin a thousand times before your eyes, love him more than me so that you may draw him to the Lord; and always be merciful with brothers such as these.[36]

It is clear that the pivotal moment in Francis' conversion process was not the encounter with the leper in the plains below Assisi or the dramatic rejection of his father as Francis stood naked before the bishop and his relatives in the town square. For Francis it was another moment, the time that God gave him brothers, as he writes —

> And after the Lord gave me some brothers, no one showed me what I had to do, but the Most High Himself revealed to me

---

[34] *The Praises of God and the Blessing, The Saint, op.cit.,* p. 109.

[35] I thank Regis Armstrong for these insights found in "If My Words...,"*op cit.,* p. 83.

[36] *Letter to the Minister* 9-11, in Regis J. Armstrong, J.A. Wayne Hellmann, and William J. Short, (eds.) *The Saint - Francis of Assisi: Early Documents.* Vol. I. ((New York: New City Press, 1999), 97-98.

that I should live according to the pattern of the Holy Gospel. And I had this written down simply and in a few words and the Lord Pope confirmed it for me.[37]

So dramatic was this gift that, from that moment onwards, Francis never again referred to himself simply as "Francis," but always as "*brother* Francis." In his writings, he used the title "brother" more often (306 times) than any other title except "Lord" (410 times).[38]

Brotherhood transformed Francis' vision of himself and his vision of the world. Fraternity, the call to be brother in this world, was his primary response to the holy gospel and it was the mode of evangelization that he believed would transform society and heal a world torn apart by avarice, greed and violence. In Francis' mind, every creature on the face of the earth participated in this fraternal system. Fraternity embraced all creation, giving Francis the reason and the joy to speak of "brother" Sun, "sister" Moon, "brother" Wind and "mother" Earth.[39] Francis was able to maneuver this embrace of a cosmic fraternity because he understood with stunning clarity the humility of God that originated and sustained it.

Francis understood, first and foremost, that the nature of the Living God is neither dominating nor depriving. God is, rather, relational and humble in a way that graciously opens all human hearts to relationship and all creatures to mutual interdependence. John Corriveau roots the Franciscan insight about fraternity in the relation between power and humility in God. He cites St. Bonaventure's insight that "God's power *is* his humility; God's strength *is* his weakness; God's greatness *is* his lowliness."[40] Corriveau proposes the intimate relationship in God that gives rise to the scope and range of social transformation, when he describes the Trinity

---

[37] Cf. *The Testament* (1226) in Armstrong, *The Saint, op. cit.,* p. 125.

[38] John Corriveau, "The Courage to be Minors," *Circular Letter 22* (October 4, 2003), no. 1.2.

[39] *The Canticle of the Creatures (1225)* in Armstrong et al., *The Saint, op. cit.,* p. 113-114.

[40] See St. Bonaventure, *Itinerarium Mentis in Deum,* VI, 5.

as a "free communion of persons without domination or deprivation."[41]

At the Fifth Plenary Council held in Brazil in 1986, the assembly of brothers ratified fraternity as a "primary value"[42] and
affirmed the Capuchin vocation "as brothers to all people and
creatures" but expressed this in somewhat external terms, such as
a "*message* of fraternity and community spirit" and a "*spirit* of welcome and solidarity." (emphasis added, 2.8). It is in Circular Letter
11, in which John Corriveau quotes John Paul II's "exceptionally
important declaration regarding the nature and mission of our Order within the Church," that one is left without doubt about the
purpose of Capuchin-Franciscan life. Evangelical fraternity is the
key to understanding the life and mission of Capuchins. And the
essential elements of that evangelical fraternity are sixfold:

- A fraternity of lesser brothers – servants to the world.
- A contemplative fraternity.
- A poor and austere fraternity.
- A fraternity inserted among the poor.
- A fraternity dedicated to justice, peace, and respect for nature.
- A fraternity filled with human warmth.[43]

The clarity and precision of this central focus on the fraternal
identity, mission and purpose of the Capuchin Order at that time
(and not earlier) has much to do with a succession of Church documents on the identity and mission of the Church itself. John Corriveau cites three in particular: (1) The new ecclesiology of communion developed at Vatican II and deepened in the teachings of
Pope Paul VI and John Paul II, particularly in *Novo Millenio Ineunte*;
(2) The 1994 document issued by the Congregation for Institutes
of Consecrated Life and Societies of Apostolic Life (CIVCSVA)

---

[41] The quote is found in Corriveau, *The Courage to Be Minors, op. cit.*, no.1.1, and originally found in David B. Couturier, "Minority and Poverty Eradication: The International
Dimensions of Christ's Compassion in 21st Century Franciscan Communities," (May 25,
2003), accessed: www.fi-na.org/prov.html.

[42] *Our Prophetic Presence in the World* (September , 1986) in Regis J. Armstrong, ed., *The
Path of Renewal: The Documents of the Five Plenary Councils and the First Assembly of the Order
of Capuchin Friars Minor.* (n.d.)

[43] Corriveau, *Circular Letter 11* (February 2, 1997), no. 1.3.

entitled, *Fraternal Life in Community* and (3) The Apostolic Exhortation, *Vita Consecrata,* published in 1996.[44] It is the development of an ecclesiology of communion that has led to an evolution in the understanding of religious communities in the Church and the declaration that fraternities exist as a "home and school of communion" that live as a "warmly human and welcoming point of reference for the poor and for those who sincerely search for God."[45]

Summarizing the Order's reflection on its Capuchin and Franciscan roots in the light of these developments, Corriveau underscores the "profound re-visioning" of the Order's mission in the world that is taking place. Noting that Gospel brotherhood is "the Franciscan incarnation of the theology of communion," he boldly affirms the centrality that fraternal life must play in the mission of the Order. He writes,

> It can no longer authentically be asserted that the Order's principal role is to serve its various ministries, but rather: 'Saint Francis founded the fraternity of the Order of Minors which would bear witness to the reign of God by a sharing of life and by preaching penance and peace through example and word (Constitutions 3.1).[46]

We turn now to the "profound impact" this insight has had on the Order's understanding of its identity and on poverty, the global economy, minority, itinerancy, service, spirituality and witness. We will see how it leads to the development and description of the concept of the "fraternal economy."

"MANY TROUBLING QUESTIONS"

The first eight Circular Letters that emerged from the General Minister of the Capuchin-Franciscan Order from September 1994

---

[44] Corriveau, *Circular Letter 20* (March 31, 2002), nos. 1.1 and 1.2.

[45] The Letter of John Paul II to the General Minister, September 18, 1996, *Analecta OFM Cap.* 112 (1996) p. 565.

[46] Corriveau, *Circular Letter 20, op. cit.,* no. 1.4

through December1995 do not reveal the dramatic insights that are ready to explode on the fraternal scene. Their themes are important; they are largely spiritual and sometimes pious.

The first circular letter is a relatively short reflection (2¼ pages) on the occasion of the approaching feast of St. Francis in 1994. Rooting itself in the insight of the V Plenary Council of the Order (PCO V) that "the point of view of the poor is the privileged position from which we, his sons, consider and proclaim" Franciscan values, Corriveau posits that "Francis and our Franciscan heritage speak very prophetically to our world today." He takes one paragraph to explore the deficits and dangers of the global economy and one paragraph to expose the numbing, random violence touching every corner of the world. He concludes with a swift call to take to heart in a new and hopeful manner the "point of view of the poor... reconciliation and respect for creation."[47]

The second circular letter is a chronicle of the General Minister and Definitory's fraternal plan and vision of the task for governing and animating the brotherhood in the sexennium before them.[48] Released at the time of the Synod of Bishops meeting in Rome to discuss the charism of consecrated life, the document gives no hint of the dramatic impact that the results of that the upcoming Synod will have on the Order's understanding of communion and solidarity. In fact, the letter ends curiously, without reference to the community's fundamental fraternal charism.[49] It concludes, "Ours is a call to personal and communal engagement in prayer, service and reflection in a manner that will maintain the vitality of our Capuchin vocation and identity."[50]

The third circular letter is another very short epistle published on November 1, 1994, in anticipation of the Christmas season. Meditating on the theme of light and darkness in the prophet Isaiah, Corriveau proposes a hopeful but highly personal message

---

[47] *Circular Letter 1* (1994), p.8.

[48] "General Definitory" is the official term of the "General Council" assembled to assist the General Minister in the government of the Capuchin Order, cf. *Constitutions* (1990) 8: 120.

[49] One can say that it is curious, since the letter is published on the Feast of St. Francis (October 4, 1994), during the time of the Synod of Bishops discussing the charism of the consecrated life and there is no mention of Francis or the charism he left the Order in the whole text. The document is a technical and organizational treatise.

[50] *Circular Letter 2* (October 4, 1994), p. 12.

that "from the very heart of your darkness, you will find and name your light."[51]

Circular Letter 4 begins and sustains a meditation on contemporary forms of political violence. It develops an extended reflection on the experience of violence in the personal lives of friars and in the fraternities of the Order and exhorts friars to "acknowledge the sources of violence in our hearts."[52] It points to various forms of institutional violence emerging in contemporary society but limits its focus to challenging friars to have the courage to face the sources of violence within their own hearts.[53] Corriveau poses the question as to how friars can subscribe to institutional forms of violence, militarism and ever more repressive forms of incarceration and capital punishment. He brackets out any structural or systemic cause[54] and appears to leave individuals with the personal form of the question or examen, "or are these simply signs of our fears and our sense of futility?"[55]

Circular Letter 5, published just three months later, takes up the theme of violence once again. Picking up from *Circular Letter 4's* caution against gazing at the world with "pointless images," Corriveau offers his readers in the fifth circular letter an alternative image to the picture of a "hatred so malignant that only murder on a grand scale can satisfy it." The image he offers is the "firm but compassionate love of St. Francis" in his encounter with the terrifying wolf of Gubbio.[56] Corriveau moves the issue of violence from within the friar to the very center of fraternal life when he states:

---

[51] *Circular Letter 3* (November 1, 1994), p. 13.

[52] *Circular Letter 4* (February 23, 1995), no. 5.

[53] *Ibid.,* 3.

[54] For an extended analysis of these social, institutional, or structural forms of sin, cf. Bryan N. Massingale, *The Social Dimensions of Sin and Reconciliation in the Theologies of James H. Cone and Gutavo Gutierrez* (Rome: Academia Alfonsiana, 1991).

[55] *Ibid,* 5.

[56] *The Deeds of Blessed Francis and His Companions,"* in Regis J. Armstrong, et al., (eds.) *The Prophet: Francis of Assisi: Early Documents* (New York: New City Press, 2001), pp. 482-485.

All too often we allow the "wolf" to dwell in our very midst: passive aggression, violent denunciation, alcohol and drug abuse, racism, sexual abuse and abusive ridicule.[57]

In October, 1995, Corriveau published *Circular Letter 6* in preparation for the 1996 Congress on "The Lay Expressions of the Capuchin Vocation." In that letter he reaffirmed the Constitution's principle that all the brothers of the Order are equal [58] and aligns himself with the position assumed by various General Chapters (1982, 1988 and 1994) that, while all friars are equal and share the same vocation, lay friars and priest friars have different callings in the Church. The Congress was designed as the first opportunity for lay brothers to reflect on the common Capuchin vocation to fraternal life from an international perspective.[59] Corriveau encourages its work and addresses some initial questions.

Circular Letter 7 is devoted to "shrines and popular devotion in our Capuchin Tradition" and was written in celebration of the 7th Centenary of the Shrine of Loreto (Italy).[60] *Circular Letter 8* is another Christmas letter that encourages fraternities to be filled with joy and to recognize the signs of God's love for creation in a world "blind to its beauty."[61]

The publication of *Circular Letter 9* signals a new seriousness and a level of concern that seem to be missing in the previous eight circular letters. The letter is written immediately after two weeks of meetings and reflections, on the part of the General Definitory, and is a summary of the experiences of the General Minister and his Definitors, after 18 months of continuous travel and meetings with brothers in the 80 out of the 150 different circumscriptions of the Order. The document is a statement of "concerns and challenges" in the closing years of the millennium.[62]

---

[57] *Circular Letter* 5 (May 18, 1995), no.4.2.

[58] *Constitutions* 84.3.

[59] Corriveau notes in his Circular Letter that 100% of the participants at the General Chapter of 1982 were clerics. The Congress of 1996 was designed as a meeting of the entire Order where 75% of the participants were lay brothers, cf. *Circular Letter* 6 (October 13, 1995), no. 3.1.

[60] *Circular Letter* 7 (October 30, 1995).

[61] *Circular Letter* 8 (Christmas, 1995), no. 2.2.

[62] The letter was published on February 2, 1996.

In a statement that is stunningly clear and direct, Corriveau writes that "fraternity is not only the gift we offer to one another, *it is our privileged manner of announcing the reign of God!*"[63] There is no avoidance of the centrality of fraternity to the identity and mission of Capuchins nor is there any overly personalized interpretation of its challenges. Right from the beginning of the letter, Corriveau wishes to address the communal, social and structural aspects of fraternity: "the quality of common prayer, ... fraternal understanding,...the signs of the times in local chapters, collaboration in ministry, living common life with nothing of our own, our presence and commitment to the poor and all other values of our gospel life."[64] He notes that "living the evangelical ideal of poverty always remains a challenge and a call to reform" and he writes that the Constitutions of the Order give ample and concrete expression to this ideal as it is to be lived in individual lives. But, his interest and his focus are now (and will be for the next eight years) on the communal, social and structural dimensions of that ideal. The reason he gives at this stage for this shift in focus is direct: "there are many troubling questions concerning the communal and institutional expression of our evangelical ideal of poverty which are not addressed or which are inadequately addressed in the Constitutions."[65]

It is as if the General Minister and the Definitors came home from their many travels and learned, like the disciples whom Jesus had sent out on their first apostolic mission, that they could not exorcise all the demons they encountered by the ordinary means of individual conversion. They needed to address the problems and challenges facing the international fraternity in a new way. A simple list of the "troubling questions" provides perspective on the scope of the issues emerging from the Order's acceptance of evangelical fraternity and gospel brotherhood as the central and defining mission of the Capuchin Order:

- Where there are provinces (mostly in the northern hemisphere) that habitually experience a modest surplus of in-

---

[63] *Circular Letter 9* (February 2, 1996), no. 2.1.

[64] *Ibid.*, no. 2.1.

[65] *Ibid.*, no.4.1.

come over expenditures to be held over for the next year, what does it mean in those many circumscriptions in the southern world where there is a habitual, large deficit in the ordinary income of the circumscription?

- What provisions are needed and permissible to assure adequate health care for the sick and elderly in a world that lives by widely different and unequal provisions of social assistance?
- When investments are such a needed element of security to fund initial formation programs, what type of investments are consistent with the Capuchin ideal of evangelical poverty?
- How does the ideal of poverty influence and condition the way we minister, when experience indicates that the "diversity of ministry often leads to a wide diversity of lifestyle, even between brothers and fraternities of the same province."[66]

The implications of a "gospel brotherhood" and the "same vocation" shared by all are noted in the apparent structural discrepancy between circumscriptions of the Order that have and those that do not. A changing demographic reality (i.e, the rapid growth of the Order in the Southern Hemisphere) combined with a more clearly focused acceptance of the evangelical-fraternal nature of the charism bring into relief a troubling situation – "past structures of financial solidarity were built upon concepts of juridic dependence. Provinces were financially responsible for custodies or missions entrusted to their care. An increasingly large portion of our international brotherhood is in need of financial assistance... these circumscriptions no longer retain juridic or even traditional ties with regions of the Order which have the capacity to assist them."[67] Corriveau asks the logical but difficult structural question, "How can new structures of international solidarity be created which do not denote dependence... how can we give inter-

---

[66] *Ibid.,* no. 4.2.
[67] *Ibid.,* no. 4.3.

national witness to the principle of the Rule: '*Wherever the brothers may be... let them show that they are members of the same family.*' *VI.7.*'[68]

In the same vein and with an eye to the structural discrepancies being revealed in a worldwide fraternity that claims unity and the same vocation, Corriveau asks about the burdens on extremely poor regions of the Order when they have to compete with the structures and standards created for brothers in the economically developed areas of the world. He poses a question about what one might call the true globalization of the charism when he asks how the expressions of common life in the Order could be enriched by Asian and African models of family life, as opposed to the standards and values that emerge from predominantly individualized (egocentric) models of socialization in the West. After posing these questions, Corriveau announced the convocation of a Plenary Council of the Order to be held in 1998 (PCO VI) to address these questions. Universality, equality and fraternity will be brought to bear on the way friars live and serve and will challenge inherited assumptions about the structures and organization of the gospel life they are leading.

It is in *Circular Letter 11* that Corriveau gives a hint and an initial insight into how communities with wildly different histories and divergent economic trajectories might begin to solve or at least fraternally address their issues of diversity and disparity. He writes, "Minority makes it possible for persons with differing gifts and widely diverse responsibilities within the church and society to live as equals united in true brotherhood."[69] The topic of minority and itinerancy will be addressed seven years later at the VII Plenary Council of the Order.[70]

A DIVINELY INSPIRED ECONOMY

Two years after the Holy Father had solemnly declared the *fraternal* purpose and mission of the Capuchin-Franciscan Order, friars were asked to contemplate how to live poverty institutionally

---

[68] *Ibid.*

[69] *Circular Letter 11* (February 2, 1997), no. 2.1.

[70] *Our Fraternal Life in Minority, VII Plenary Council of the Order* (Assisi: March 1-27, 2004)

and in a way that advanced unity, promoted equity and transparency, and led to a realistic and joyful peace for all. In *Circular Letter 13*, "Living Poverty in Fraternity: A Reflection on the Sixth Plenary Council of the Order," Corriveau lays the theological foundation for institutional expressions of poverty, demonstrates how dependence actually leads toward (not away from) social harmony and traces the history of the problem of communal poverty in the Order, since the 1950s. He lays much of the groundwork for a task that will be taken up a few months later at the Plenary Council itself.

Three steps are particularly instructive for our purposes of trying to understand the "divinely inspired economy" of which Corriveau writes. The first is an enunciation of the threefold conviction which formed the basis of Francis' attitude toward poverty. Corriveau retrieves them from the work of Thaddee Matura, OFM:

1. Every good thing comes from God and must be attributed to God.
2. *The only thing we can rightly appropriate to ourselves is our own sinfulness.*
3. *We should joyfully bear life's sufferings as a participation in the cross of our Lord Jesus Christ.*[71]

Poverty, humility, dependence, service and peace all intersect at the crossroads of God's generosity and gracious goodness. Francis insists on a communal embrace of material poverty because it is the surest way he knows to advance peace and sustain the fraternal relationship he has with his brothers, his world and, indeed, with all creation.

As noted above, Francis' early life experiences were drawn in the blood and the greed of a society hungry for power and steeped in violence. His economic choices are a conscious and critical manifestation of his intention to preserve the fraternal vision of the world that he had gotten as a grace "after the Lord had given (him) brothers." In the *Legend of the Three Companions*, when the bishop

---

[71] *Circular Letter 13*, no. 2.2. (The original is found in Thaddee Matura, OFM, *Francis of Assisi: the Message of His Writings*, p. 130.)

remarks that Francis' life seems so inordinately and unnecessarily difficult without material possessions, Francis makes the connection for the bishop between wealth and violence:

> If we were to have possessions we would also have to have weapons to defend ourselves. Wealth leads to arguments and lawsuits, and in many ways would only hinder us from loving God and loving our neighbor. That's why, in this life, we do not want to have material possessions.[72]

The second step that Corriveau attempts is to "bridge the centuries;" he wants to do more than simply photocopy Francis' 13th century experience of poverty onto the 21st century. Capuchins cannot duplicate the poverty of Francis because we live in different economies and social contexts. The task for friars is more complex than a simple fundamentalist or literalist transposition. Capuchins have to understand the ideal of fraternity and apply it faithfully so as to create a "divinely inspired economy" that takes into account both the positive and negative aspects of the society around them. Corriveau finds the dividing line between the generally accepted social definition of the economy current in the world today and a Franciscan interpretation of social relations and poverty to lie in the understanding and acceptance of "mutual dependence." He uses the "virtue of solidarity" as enunciated in John Paul II's Encyclical, *Sollicitudo rei socialis,* as his hermeneutical key.[73]

In *Circular Letter 13* Corriveau finds that "capitalism proposes competition as the best response to protect and administer scarce resources." In a capitalist economy, resources are scarce by definition and men and women are forced to compete for advantage and control over those resources. On the other hand, from a Christian point of view and from a Franciscan perspective, the children of the world are not competitors under a stingy God. They are brothers and sisters to one another and recipients (and thus, by gracious extension, donors themselves) of the gifts from an inexhaustibly good and wonderfully gracious God. The sign of this confident worldview lies in the historical practice of Franciscan begging.

---

[72] *Legend of the Three Companions,* 33, cited by Corriveau, *Circular Letter 13,* no.3.1..
[73] John Paul II, *Sollicitudo rei Socialis,* (Rome: December 31, 1987.)

Through begging, friars give dramatic witness that they can put their absolute confidence in a good and gracious God and in the generosity of their neighbors. They do not need to substitute the confidence forged in grace with the "idolatry" of self-sufficiency or replace it with greed and personal power. It was the belief of Francis and Clare that, in this way, they had found the route to a more, not a less, secure form of life by entrusting themselves in humility and minority to the love expressed in grace and fraternity.[74] The paradox of radical Franciscan poverty lies in its ability to create more, not less, peace and security.

The third step that Corriveau takes is to present a short history of the problem of communal poverty in the Order since the 1950s. We need to make, for our purposes, only three points to illustrate the challenge the Order faces in creating a "divinely inspired economy" across the 95 countries in which it lives.

The first is that, up until the 1950s, the Order was largely centered in Western Europe and North America, with 91% of all circumscriptions located there. Common life was relatively uniform and easily regulated. The friars lived like the working poor of Europe, that is, from the fruits of each day's work for the immediate necessities of life. Friars did not earn salaries or garner pensions. They lived off the donations and offerings given for their services as preachers and confessors. They relied on questing and begging to supply for their mostly immediate needs.

Another aspect is that life changed dramatically for the friars from the 1950s through the 1970s. Corriveau cites a few of those sociological changes that impacted the Order. First, the economic wealth of the world multiplied after the Second World War, most especially in North America and Western Europe, leaving a widening chasm between the North and the South. Second, public welfare and social assistance programs (for the sick and elderly) were expanded, giving whole groups of people a social security into the future that had never been experienced before. Third, the class of the "working poor" disappeared and, with it, the Capuchin

---

[74] The radical difference between Franciscan and some modern searches for new economic paradigms, i.e. the communitarian ethic of social theorists like Amitai Etzioni, lies in the role that humility, minority and the self-transcendence of the Cross does or does not play in secular social dynamics. Cf. Etzioni, *The New Golden Rule: Community and Morality in a Democratic Society* (New York: Basic Books, 1986).

connection to an inherited form of communal poverty. Friars in North America and Western Europe, with significant differences based on the varying national social arrangements, earned salaries and stipends. They made use of insurance policies and pensions. They held stock, invested donations and increased their earnings by playing the stock market. As Corriveau notes, "the brothers were no longer evidently and directly dependent upon the people for their support."[75] In a dramatically new way, the friars experienced a sense of social entitlement, even as there was a rapid deployment of ministries to serve those who dropped from the disappearing class of the working poor into the realm of the desperately poor. In this period, the gap between the rich and the poor becomes dramatically more evident within Provinces and across them.

From the 1970s until the present, we find a dramatic demographic shift in the Order. By 1997, 30% of the brothers of the Order live in Asia-Oceania, Africa and Latin America. More than 50% of the brothers are juridic members of circumscriptions outside Western Europe and North America. The creation of wealth continues in the North and the economic gap between Provinces in the Northern and Southern Hemispheres widens. This is due to endogenous and exogenous forces. Poverty became globalized due to the crushing weight of unserviceable world debt and the emergence of powerful regional world blocks. Within the Order, it widened because of the rapid population growth in communities of the Southern hemisphere (i.e. Latin America and Africa) that created new and independent jurisdictions and severed the old solidarity between "mother provinces" and "dependent daughter-jurisdictions." Without dialogue and international fraternal agreement, the "divinely inspired economy" with its message of peace and the promise of a "cosmic fraternity" would founder on the jagged rocks of structural injustices.

THE PURPOSE OF POVERTY IS RELATIONAL

Globalization today is not working for many of the world's poor. It is not working for much of the environment. It is not working for the stability of

---

[75] *Ibid.,* 7.3.2.

the global economy. The transition from communism to a market economy has been so badly managed that, with the exception of China, Viet Nam, and a few Eastern European countries, poverty has soared as incomes have plummeted.[76]

In many ways, the globalization of the fraternal charism in the Capuchin Order was facing a severe test when friars from around the world gathered for the Sixth Plenary Council in Assisi on September 7, 1998. The task before them was to understand clearly enough the social trends and demographic shifts of our times and weigh them in the spiritual light of gospel brotherhood. They needed to do this in such a way as to clarify the communal, structural and institutional dimensions of evangelical poverty. Their task was to resolve in some way, through fraternal dialogue, the troubling questions that emerged in *Circular Letter 9* and the institutional obstacles to the "divinely inspired economy" presented by John Corriveau and his definitory in *Circular Letter 13*.

From the beginning of their discussions, the friars accepted the grace of gospel poverty as a "valid alternative for our times," an economic "system" they described as a "more genuinely human way: with its values of simplicity, gratuitousness, the will to serve, respect for persons and for creation."[77] Perhaps the central insight to emerge from the Plenary Council lies in Proposal number 6, where the delegates remind the Order that the economic choices of Francis and his early companions were not haphazard but, indeed, a concrete and critical assessment of the religious and social context of their times.

According to the delegates, the early Franciscans understood only too well, the avarice and greed that shaped and conditioned the communities in which they lived. They realized the fear that endless wars induced and the insecurity that derived from the ambition and competition of their contemporaries. Their economic choices were a radical claim on the protection of their brotherhood. They saw their extreme form of poverty not as an enticement to severity and insecurity. Just the opposite, they realized that

---

[76] Joseph E. Stigltiz, *Globalization and its Discontents* (New York: W.W. Norton, 2002), p. 214.

[77] Cf. *Proposals: Living Poverty in Brotherhood.* VI Plenary Council of the Order (Rome: OFMCap., 1998), no.7.

when brothers can "confidently make known their needs" and seek forgiveness when they had sinned from the tender (maternal) love of a leader placed over them, they experience freedom, joy, creativity and peace. As John Corriveau later interprets this insight, "it was a conscious choice for a more fraternal world, a more human world."[78] The brothers chose absolute poverty to increase their security, not lower it. They knew that Assisi was trying to build its security on the (violent) appropriation of land and power by the wealthy few at the exclusion of the destitute many. Francis and his companions were determined to create a new foundation for human security and freedom, basing themselves on economic principles that included the non-use of money, the non-appropriation of goods, manual work as the ordinary means of support and a recourse to alms to supply for one's needs.

The delegates at the VI Plenary Council made it clear how engaged Francis and his early companions were in the economic realities and social conditions of their time. The market economy of the 13th century was forged in the tragic battles between the *majores* and the *minores*, the "mania for trade" and the bloody hope of "coming revenge."[79] Noting the equally, if not more pronounced, destructive social implications of our own market economy, the delegates called on the international fraternity to protect their grace-filled identity as "lesser brothers" and to practice a more obvious form of justice and peace in today's global economy. The delegates based this call on the Constitutional norm, "The minimum necessary, not the maximum allowed." (Constitutions 67.3) A new economy is to be based on compassion, not competition, and on mutual dependence not ambitious greed.

Recently, Joseph Stiglitz, winner of the 2001 Nobel Prize in Economics, catalogued the many discontents and dangers with globalization today.[80] His assessment is that the (mis)management of globalization takes the world to a dangerous crossroad. The reason he cites is that international, commercial standards today are inflexible and absolute, unaware and unbending toward local

---

[78] See our analysis of this insight, in our chapter on "The Development of the Fraternal Economy" in this work.

[79] Fortini goes on at length about the tenacious hatred and greed that fueled social relationships in the Assisi of Francis' day. Cf. Fortini, *op.cit.,* pp. 38-76.

[80] Stiglitz, *op.cit.*

needs and regional challenges. Beyond that, financial interests alone matter at the International Monetary Fund and World Trade Organization, he says, even as evidence mounts that their universal policies of applied market fundamentalism (i.e. of capital market liberalization, for example) are only increasing social turmoil and giving rise to massive inequities.[81]

Stiglitz maintains that the creation of wealth cannot be the end all and be all of economic policies. There are other values (critical to the security and health of a people that must be respected.) What is needed, he says, is not technical efficiency but "globalization with a human face," a more sensitive, local and relational interpretation and application of international market policies.[82] The delegates at the VI Plenary Council determined, with far less economic sophistication or sophistry, that globalization must be about more than the creation of wealth and the increase of profits. In Proposal 21 they urged that "fraternal communion and interdependence should inspire and determine... our interaction with the world, particularly the world of the poor."

THE ELEMENTS OF A FRATERNAL ECONOMY

In a talk on "Formation to Franciscan Capuchin Values in Post Novitiate," Corriveau admits that the expression "fraternal economy" does not appear in the Constitutions or even in the propositions of the Sixth Plenary Council. And yet he states that the Plenary Council actually began a process of elucidating the conscious and clear economic choices facing friars today "in order to create among the brothers and the peoples they serve a 'fraternal economy' whose purpose is the enhancement of communion rather than the protection and increase of wealth."[83]

The term emerges first in Corriveau's *17th Circular Letter* when he lays out the principles for a Franciscan, fraternal economy, a concept he sees emerging in the proposals from the VI Plenary Council. Rooted in the absolute conviction of communion, mutual

---

[81] *Ibid.,* pp. 214-252.

[82] *Ibid.,* p. 247.

[83] John Corriveau, "Formation to Franciscan Capuchin Values in Post-Novitiate," (Assisi: Convention on the Post-Novitiate, September 14, 2004).

interdependence, and goodness of God, the Sixth Plenary Council constructed four mutually related principles for the development of the fraternal economy.

The first concerns work as a "primary source of support." (Proposal 14) The second concerns the continuing importance in the Capuchin-Franciscan tradition of questing and alms. It reads that, when their work does not suffice, the brothers are to turn confidently to the table of the Lord. But they are warned that "no province has the right to ask of another that which the labors of its own brothers and the alms of its own people can provide." (Proposal 24d)

The third principle refers to equity when the "table of the Lord" does not suffice. It holds that "equity requires that each province have the capacity to respond to the needs of its brothers and ministries in ways that are tailor-made to its own culture and people." (Proposal 24c)

And the final principle relates to the possibility of investments and financial reserves that are justified only "in cases of manifest necessity." (Proposal 29)

Interestingly, the delegates focus their attention not on the personal use of funds but on the "fraternal administration" of them. They are concerned about the structures of the Order. It is important to note that the delegates did not conceive of administration simply under the rubric of efficiency and management. On the contrary, they held that, since the Capuchin Order is a "home and school of communion," an evangelical fraternity and gospel brotherhood, the primary goal of administration could never ultimately be about the maximization of profit and the increase of wealth. In keeping with our evangelical identity, the goal of fraternal administration is the building up of relationships and the growth in communion. Proposals 29 through 45 delineate three principles that guide this fraternal administration: transparency, participation and equity.

In a communion mentality of economics, transparency in all financial matters "expresses and facilitates brotherhood and solidarity among all the constituent parts of the Order." (Proposal 30) Participation widens the circle of influence and decision-making to include the least of the brothers in the building up of the fraternity. And, where communion is the ultimate objective of administration, the principle of equity insures that the diverse and various needs of the brothers will be met at the local level without privilege and with equal concern.

The insights of the VI Plenary Council are capped in a simple but stunning phrase – "Franciscan spirituality must direct and permeate even our administrative structures."[84] According to VI PCO, the birth of the fraternal economy in the Order demands an effective solidarity between local fraternities and the transformation of all social (and even clerical) ministries that create division and are, even in part, exercises of dominating or depriving power.

In several of his Circular Letters, Corriveau completes the framework for the fraternal economy by illustrating the spiritual dynamics that under-gird it. We turn briefly to that reflection now.

THE SPIRITUALITY OF THE FRATERNAL ECONOMY

In *Circular Letters* 18-21, Corriveau returns and, in fact, completes the spiritual insights about evangelical fraternity and the "fraternal economy" that he began in *Circular Letter 8*, the letter before the emergence of those "troubling questions" facing the brotherhood. In *Circular Letter 18* he focuses his attention on the personal prayer of brothers.

It is, as if having concluded the major insights of a revolutionary concept and ecclesial upheaval, Corriveau would have the brothers understand that the communion we seek, the solidarity we propose, and the fraternal economy we hope to build will not and cannot be constructed by human effort alone. Communion is, as it were, the complement of contemplation.

That insight has been implied throughout the corpus of the Order's "social encyclicals" and circular or evangelical letters. Put another way, the development of equity and the exercise of administration in the Order and, indeed, in all of society are not simply geared toward a more efficient set of relationships and a fairer distribution of goods. As stated throughout this chapter, the goal of the fraternal economy is communion with God and solidarity with one's neighbor. It is achieved, in Franciscan life, by

---

[84] *Circular Letter 17* (March 3, 2000), n. 7.

the kenotic and self-transcending love of a humble friar intent on being a "lesser brother" in a mutually interdependent world. Since we are about an immersion in the "mystery of communion," it is clear that we will never reach the fraternal economy perfectly and its approximation will be achieved only by the forgiveness of sins, reconciliation and peacemaking. The call to fraternal communion, which is our evangelical call to holiness, requires contemplation and "is accepted and can be cultivated only in the silence of adoration before the infinite transcendence of God." *(Vita Consecrata,* n. 32) For this reason, the VI Plenary Council makes an important distinction between work and activism and recommends that work be an outpouring of love that flows from prayer and not an avoidance of the hospitality and silence one must find in the presence of the living God.

One notices a pattern that seems to have developed in the *Circular Letters,* one that has three steps: an individual foundation is laid, social implications are explored, and then the communal insights are returned to strengthen individual motivation and progress. One sees this in the early *Circular Letters,* especially in the first five or so letters where Corriveau spends a considerable time focusing on a "personal reminder" to live the Rule with (1) "utmost fidelity and wholehearted enthusiasm," (2) a gentle call for friars to engage in prayer, service and contemplation, (3) to find their personal light in the darkness, (4) to acknowledge violence in their hearts (5) and recognize the "wolf" that lurks in our midst.

In *Circular Letters 9-17,* Corriveau addresses with enormous energy and skill the "troubling questions" surrounding the institutional aspects of evangelical fraternity. Aware that he had laid the groundwork for a personal appropriation of gospel brotherhood in his reflections on peace, nonviolence, light, popular devotion and the thirst for God, Corriveau now lays a final stone of support for his grand project of institutional reform with his thoughts on compassion rooted in prayer and contemplation.[85] Having exposed the "many troubling questions" surrounding the communal and institutional expressions of our evangelical life, he turns the friars' attention first to humility in *Circular Letter 10,* lays the theological foundations and elements for the fraternal economy in *Circular*

---

[85] Corriveau does this in *Circular Letter 12, op. cit.*

Letter 11, and shores up the structure again with a spiritual reflection on the compassion and peace, achieved by a simple lifestyle, assuming the vantage point of the poor, rejecting violence and joyfully discovering the means of reconciliation in our world.

After the long excursion into the dynamics surrounding the institutional expressions of our evangelical life, Corriveau stabilizes the fraternal enterprise with two *Circular Letters* (18 and 19) on prayer (one personal and the other, liturgical). In *Circular Letter 20,* he reiterates and solidifies the insights around the evangelical fraternity and the fraternal economy and in *Circular Letter 21* he provides further spiritual support by returning, once again, to the theme of humility and kenosis. Corriveau is laying the theological groundwork for the VII Plenary Council on minority and itinerancy. He reprises certain themes: compassion, kenosis, the humility of the cross, beauty, and peace but puts them up as counterweight to an emerging "culture of arrogance" in our world.[86] As if to reiterate in process what he has consistently throughout his Letters stated in principle, he asks the friars concluding their read of this letter to pause and to read it through again. He asks them to focus this second time, in the ancient tradition of the *lectio divina,* on the Word of the Lord, the words of Francis, Celano (Francis' biographer) and St. Bonaventure, rather than on his commentary. It is clear from the methodology we have come to witness in Corriveau's writing that he is laying the contemplative foundation for a powerful social and cultural analysis.

Circular Letter 22 begins and ends with a Trinitarian insight that the inner life of God is wonderfully described as a "free communion of persons without domination or deprivation." The arc begins with the insight that "humility opens hearts to experience relationships" (and God's humility is the key to Franciscan development) and ends with a statement about the fraternal economy:

> These 'new ways of understanding and living relationships' with the poor can result when the principles of the fraternal economy – participation, solidarity and transparency – create minis-

---

[86] *Circular Letter* 21 (April 18, 2003).

tries which empower the poor in relationships 'without domination or deprivation.'[87]

The "excessive love" of God demonstrated in the self-emptying love of Christ Crucified shows itself in the minority of Francis,
his desire to be a lesser brother in all things. It gave him the power
and strength to abandon his social position of privilege, to form
a communion of brothers without domination or deprivation, to
engage in a mutually respectful collaboration of gifts in fraternity
and not only to obey authority but also to reverence it. The justice
of a fraternal economy begins with "restored relationships" borne
of forgiveness and reconciliation and the ceding of arrogance for
the development of a culture of peace.[88]

THE SOCIAL CATECHESIS OF THE FRATERNAL ECONOMY

Before concluding our overview of the development of the
concept of the fraternal economy, it would do us well to review
what might be called the "social catechesis of the fraternal economy," as this is being developed in the Plenary Councils of the Capuchin Order and the Circular Letters of its General Minister. By
this we mean to explore the practical lessons and pastoral insights
that are beginning to emerge at the social, relational or structural
level in the theological and spiritual teaching of the Order in the
documents we have been reviewing.

In a chapter of this size, it is impossible to detail all of the
components involved in a concept as original and yet as dense as
the "fraternal economy." But, it is clear that the enumeration of
such a reality calls for a re-interpretation of some fundamental and
inherited social and economic categories of Capuchin life.

It is not unfair to state at the beginning that the texts we have
been discussing presume that the early sources of the Franciscan
Order are significantly engaged in and formative of the social and
economic questions of their day. They assume that friars today
should be similarly connected to their own. Although it may be

---

[87] *Circular Letter 22* (October 4, 2003).

[88] Corriveau develops his ideas about arrogance in *Circular Letter 21*, n. 7.2.

too soon to claim a field for "Franciscan economics," research indicates a powerful tradition, now being excavated, that engaged the difficult and problematic social questions of ownership, jurisdiction, law, money, the use of goods, power and politics, property and freedom from the very beginnings of the Franciscan experiment.[89]

The Franciscan tradition, with its meditations on poverty and the proper use of things in this world, sets out what has been called a "penitential humanism" that coheres around the central evangelical insight about the goodness of God and the utter dependence of the human person on the generosity of God in this world, i.e. *sine proprio.* [90] Joseph Chinnici outlines the elements of this tradition of "penitential humanism" as: (a) a global or universal vision of humanity; (b) the vindication of the dignity of the human person in the context of all forms of social violence; (c) a new model of what it means to be "holy" that is directly tied to the most basic elements of life, i.e. the city, the economy, work, behavior and participation in government; and (d) a new social ethic whose goal is the embodiment in social life of "being brother, being sister" and the formation of a civic *fraternitas.*

What we see developing in the social teachings of the Capuchin Order in the years 1994-2004 may be described as a kind of "providential humanism" that seeks a similar prophetic engagement with the troubling social dynamics of the day, especially escalating violence and the growing and dangerous gap between those who have and those who do not in the aggressive consumerist capitalism of the late 20th and early 21st centuries. We call it a "providential humanism," since it begins with a fundamental conviction about the goodness of God and the sustaining power of that generosity even in the lapsed and fragmented condition of the human person in contemporary society. The providential humanism in Capuchin social teaching picks up the central elements of the tradition (i.e., a universalist vision, the civic *fraternitas,* etc.) but

---

[89] Michael Cusato, "Commercium: From Profane to the Sacred," in Jay M. Hammond, (ed.) *Francis of Assisi: History, Hagiography and Hermeneutics* (Hyde Park, NY: New City Press, 2004), pp. 179-209;

[90] Joseph Chinnici, "Penitential Humanism: Regarding the Sources to Develop a Franciscan Urban Spirituality," in Roberta F. MicKelvie, (ed.) *Franciscans In Urban Ministry* (St. Bonaventure, NY: The Franciscan Institute, 2002), pp. 109-128.

extends it a step further by highlighting that the civic *fraternitas* is created by humility (a self-emptying love) borne out of confidence in the absolute goodness of God and the security that is formed by the generous and full donation of oneself (as reflexive action) and all one's property to the service of one's brothers and sisters. What "the providential humanism" of Capuchin social teaching supplies is simply, perhaps, a stronger accent on and elaboration of the (social) security that derives from evangelical poverty and not a critique of the other elements we have noted above.

The social catechesis of the fraternal economy is a practical engagement and dialogue between theory and praxis. Corriveau begins his meditations on evangelical poverty and the development of the fraternal economy in the light of "troubling questions," a problematic social situation, a change in juridic dependence that leads to inequity in the fraternity. In many ways, this is how friars typically renew and reform their understanding and practice of evangelical poverty. Incidents lead to insight. Social circumstances unravel agreed upon structures and challenge the friars to discern the signs of the times in the light of their inherited vision of a universal fraternity. Their actions demonstrate a reasonable flexibility and a creative adjustment to the fraternal exigencies of real life. This practical engagement with evangelical poverty provokes critical questions that constantly involve the friars in questions of commerce, politics and economics. The "troubling questions" that gave rise to the Capuchin Order's meditations on evangelical poverty forced friars to re-evaluate their international situation and to address anthropological issues at the core of economic matters. Among them are:

- How do friars live in an unequal and, at times, unjust world?
- How do they use the goods of this world and how do they manage their time, talent and resources?
- What do they do with surplus? How do they invest? How do they understand their relationships and obligations with one another across provincial boundaries and international borders? What is their response to the rise of globalization and its discontents?

Clearly, their meditation provides a blueprint and a framework for action. First, there is to be no disengagement from the world. Economic questions, class differences and the inequities that derive from a divided world are not to be avoided or brushed aside. Francis' own conversion to the human, which began when Francis overcame his revulsion, accepted the leper and brought him into his world as "brother," set into motion a new social ethic that would pull in all peoples, friends and enemies, and indeed all creation into the cosmic fraternity of gospel love.

Secondly, with regard to the inequalities and deficits that attend the human condition, Francis proposes what he believes to be a more solid foundation for peace and security than the inevitable resort to avarice and the brutal restraint of arms on the part of his contemporaries. His conviction revolves around the potency of poverty as a relational dynamic, believing that the voluntary ceding of one's demands for priority and privilege in favor of self-sacrificing love, under God's gracious dominion, is a more fruitful and creative solution to the human quest for social harmony.

Thirdly, the Capuchin's social catechesis begins to engage the inevitable question of profit, surplus, the just wage, the just profit and the propriety of investment in a world characterized by amazing diversity but also stunning disparity. Friars can no longer avoid the gnawing questions of privilege structured into the conventions, customs and systems of fraternal exchange of goods, services and personnel within the Order and in the world in which they live. The old order of juridic dependence has broken down and, in the face of economic globalization and the universalization of charism, it must be replaced by a new system of economic solidarity that will impact the identity and action of each friar and fraternity, their understanding of mission and their relationship to authority.[91] No wonder Corriveau has called this development "revolutionary."

---

[91] Left largely untreated in the Capuchin discourse is the question of "authority," who decides and how are decisions arrived at in this new fraternal economy. Corriveau begins a treatment of this difficult question in his 21 Circular Letter but the topic is of such importance that one could recommend an analysis of the "political philosophy of the fraternal economy."

SUMMARY

In this chapter, I have tried to provide the background needed to appreciate the insights of the "fraternal economy," as it has
been developed in the recent *Plenary Councils of the Order and the
Circular Letters of John Corriveau* (from 1994-2004). This was done
through (1) a brief analysis of the economic models that condition
and shape the contemporary world and (2) an extended exposition of the concepts, themes and images leading up to the expression of the "fraternal economy" in Capuchin literature. We noted
that the "fraternal economy" stands in contrast to the prevailing
"market economy" of the day. It is rooted firmly in a theology of
communion and solidarity that has recast the Order's understanding of its fundamental mission and purpose in the modern world.
The Order no longer understands its identity and action in the
world in clerical or even ministerial terms. The Order exists in the
Church and on the margins of society for fraternal evangelical witness, to create fraternity and brotherhood in the world (especially
where there is apparently none) and to reveal the cosmic unity of
all things in Christ.

As we have noted, this can only be begun in humility and minority in the Order by brothers immersed in contemplative prayer
and committed to a joyful embrace of their brotherhood and the
readiness to be formed by grace into a free communion of persons
without domination or deprivation. This is not a solitary venture
or a private enterprise. The fraternal economy is a personal and
fraternal commitment. It is an organizational reality with personal,
interpersonal and structural dynamics. An individual cannot accomplish the Franciscan mission on his or her own. The development of a true Franciscan presence in the world takes collaboration and mutual dependence, courageous choices of minority,
redeemed and reconstituted relationships, authority without domination, service characterized by humility and a life exercised on the
social periphery.[92]

The fraternal economy is essentially a new way of being and
acting in the world today. It stands as a clear, albeit vulnerable,
alternative to the market economy that rules the day. Its rules are

---

[92] This list emerges from the Proposals of the VII Plenary Council (March 2004),
n.6.

not the competition, ambition and greed that drive the market fundamentalism of contemporary economics. The fraternal economy is rooted, paradoxically enough, in freely chosen and mutually engaged poverty. It is exercised by a community intent on the gracious experience of brotherhood, found in its communion with God in the Spirit of the Christ crucified in self-emptying love for the world.

We turn now to a psychological analysis of religious vocation and an application of its theory and existential confirmations to our theme of the fraternal economy.

CHAPTER SIX
TOWARD THE PSYCHODYNAMICS OF
GOSPEL BROTHERHOOD

There are several reasons to subject our theme of "the fraternal economy" to a psychological analysis. First, as already been noted, it is rare that actions on behalf of justice in the Church are mined for the "psychological complexities" of the act of faith that does justice. Theologians, even those strongly committed to exposing the social dimensions of sin and reconciliation, rarely treat the psychological obstacles that hinder the liberation process and the psychological competencies that would advance it. Avery Dulles observed:

> In the liberation theologies I have read, there is no adequate study of the psychological complexity of the act of faith. Liberation theology has been in dialogue with sociology and economics but not to the same extent with the disciplines that seek to penetrate to the inner depths of the human spirit.[1]

As a confirmation of this lack, Bryan Massingale, in a doctoral dissertation on the social dimensions of sin and reconciliation in the thought of two premier theologians of liberation (James Cone and Gustavo Gutierrez), concludes that neither of these theologians take the psychological complexities seriously enough. He writes,

---

[1] Avery Dulles, "The Meaning of Faith Considered in Relationship to Justice," in John C. Haughey, (ed.) *The Faith that Does Justice* (Ramsey, NJ: Paulist Press, 1977) 39-40.

While there is some attention given to the psychological effects that internalizing a culture's pejorative evaluations has upon the oppressed (e.g., passivity, docility, and self-hatred) – Cone seems to be more interested in this than Gutierrez – this is not a major concern for either theologian. Nor is there much advertence to the psychological obstacles that would impede the development of a stance of solidarity with the poor on the part of the privileged segments of society.[2]

Secondly, providing for and exposing, in some fashion, the psychological dimensions of the fraternal economy allows a more ample and thus more complete, if not more complex, picture of moral agency in the world. As Gregory Baum has indicated, there are two dimensions of action involved in the promotion of justice or in its obstruction.[3] There is the voluntary dimension and then there is the nonvoluntary dimension.

The *voluntary* dimension of justice concerns those structures or options that are the result of freedom and awareness. They are the actions that are the consequence of purposeful intentionality and conscious determination in the pursuit of that which is good or in the performance of that which is evil. It is the arena, for example, in which individuals and communities choose to do the good, avoid evil (individually and communally) and take responsibility for the defects in the construction of the just society, because they see and understand what is going on in and around them. It is also the arena in which individuals allow themselves to be taken in by false claims, drawn into acts that are discriminatory, or led (consciously and with their own complicity) into situations that are unfair and unethical. In our terms, the voluntary dimension of the fraternal economy would be all those measures that are the result of friars' conscious efforts, determined choices, considered intent and desired awareness to build brotherhood in community or, on the other hand, obstruct communion in the world. But, there is another dimension that is more rarely treated, i.e. the nonvoluntary.

---

[2] Bryan N. Massingale, *The Social Dimensions of Sin and Reconciliation in the Theologies of James H. Cone and Gustavo Gutierrez* (Rome: Pontificia Unversitas Alphosianum, 1991), p. 490.

[3] Gregory Baum, "Structures of Sin," in Gregory Baum and Robert Ellsberg, (eds.), *The Logic of Solidarity* (Maryknoll, NY: Orbis Books, 1989), p.110-117.

The nonvoluntary dimension refers to that level of agency and action that, in some sense, precedes our participation and, in unconscious and unintended ways, conditions the voluntary aspects of our intentions, our expectations and our desires. That is to say, we come to moral dilemma and situations of injustice that have their own social history and a moral baggage that precedes us, a trail of assumptions, intentions, meaning and purpose that is often outside our knowledge, advertence or even conscious acceptance. We are conditioned by contexts and circumstances of which we may be largely unaware. We may be bound to situations about which we have little or no understanding, consent, or choice. The nonvoluntary dimension so resides at a level below the surface of consciousness that even patently immoral and unjustifiable actions may appear normal and may continue beyond question. In fact, these actions are often justified by reasonable explanations and defended by a persuasive commonsense through the psychological dynamics and organizational maneuvers of groups who may remain largely unaware of the tactics they are using and the reasons why they are using them.

A psychological analysis of the fraternal economy allows us entrance into this venue of the voluntary and involuntary dimensions of evangelical poverty. It allows for a more persuasive engagement of the range of expectations and desires, both individual and social, which are at play when brothers seek to promote gospel brotherhood in the world. A psychological analysis of the "fraternal economy" allows us to enunciate more completely the ideals of gospel brotherhood and the communion of all creation and to consider as well the resistances to them.

Another reason to subject our topic to a psychological analysis is that we are trying to understand the vocation of the Franciscan friar, his call in the world today, as a commitment of the whole person. Because of this, we are bound to treat the friar within the full range of his capacities and potentialities. We cannot reduce the friar as a human person to a sociological description, i.e. the "economic man" of 19th century classical economic liberalism. A friar is even more than the exogenous or social forces that condition and provide context for his actions. He is more than the "consumer" or "producer" categories used to describe individuals in the economic world. His needs are not circumscribed by the supposed infinite range of desires promoted in contemporary advertising strategies.[4] As Karl Rahner has reminded us, there is a self-transcendent remainder in the human person that, even unconsciously and anonymously, seeks, desires, hopes in and trains its sights on and is never satisfied unless and until one abides in the infinity of God.[5] We need a fuller description of the motivations and desires that course through the veins of the modern person and such a description must include a finely tuned elucidation of the mechanisms that translate these desires into action or frustrate these motivations into apathy.

At the same time, we cannot reduce the friar or any person solely to a spiritual or theological description, if by that we have excised or bracketed out for supposed "religious" purposes the horizon of expectations, needs and desires that reside in the human heart, sometimes below the screen of consciousness.[6] A psychological analysis of the fraternal economy will be, by definition, a partial description of the human person. And yet, it can and ought to be a critical exploration of the dynamics that are at play when friars choose to promote a more just society in the world today.[7] A psychological analysis can expose some of the motivations that drive the intention for evangelical fraternity and gospel brotherhood, at the conscious and unconscious levels of the human person. It may also reveal those motivations that seek to obstruct, resist, delay, deny or otherwise stall the fulfillment of even deeply held and loudly proclaimed values for the fraternal economy.

A third reason to develop a psychological analysis of the fraternal economy is because the issues attached to it and the concerns contained within it are fraught with deep emotion and considerable feeling. The concept we are considering is "revolutionary" and calls for a "profound conversion" of individuals and their

---

[4] Roger Rosenblatt, *Consuming Desires: Consumption, Culture and the Pursuit of Happiness* (Washington, D.C.: Island Press, 1999) and Vincent J. Miller, *Consuming Religion: Christian Faith and Practice in a Consumer Culture* (New York: Continuum, 2003).

[5] Karl Rahner, SJ, *Theological Investigations, VI,* (New York: Seabury Press, 1974) pp. 178-196. For another perspective on the theocentric self-transcendence of the human person, cf. Bernard Lonergan, SJ, *Method in Theology* (New York: Herder, 1973), p. 110.

[6] The philosopher, Henry Ey, writes: "to be conscious and to be unconscious are two complementary modes of the ontological structure of… every human being," in H. Ey, *Consciousness* (Bloomington and London: Indiana University Press, 1978), p. xix.

[7] For a critical understanding of the belief in a just world, cf. Melvin J. Lerner, *Belief in a Just World: A Fundamental Delusion* (New York: Plenum Press, 1980).

communities. It seeks nothing less, as we have seen, than a replacement of a long and established economic (and relational) system built on suspicion, corruption and division with one that promotes communion and trust by acts of profound humility, generous service and the willingness to forgive the sins of others. As we know from the struggles against apartheid and racial segregation, social change and economic transition do not come without a significant psychological price.[8] They often evoke primitive emotions that are displayed as irrational fear, deep concern, furious rage and outright denial.[9] They are also often defended by powerful rationalizations, justifications, projections and denial.[10] These are part of the "psychological complexities" of the faith that does justice that are often ignored in treatments of social concern in the Church. Our analysis hopes to open up this arena, within the reasonable limits and scope of our study, so that we can understand more clearly not only the ideals that motivate the development of the fraternal economy, but also perhaps the unconscious desires.

The fourth and final reason to consider a psychological analysis of the fraternal economy is because the Capuchin Order is at the beginning of a significant transition in its self-definition. The fraternal economy is, as Corriveau has noted, a "new way of relating economically and socially."[11] The "fraternal economy" introduces a new challenge to formators who are called to help young men in their charge to move in the direction of this newly claimed value. In this work, we are considering the *formative* challenges contained in this revolutionary call. We wish to highlight, among other things, the educational or training dimensions involved in this conversion. There are four levels to the formation in the human person called into vocation: the intellectual, the pastoral, the spiritual and the human.[12] Our psychological analysis attends primarily,

---

[8] But this price is rarely analyzed, cf. James H. Cone, *God of the Oppressed* (New York: Seabury Press, 1975) and Isaac Prilleltensky and Geoffrey Nelson, "Power, Well Being, Oppression and Liberation: Points of Departure," in their book, *Doing Psychology Critically: Making a Difference in Diverse Settings* (New York: Palgrave Macmillan, 2002), pp. 5-20.

[9] Bryan N. Massingale, "Anger and Human Transcendence: A Response to a 'Rahnerian Reading of Black Rage,'" *Philosophy and Theology* 15 (2003), pp. 103-115.

[10] A perceptive analysis of the characteristics of social sinfulness is found in Massingale, *op.cit.*, pp. 132-142.

[11] John Corriveau, "Formation for Capuchin Values," (2004) *op. cit.*, p. 1.

[12] J. Ridick, "Preparing Priests: The Road to Transformation," in Franco Imoda, SJ, (ed.) *A Journey to Freedom: An Interdisciplinary Approach to the Anthropology of Formation*

though not exclusively, to the latter, providing a richer description of the stages of growth, the moments of transition, and the dynamics of internalization (versus compliance) in the individual and in the community that professes its allegiance to promoting this value in the world today.[13]

With these reasons in place, we turn our attention to the exposition of a theory of religious vocation that may shed light on the psychological dynamics involved in the development of the fraternal economy.

A PSYCHOLOGICAL THEORY OF RELIGIOUS VOCATION

In 1976 a team of religious researchers, led by (the late) Fr. Luigi M. Rulla, S.J., was awarded the *International Quinquennial Prize for the Scientific Psychology of Religion* by the International Association for the Psychology of Religion in Brussels.[14] This was no small feat for a team of clinical psychologists who had, only five years before, founded the Institute of Psychology at the Pontifical Gregorian University in Rome, with great difficulty and not without significant suspicion and opposition at the highest levels of the Church.[15]

Their research on the psychological structure of vocation and the intrapsychic dynamics that motivate entrance, perseverance and departure from priesthood and religious life had begun in doctoral dissertations each had completed at the University of Chicago.[16] It blossomed first in an original statement of their theory of

---

(Leuven: Peeters, 2000), pp. 185-214.

[13] For a developmental understanding of vocational growth, cf. Franco Imoda, SJ, *Human Development: Psychology and Mystery* (Leuven: Peeters, 1998).

[14] The other members of the team included Fr. Franco Imoda, S.J. and Sr. Joyce Ridick, SSC.

[15] The suspicion and opposition is chronicled in an article by Herve Carrier, SJ, rector of the Gregorian University at the time of the Institute's founding, in his article, "Twenty-Fifth Anniversary of the Institute of Psychology," Franco Imoda, SJ, (ed.). *A Journey to Freedom: An Interdisciplinary Approach to the Anthropology of Formation* (Leuven: Peeters, 2000), pp. 9-12.

[16] Joyce Ridick, SSC. *Intrapsychic Factors in the Early Dropping Out of Female Religious Vocationers.* Unpublished Ph.D. dissertation, University of Chicago, 1992; Franco Imoda, SJ, *Sociometric Status and Personality in Training Centers for Religious.* Unpublished Ph.D. dissertation, University of Chicago, 1971; Luigi M. Rulla, SJ, *Psychological Significance of Religious Vocation,* Unpublished Ph.D. dissertation, University of Chicago, 1967.

religious vocation ("the theory of self-transcendent consistency") published in 1971 by Fr. Rulla.[17] It was followed five years later by a book that put their theory to the test in a series of empirical studies that probed the motivations of candidates to enter, persevere or leave religious communities and seminaries in Europe and the United States.[18] That theory and its empirical confirmations were developed over the course of more than thirty years of research and clinical investigation at their cross-cultural consultation center for psychotherapy, clinical diagnostics and vocational growth therapy *(Centro di Consultazione)* in Rome.

In 1986, Rulla, Ridick and Imoda published a new two-set volume of theory and existential confirmations that expanded on their original conclusion. It now proposed that their research not only uncovered the psychological processes leading to effective perseverance in religious and priestly life, but that it also laid the foundation and was the confirmation of the psychological structures of the vocational journey of the Christian life, in general.[19] Rulla suggested in his 1986 volume that the psychological structure he had uncovered might well be the general or foundational anthropological framework for all human dynamics:

> In this regard note that, while in previous publications the theory considered only the priestly or religious vocation, the approach taken in the two volumes of the present study holds for the vocation of *all* Christians, since, in an ontological sense, it holds for the human person as such.[20]

In presenting his theory of the "anthropology of vocation," Rulla contends that the structural method adopted in their theory and practice amounts to a mechanism of investigation and ther-

---

[17] L.M. Rulla, SJ, *Depth Psychology and Vocation: A Psycho-social Perspective* (Rome: Gregorian University Press, and Chicago: Loyola University Press, 1971).

[18] Luigi M. Rulla, SJ, Joyce Ridick, SSC, and Franco Imoda, SJ, *Entering and Leaving Vocation: Intrapsychic Dynamics* (Rome: Gregorian University Press, and Chicago: Loyola University Press, 1976).

[19] Luigi M. Rulla, SJ, *Anthropology of the Christian Vocation, Vol. 1. Interdisciplinary Bases* (Rome: Gregorian University Press, 1986); Luigi M. Rulla, SJ, Joyce Ridick, SSC, and Franco Imoda, SJ, *Anthropology of the Christian Vocation, Vol.II. Existential Confirmation* (Rome: Gregorian University Press, 1989). From here on in, we will refer to these two volumes as ACVI and ACVII.

[20] Rulla, *ACVI, op.cit.,* p. 307.

apeutic intervention that is trans-situational and trans-cultural.[21] This universal applicability is based on (1) the fundamental drive for theocentric self-transcendence in every human being; (2) the basic dialectic in each person between what we hope to be (the "self as transcending") and what we have become (the "self as transcended); (3) the qualitative difference between self-transcendent and natural values which are ontologically inherent in human nature.[22] Departing from the premise and assumption held by this research team that the theory of self-transcendent consistency and anthropology of vocation are indeed applicable across situations and cultures, we will apply them to the emerging "situation" of the fraternal economy in the Capuchin-Franciscan Order. But, first, we must offer the main lines and general direction of the research.

Clearly, we cannot hope to present their system to the reader in all its finely tuned details or to replicate their intricate series of empirical trials, without subjecting the reader to the more than 1,000 pages that their final two volumes alone take up. We can, however, offer a careful summary that faithfully presents the methodology and conclusions of what Rulla himself has called "a more comprehensive Christian anthropological vision."[23] We turn now to a look at the drive toward self-transcendence in the human person and the dynamics that promote and those that hinder its realization.

THE DRIVE TOWARD SELF-TRANSCENDENCE IN GOD

The pivot and core of Rulla's theory and his vision of the vocational call of each person in Christ is the inexorable (and ontologically prior) drive of the human person toward God. The human person exists for God and can never truly be satisfied unless and until that person presents himself or herself fully and integrally, in a totality that encompasses each and every part of one's human life, into the hands of the living and

---

[21] *Ibid.*, p. 334.

[22] Rulla arrives at this conclusion from a lengthy and detailed interdisciplinary investigation of works by Lonergan, Rahner, Wojtyla, Ey, Ricoeur, von Hildebrand, Mondin, deFinance among others. Cf. Rulla, *ACVI*, pp. 1-334.

[23] L.M. Rulla, SJ, "Towards a Christian Anthropology," in Franco Imoda, *A Journey to Freedom, op.cit.*, p. 227.

loving God of all creation. Rulla is fond of quoting the philosopher, Bernard Lonergan, on this point:

> The question of God, then, lies within man's horizon. Man's transcendental subjectivity is mutilated or abolished, unless he is stretching forth towards the intelligible, the unconditioned, and the good of value. The reach, not of his attainment, but of his intending is unrestricted. There lies within his horizon a region for the divine, a shrine for ultimate holiness. It cannot be ignored. The atheist may pronounce it empty. The agnostic may urge that he finds his investigation has been inconclusive. The contemporary humanist will refuse to allow the question to arise. But their negations presuppose the spark in our clod, our native orientation to the divine.[24]

This capacity for a theocentric or God-centered self-transcendence and the corresponding but fully graced call that God freely offers to each person is a distinguishing mark of the psychological project undertaken by Rulla and his colleagues. As Browning notes, most psychological endeavors and personality theories employ what he calls deep narratives or "metaphors of ultimacy," but they remain only implicit. He says, "… their psychologies… have religious horizons for which they give no explicit scientific account."[25]

Rulla and his colleagues, on the other hand, openly discuss and make critically central the conscious intentionality of all persons to transcend themselves towards that which is ultimately true, good and beautiful. Rulla grounds his theory first in a cognitional self-transcendence, whereby individuals go beyond themselves intellectually to come to knowledge.

> The person thus comes to know not just what appears, nor what is imagined, nor what is thought, nor what merely seem to him (sic) to be so, but that which *is* so. To know what really is so is to go beyond the subject and transcend the subject, reaching

---

[24] B. Lonergan, SJ, *Method*, p. 103. [Neither Lonergan or Rulla use gender inclusive language. We apologize to the readers.]

[25] Don S. Browning, "Can Psychology Escape Religion? Should It?" in Franco Imoda, *A Journey to Freedom*, *op.cit.*, p. 44.

that which would still be, even if this particular subject did not exist.[26]

But, there is a second level of transcendence in which we come to know, to desire and to do that which is truly good, beyond all merely personal interests, preferences, pleasures and satisfactions. This is the further step of moral self-transcendence.[27] It is succeeded (or superceded) by a third level, which is the self-transcendence of love, whereby the "isolation of the individual is broken, and he [sic] functions not only for himself but also for others."[28] Here love moves from intention to action, influencing our decisions and deeds. It is the self-transcendence that reaches out to fellow human beings in empathy or charitable action. It is the care that respects the needs and seeks the fulfillment of responsibilities to spouse or children. It is also the positive and caring attention to humanity and the common good which seeks the benefit and welfare of others locally, nationally or globally. And then, there is our love for God, which is nothing other than the gift of God's love for us, which becomes a free, self-donation. It is otherworldly in that "it does not admit conditions, qualifications, restrictions, or reservations."[29]

This is the foundation and centerpiece of Rulla's psychological system, one that distinguishes his theory and practice from others who limit or reduce the intentions and desires of humanity to the purely natural, material or even simply social world around us. There is a teleological reach to Rulla's initial theoretical frame and a thrust that reaches all the way to the Infinite. Rulla and his colleagues have tried to compose an analytical system of psychodynamics that factors in and does not exclude the farthest reaches and the deepest meaning of humanity's hunger for that which is really real, truly beautiful, and ultimately good. As de Finance has indicated, "It is... the absolute Other and nonetheless the source of my very being – who gives me to myself and yet tears me from

---

[26] Rulla, *ACVI*, p. 144.

[27] Tim Healy, SJ, "The Challenge of Self Transcendence: *The Anthropology of the Christian Vocation* and Bernard Lonergan," in Franco Imoda, *A Journey into Freedom, op.cit.*, p. 70-115.

[28] Rulla, *ACVI*, p. 144.

[29] *Ibid.*, p. 145.

myself; it is (that) presence which puts into me a principle of interior tension and of passing beyond myself."[30]

At the same time, Rulla's theory admits of a fundamental *dialectic* in life. There is not only thrust in human existence, there is a drag. There is not only reach; there is also hindrance. While there is a fundamental freedom in the human person that excludes determinism and opens up in them the possibility of choosing that which is true and of value in itself, there is, at the same time, "an opposition of motivational forces, which is inherent in the motivational system of the human person."[31] It is the tension between the immediate and the transcendent, that which is (sensually or emotionally) satisfying in the here and now and that which is rationally important in itself, beyond immediate satisfaction.[32]

Rulla posits then two fundamental anthropological realities, two data of psychological significance. The first is the *self-transcending* dimension of life that draws us forward to the farthest limits or, better yet, potentialities of the Infinite through knowledge, will and love. The second is the *self-transcended* dimension of life, "the forces of ambiguity" that hold us back, weigh us down, bend us backwards and constitute an obstacle, even if unintended, to the freedom to live out the anthropological tendency to theocentric self-transcendence. These are the anthropological realities of life. This is the situation and the dramatic stuff in which human freedom and authenticity operate.

Rulla and his colleagues further contend that this anthropological struggle creates over time, both gradually and spontaneously, two structures in the personality.[33] In the choices that we make in early childhood and youth (and even through the unseen and unconscious adaptations made over time) because of the influence of values, attitudes and needs, each person constructs a human personality made up of two inter-related structures. First, there

---

[30] J. DeFinance, *Essai sur l'Agir humain.* (Rome: Gregorian University Press, 1962), p. 191.

[31] Rulla, *ACVI,* p. 150.

[32] For the distinction between rational wanting and emotional wanting in Rulla's theory, cf. Rulla, *Depth Psychology and Vocation* (Rome: Gregorian University Press, 1971), pp. 31-34.

[33] For an extensive reading of the developmental theory underlying the anthropology of the Christian vocation, cf. Franco Imoda, *Human Development: Psychology and Mystery* (Leuven: Peeters, 1998).

is the part of the self that in fact grows in self-transcendence, or resists it consciously or unconsciously. This is the part of the self that is built up over time, the constellation of values, attitudes and needs that have become, with various intensities and at different levels of consciousness, the motivational organization of the self. Rulla calls this *'the actual self.*[34] There is, however, a second structure (interacting with the first) that is called the *"ideal self"* and this refers to the "part of the subject that *wants* to grow more and more, that *wants* to progress towards knowledge, the good, and love, as far as fullness and perfection."[35] This is part of the self that is beyond the immediate and the available in the here and now. It can critique "primary processes," because it is an area of personality whose judgment can appraise the limits and forego the immediate benefits of a situation at hand.

Rulla adds two substructures to this construction of the Christian personality. First, the ideal self is made up, in his system, of a *personal self-ideal* (SI), consisting of the (proclaimed and consciously held) ideals that a person wants for himself or herself, and of an *institutional ideal* (II), made up of the perceptions or understanding that one has of the values/ideals which are proposed to him/her in the community to which one seeks to belong. Secondly, in the actual self we find what Rulla designates as the *manifest self* (PB or "present behavior") and the *latent self* (LS). The "manifest self" consists of the knowledge that individuals have of themselves and their actions. It is their understanding of themselves at present, in the here and now. The "latent self" consists of those characteristics that individuals have in themselves but without awareness of them. It is the side of the personality where emotional needs and attitudes, for example, can play out defensively, that is, out of sight of one's conscious awareness, consent or choice.

It is clear from this very brief introduction to a complex system of thought that ambiguity and tension are an inevitable part of the drama of human and religious growth. There is, in Rulla's thought, a fundamental dialectic within and between the structures of human personality. On one side is the structure of the ideal self that tends (through consciously held ideals and values) towards un-

---

[34] Rulla, *ACVI, p. 167,* and in *Depth Psychology and Vocation* (Rome: Gregorian University Press, 1971), p. 35-37.
[35] Rulla, *ibid.,* p. 166.

limited self-transcendence. It is the side of the self that yearns to become. It is the structure on which the call of God for unlimited freedom, truth and love depend for actualization. On the other side is the structure of the actual self, the reality of what we have become and have made of ourselves for ourselves, through the accumulation of conscious adjustments and unconscious adaptations. Human growth and development happen in the arc between this "self as transcending" and this "self as transcended," between the structures of the ideal self and the structures of the actual self.

We have alluded to the unconscious several times. We need not offer, for our purposes, a comprehensive justification of Rulla's utilization of this dimension of human personality. We need only note that his reasoning is extensive[36] and gives weight to his understanding of the fundamental ambiguity in the motivational system of those who enter, persevere or withdraw from vocational life.

Thus far we have stressed the *structural* aspects of Rulla's theory of self-transcendent consistency. When considering the structure of personality (which is a more or less permanent and consistent psychodynamic edifice that has been built up over time), we are speaking of two entities developed over the course of one's history: the ideal self and the actual self. The ideal self is that part of the personality consisting of what a person wants to be or become – that which a person desires or hopes for oneself. The actual self consists of what a person really is (whether he or she knows it or not) and the way that a person habitually acts.

Within the personality structure, there are also *contents* – the building blocks of Christian personality, if you will, of values, attitudes and needs. Relying in part on Rokeach, Rulla considers values as enduring abstract beliefs of a person about ideal end states of existence or ideal modes of conduct.[37] Utilizing the philosophical work of deFinance especially, Rulla distinguishes between objective and subjective values and makes a crucial distinction in the vocational life between (revealed and objective) self-transcendent values[38] and merely natural values (i.e., prosperity or misery, per-

---

[36] Rulla, *ACVI*, Chapter 6, "The Conscious and Unconscious," pp. 78-116.

[37] M. Rokeach, *Beliefs, Attitudes and Values: A Theory of Organizations and Change* (San Francisco: Jossey Bass, 1968.)

[38] From his theological análysis of the documents of Vatican II, Rulla identifies two terminal objective values for religious life (imitation of Christ and union with God) and

sonal success or failure). [39]It should be clear by now that, according to Rulla, religious or vocational life would tend by nature to be a graced response to self-transcendent values, since they "engage the exercise of the freedom of the whole person towards the self-transcendence for theocentric love; while natural values are a measure of the person in specific areas, (e.g., whether he is rich, handsome or intelligent, etc.) (S)elf-transcendent values provide a criterion for judging if the person in his totality acts well or badly."[40]

Rulla defines the second content of the personality, *needs*, as "action tendencies resulting from a deficit of the organism or from natural inherent potentialities which seek exercise or actuality."[41] They are innate inclinations or sources of motivation that appear to be universal. Rulla uses the typology developed by H.A. Murray both in his theory and in the statistical confirmation of it.[42] In that typology, needs are universal and innate, for example, the need for nurturance, aggression, sexuality, and dependency. Needs can be expressed through our attitudes: a need to be aggressive can be expressed in an attitude of wanting to constantly compete with others or get even with authority figures. Needs do not have to appear in the clear light of consciousness. Sometimes early life experiences may have made some needs unacceptable to the person, thus inviting the construction of defenses or other forms of resistance.[43] It should be noted that Rulla, using Murray's typology, considers the following needs as fundamentally vocationally dissonant: abasement, aggression, defendence, exhibition, harm-avoidance, sexual gratification, and succorance.[44] They work (by definition) at cross-purposes to the objective terminal and instrumental values of religion.[45]

---

three instrumental values, namely poverty, chastity and obedience. Both are objective self-transcendent values. Cf. Rulla, *Depth Psychology, op.cit.,* pp. 69-73.

[39] Rulla, *ACVI,* p.158-163.

[40] *Ibid.,* p. 162.

[41] Rulla, *Depth Psychology, op. cit.,* p. 31.

[42] H.A. Murray, *Explorations in Personality* (New York: Oxford Press, 1938).

[43] Rulla, Ridick and Imoda, ACVII, pp. 173-174.

[44] Rulla, *ACVI,* p. 313.

[45] This is not to suggest that, in Rulla's theory, that one can simply dismiss the presence and function of emotional needs in the personality. The matter is one of integration and internalization, rather than mere compliance, with the emotional needs operative in one's life. Cf. Rulla, *Depth Psychology, op. cit.,* pp. 149-150 and 358-361.

The last content used in the construction of the Christian personality is attitudes. Relying on Allport and McGuire, Rulla defines attitudes as "…a mental and neural state of *readiness to respond*, organized through experience, exerting a directive and/or dynamic (level of energy) influence on mental and physical activity."[46] Whereas needs tend to be innate and universal, attitudes appear to be an acquired and a more personal source of motivation. They are action-tendencies to respond in a certain manner under certain conditions. For a dynamic understanding of attitudes, it is helpful to remember that attitudes are fluid or flexible in the motivational system. As a readiness to respond in a particular situation, an attitude can be developed to serve one's values or to advance one's emotional needs, even if unconsciously. Therefore, following Katz, it is critical to know not only the content of an attitude but also its various functions in the personality.[47]

Having outlined the teleological thrust of Rulla's theory and that of his colleagues, Imoda and Ridick, and having demonstrated the general pattern of the content and structure of their theory, we can return to a critical insight touched upon above, e.g., the ambiguity of the motivational system.

Rulla, Ridick and Imoda have concluded that, while the goal of Christian life is clear (e.g., a self-transcendent theocentric love), the mechanisms and dynamics that serve that end are fraught with the potential of ambiguity, tension, conflict and inconsistency, thus compromising in significant ways, the ability of some well-meaning religious to internalize effectively the values they have consciously chosen to live. In short, the vocational life is a struggle, but qualitatively different for some.

The existence of anthropological constants of a self-transcending and a self-transcended, when combined with the real possibility of conscious (objective) values contradicting emotional needs or attitudes, especially at an unconscious level, portends the development of structures or horizons of expectations over time

---

[46] G.W. Allport, "Attitudes in the History of Social Psychology," in G.Lindzey (ed), *Handbook of Social Psychology, Vol. I.* (Reading, MA: Addison-Wesley, 1954), pp. 43-45; W.J. McGuire, "The Nature of Attitudes and Attitude Change," in G. Lindzey and E. Aronson, *The Handbook of Social Psychology, Vol. III.* (Reading, MA: Addison-Wesley, 1969), pp. 136-314.

[47] D. Katz, "The functional approach to the study of attitude change," *Public Opinion Quarterly* 9 (1964) pp. 131-146.

that are at odds or dissonant with, in some fashion and to some degree, the intended goals or values of vocational life.

Rulla, Ridick and Imoda claim to have uncovered three dimensions of psycho-spiritual life that correspond to the dialectic structures emerging from the interaction of the ideal self with the actual self.[48] Each dimension constitutes a vantage point, a horizon of expectations and desires, which condition the range of imagination and perception as dispositions of the transcending self in relationship to the values presented to the individual.[49] Because of this structural differential, people experience, judge, imagine, and evaluate situations from (qualitatively and not just quantitatively) different perspectives. They do so on a different plain of desire or horizon of expectations. The predominating or privileged vantage point in the individual offers a more or less limited range of options for the religious imagination, impacting the effective (not absolute) freedom of the individual.

In what Rulla, Ridick and Imoda call the *first dimension*, an individual has over time developed, through experience, choices and accommodations (made consciously and unconsciously), a structure of perception and awareness that allows the individual to attend, more or less consistently, to natural and self-transcendent values. It is an area and a condition of maximum freedom and choice. Because the structural alignment of motivational forces favors the ideal self (with its constellation of values and ideals) and the part of the actual self that is conscious and available to conscious awareness and disposition (i.e., the manifest self or PB), it is the area in which the individual can and does make choices that freely promote or severely limit that very freedom. It is not, therefore, an arena without tension and frustration, since the individual must make the daily choices to follow the good and to avoid that which is evil. It is the area of virtue and vice.

The *third dimension* is that zone of conflict, most often elaborated in traditional schools of abnormal psychology.[50] We need not elaborate on the origins of this third dimension of fundamental

---

[48] Rulla, *ACVI*, pp. 171-195 and Rulla, Ridick and Imoda, *ACVII*, pp. 107-116.

[49] Rulla, *ACVI*, P. 174.

[50] Jerrold S. Maxmen and Nicholas G. Ward, *Essential Psychopathology and Its Treatment*, 2nd ed. (New York: W.W. Norton, 1995).

emotional health or illness (e.g., pathology)[51] but only suggest that there are individuals who, because of history (e.g., abuse, severe post-traumatic stress or biological/genetic imbalances), live constantly within the parameters of this dimension where primitive needs can affect in a consistent and troubling manner ordinary functions of work and intimacy. In Rulla's theory, individuals who live primarily in the third dimension struggle on a regular basis with their, more or less, primitive emotional needs (e.g., abasement and dependency) and attend on a, more or less, ever present primitive defenses (e.g., paranoia, splitting, massive denial, etc.).[52]

It is the *second dimension* that is the novelty in Rulla, Ridick and Imoda's research and writing.[53] They claim to have discovered an area of personality that is neither the full freedom nor the authentic struggle of virtue and vice (with its moral designations of responsibility and culpability). Nor is it the zone of pathology and disturbance regulated under the rubric of psychological conflict and elaborated in most textbooks of abnormal psychology.[54] It is a dimension, which is neither sin nor pathology, but which has unconscious components and includes unconscious defenses regarding both natural and theocentric values. While the first dimension derives from conscious structures (between the ideal self and the conscious portion of the actual self, i.e., the "present behavior" or PB concept of oneself), the second dimension is a structure made up of conscious and unconscious elements. More precisely, it is the equilibrium between the ideal self (that is conscious) and the *unconscious* actual self. It is the struggle or inconsistency between the consciously held and publicly proclaimed values of religion and the largely unconscious segment of oneself as he or she really is, even without knowing it.

---

[51] Cf., for example, Herbert Weiner, "Schizophrenia: Etiology," in Herbert I. Kaplan and Benjamin Sadock, *Comprehensive Textbook of Psychiatry, Vol. Two, Fourth Edition.* (Baltimore: Williams and Wilkins, 1985), pp. 650-679.

[52] For an explanation of defenses, cf. William W. Meisner, SJ, "Theories of Personality and Psychopathology: Classical Psychoanalysis," in Kaplan and Sadock, *Comprehensive Textbook, Vol.I, Fourth Edition, op. cit.*, pp. 388-390.

[53] Rulla, Ridick and Imoda, *ACVII*, pp. 173-178, 180-181, 193-195, 284-298.

[54] O. Kernberg, "Neurosis, Psychosis and the Borderline States," in *Comprehensive Textbook of Psychiatry.* H.I. Kaplan, A.M. Freedman and B.J. Sadock (eds.) (Baltimore, MD: Williams and Wilkins, 1980), pp. 1079-1082.

As Rulla indicates, there is no immediate question of virtue or sin in the second dimension. Nor is there a determination of moral good or evil, because freedom and responsibility are more or less limited by the unconscious. What we have here is the development of a perceptual structure of attention and a somewhat restricted horizon of expectations and desires that make the living out of publicly proclaimed values chronically difficult and frustrating, but not impossible. In the second dimension, one is not seeing the fullest range of one's theocentric potential in its clarity and full light. That is because it is often, and with varying degrees - depending on the inconsistent needs at play - obscured by pressing emotional considerations (needs and desires) and their defenses, even without awareness and much cognitive dissonance.

As stated above, this is not a question of sin or pathology. It is, as Rulla describes it, a "dimension of non-culpable error" and inconsistencies that can impact one's effectiveness in ministry and service but, because of its unconscious roots, defies awareness, escapes reform, and can easily remain untouched by the pull of moral conscience and responsibility.

In this dimension, legitimate values are (unconsciously) translated into inappropriate agenda or convenient ideological justifications that seek personal satisfaction or accommodation. This is so even as the values of the person continue to be publicly and, in that sense, honestly proclaimed (because they are believed to be true and operative).

This is the dissonance of the second dimension. Individuals hold and publicly proclaim the self-transcendent values that are important to them and their institutions while, at the same time and in unconscious and restricted fashion, undermining the actualization of the very values they hope to be consistent and effective in practicing.

Change is difficult in the second dimension because the existence of the inconsistency is oftentimes beyond awareness as are the defensive measures used to protect the concept one has of oneself in the practice of one's beliefs. When there are multiple inconsistencies working together, in various ways, to protect the viability of an inappropriate (for vocation) emotional need, one can imagine the network of defensive adaptations and ideological justifications one can construct in order to keep one's religious or vocational life moving forward, in some fashion.

It is important to note that we do not live in only one dimension. The human person, as an integral whole, is a structured unity of all three dimensions in Rulla's theory. Every individual constructs - overtime and through the course of human development - these three structures: a dimension of conscious intention and capability to transcend oneself, *and* a dimension of ambivalence and inconsistency between consciously proclaimed ideals and subconsciously held needs, *and* a dimension of primitive emotions, drives and defenses that result in some degree of conflict. We see the world, as it were, through the lenses of three different, but inter-related, optics working in the psycho-spiritual life. The question that should interest religious leaders, therapists, formation advisors and spiritual directors is the one that seeks an answer as to the prevalence of which dimension is primarily at work in a person's life. Which is the "preferred" dimension? It is important to know which dimension predominates and which type of struggle is primarily at work in a person's motivational system (i.e., virtue/vice, inconsistencies or emotional conflicts)?

CONFIRMATION OF A PSYCHOLOGICAL THEORY

If the theory of self-transcendent consistency and the anthropology of vocation were simply hypotheses, they could easily be dismissed as probative musings and the interesting conjectures of high-minded psychologists. What has interested and intrigued researchers, however, is the existential confirmation or statistical research elaborated by Rulla, Ridick and Imoda in 1976 and then again in 1989.[55] We cannot hope to revisit, within the space and constraints of this chapter, their original research design or the psychometric procedures used to confirm their hypotheses. We refer the reader to the original texts themselves and to several authors who have followed a similar methodology.[56] We can, how-

---

[55] L.M. Rulla, Joyce Ridick, and Franco Imoda, *Entering and Leaving Vocation: Intrapsychic Dynamics* (Rome: Gregorian University Press, 1976) and *Anthropology of the Christian Vocation, Vol. II* (Rome: Gregorian University Press, 1989).

[56] Marie Eugene D'Almedia, *Psychological and Spiritual Factors in Formation.* Unpublished Ph.D. dissertation, Gregorian University, Rome, 1992; Anna Bissi, *Vocation and the Stages of Love.* Unpublished Ph.D. dissertation. Gregorian University, Rome, 1990; Kieran McCarthy, *Psychological Factors in Obedience.* Unpublished Ph.D. dissertation, Gregorian

ever, briefly outline their methodology and draw out their major conclusions in a way that is both fair to their exacting experimental design and the needs of our work here.

Briefly stated, the subjects who participated in the original experimental design were religious of both sexes and also seminarians and control groups composed of Catholic lay students, both men and women, attending Catholic colleges. The male religious and seminarians belonged to three different centers and the women religious in the study belonged to three different institutional centers. The lay students that made up the control groups attended four different universities.

Questionnaires were employed to test the various levels of psychic life and functioning, e.g, preconscious, subconscious, etc. Among them were the *Thematic Apperception Test, Rotter, Minnesota Multiphasic Personality Inventory (MMPI), the Sixteen Personality Factor Questionnaire (Finney)*, the thirty six scales of the *Modified Activities Index (MAI) and the Vassar Attitude Inventory (Webster, Sanford and Freedman)*, among others. The total number of variables studied was 162, for each session in which the tests were given. Various statistical tests were employed to evaluate the data: Chi-square, multivariate analysis of variance, the sign test, the Wilcoxon test and the significance of correlation.[57]

The tests were administered in three different sessions at three different points in the formation process (ten days after entrance; about two years later; about four years after entry). The same tests were given three times to each religious group. For the lay control group, the tests were administered at the end of the first week on campus and at the beginning of their fourth year of college.

Besides the questionnaires, two interviews were administered. The first was an interview on the dynamics of the family (Family Interview: FI) and the second was a depth interview (DI), explained as an "exploration of the nature and content of the person's inconsistencies or conflicts, to find out the degree to which

---

University, Rome, 1989; Brenda Dolphin, *The Values of the Gospel and Thematic Perception.* Unpublished Ph.D. dissertation, Gregorian University, Rome, 1991.

[57] Rulla, Ridick and Imoda, *ACVII*, p. 100.

the subject was conscious or his problems and to observe the personal characteristics of the subject."[58]

We cannot replicate here the sophistication or the breadth of the studies. We can offer, however, an example of the results, especially as they may relate to and provide insight into the psychodynamics of justice and social concern.

First of all, the research of Rulla, Ridick and Imoda shows that those who enter religious life or seminary do so on the basis of their personal ideals, that which they would like to be or become and they tend to have a more or less idealized picture of their religious congregations. Research shows that, along with this germinative mode of entrance, there is also a vulnerable motivation. The vocational motivation of 60 to 80% of candidates was marked by attitudes that were in the service of subconscious needs – attitudes that were held to satisfy or to defend against certain emotional needs. And it is specifically the dissonant needs (needs which are contrary to the essential values of Christian life, i.e., domination versus charity) that are more central to this dynamic.

For example, when seminarians were tested on their values, they showed the following characteristics: they were lower than lay people for 'making a place for myself getting ahead,' higher in self sacrifice for a better world, less looking for security, for coping for with life's problems only as they come, and for power and control over people and things. They also valued serving God by doing God's will, value service to humankind and obedience to God. When tested on the institutional ideals, they emphasized mortification and nurturance.

But, on tests that measured their subconscious needs (those revealed, for example, in the TAT), these same seminarians revealed needs for avoiding censure and failure, for autonomy, dominance, abasement, aggression and novelty. Rulla, Ridick and Imoda's summary of the prevalent conflict faced by seminarians is, as follows:

> The inconsistencies between the ideal self and the latest self are apparent: entering seminarians consciously emphasized deferent submissiveness to God and to authority and shunned competition and dominance; however, subconsciously, they present

---

[58] The methodological premises are set out in Rulla, Ridick and Imoda, *ACVII*, pp. 81-103.

greater needs for autonomy, for dominance, for aggression and- in such a context- for counteraction. Similarly, they stress the unselfish ideals of lack of concern for personal security but – in contrast – they show greater concern about abasement and have greater needs for avoidance of censure and failure. By the same token, they proclaimed readiness to self-sacrifice for a better world and indifference to tangible gains, but they present needs for dominance, for aggression, and for avoidance of censure and failure.[59]

The dynamics are similar for male religious. When male religious were tested for their values, they proclaimed deferent service, obedience, the shunning of competitive power and control. They strove less for making a place for themselves to get ahead and wish rather to serve God. To do this they are willing to forego personal security, intellectual advancement and doing what is best only for themselves. They valued self-sacrifice, self-discipline, duty and they show a higher sense of poverty, piety, mortification, responsibility and chastity in their repertoire of proclaimed values.[60]

However, on psychological tests that measure subconscious needs (e.g., TAT) and during in-depth interviews, they showed higher trends toward emotionality, dominance, avoidance of censure and failure, autonomy and aggression.[61] It is clear that these young religious are being pulled in opposite directions, at the same time. They proclaim and strive after values of deferent service, obedience and the shunning of competitive control and yet, in the latent self, present a picture of greater aggression, domination of others, autonomy and emotionality. They proclaim values and a readiness to sacrifice for a better world while, at the same time, demonstrating conflicts in the area of aggression, domination, and avoidance of criticism, etc. Rulla summarizes the findings of his original research:

---

[59] Rulla, Ridick and Imoda, *Entering and Leaving*, p. 95.

[60] These findings are discussed in Rulla, Ridick and Imoda, *Entering and Leaving, op.cit.*, pp. 98-113.

[61] *Ibid.*, p. 102-103 and, in *ACVII*, pp. 443-453 for the statistical data.

First of all, in line with the inconsistencies between humanitarian, cooperative goals, on the one hand and competitive, aggressive needs, on the other, the main conflict for both seminarians and religious is autonomy vs. shame and doubt. It would seem that for some of the seminarians and religious, the choice of religious vocation may have, in part, served the defensive function of coping with the subconscious conflict over an underlying rebellious autonomy. In committing themselves to humanitarian concerns and obedience to authority, seminarians and religious hope to be able to resolve their inconsistencies in a socially useful manner.[62]

The question obtains as to whether things get better with time and experience in religious life. Another way of posing the question is whether socialization and practice in formation lead to necessary improvement in one's ability to internalize one's deeply held values and integrate them effectively with one's emotional needs, especially those that are dissonant with those same values.

Through various statistical maneuvers that are discussed at length in their 1989 book, Rulla, Ridick and Imoda come to the conclusion that no significant change in affective maturity was found after four years of religious life:

> ... 86% of the men and 87% of the women in this group were partly or wholly unaware of their more important limitations at the time of entering the novitiate; and after four years of formation, the great majority (83% of the men and 82% of the women) were still unaware of these limitations.[63]

We can summarize the findings in the following manner. High vocational ideals are not enough to presume that individuals within a religious vocation or entering a religious vocation have an effective capacity for the values proposed by the Gospel, e.g. solidarity with the poor and compassion for the needy in the world. The social imaginations of those studied in the research conducted by Rulla, Ridick and Imoda are often enough constructed out of a compromise between vocational ideals, on the one hand, and in-

---

[62] Rulla, Ridick and Imoda, *Entering and Leaving, op. cit.,* p. 103.
[63] *Ibid.,* p. 208.

consistent (unconscious) emotional needs, on the other. It seems fair to posit that the horizon of social expectations and desires is developed, more often than not in a large percentage of cases, in reference to a solidarity with one's own inner turmoil rather than in response to the actual needs of those suffering around us.[64]

The problem here is not one of sincerity and, as noted above, there is no question of moral culpability in a majority of these cases. What we seem to be dealing with here are the tragic consequences of ambiguity in the built up structures of vocational life. The seminarians and religious studied were sincerely trying to live out their Gospel values, which they personally held and publicly proclaimed. What is clear, however, is the frequency with which dissonant and often-unrecognized needs interfere with the sincere desire on the part of religious to enter into mature, dedicated, sustained and value-centered relationships.

The resistances to solidarity and compassion, therefore, cannot be conceived of solely in sociological or cultural terms. Nor can they be categorized as moral failure or a determined and conscious ethical resistance (that is, within the ambit of sin). Resistance seems to be tied, at least in part, to dissonant and largely unrecognized emotional needs within us. Initial research indicates that this may be true for upwards of 60 to 80% of religious men and women, at least some of the time.[65]

---

[64] In the statistical research of Rulla, Ridick and Imoda, the "inner turmoil" would amount to significant emotional conflict in about 20% of the cases and to vocational inconsistency and ambivalence (due to dissonant needs) in about another 60% of the cases. Cf. *ibid.,* pp. 135-140.

[65] This was measured by the *Index of Interpersonal Orientation (IIO)* which "assesses to what extent the defensive consistencies, inconsistencies and conflicts present in the 'neutral' or 'natural' areas just described, are conditioned by inconsistencies involving vocationally dissonant variables... When there is a greater relative presence of dissonant inconsistencies which are opposed to theocentric self-transcendence (the denominator of the Index), it is logical to think that the area of social-philanthropic interest (the numerator of the Index) will show a disposition to live relations with others not in a way that is total and theocentrically self-transcendent, but prevalently according to the characteristics of a social-philanthropic self-transcendence or prevalently those of an egocentric process." Cf., Rulla, Ridick and Imoda, *ACVII,* pp. 268-277.

THE FRATERNAL ECONOMY: AN INTRAPSYCHIC PERSPECTIVE

At the Capuchin's General Chapter of 2000, in the Aula Magna of the International College in Rome and before approximately 200 Capuchin delegates from around the world, three friars from Africa stood before the assembly and made a plea that Capuchin friars would hear and attend to "the cry of the poor in Africa."[66] The significance of their statement was not so much in what they said. Clearly, the extent of the poverty and suffering in Africa has been well researched and is widely known.[67] The significance lay in that it needed to be said at all.

This is a community that has committed itself to a radical form of poverty and accompaniment of the poor, and to an all-embracing form of minority.[68] In 1986, at the Plenary Council of the Order on "Our Prophetic Presence in the World," the Capuchin delegates made this claim:

> The fact that many human beings live in extreme poverty and dependency violates the dignity and fundamental rights of the human person and of nations. It obliges us to work for the construction of a more just and egalitarian society.[69]

Then, why did the three African brothers need to remind the friars' of their peoples' suffering and to plead for interest and commitment so that their cry would be heard? At the Fifth Plenary Council, the delegates gave a hint and offered two possible explanations. The first was an analysis of a hardening of spirit and of attitudes, what the delegates called "an insensitivity":

---

[66] Beatus Kinyaiya, Ambongo Besungu, and Noel Brennan, "Clamor Pauperum," *Analecta Ordinis Fratrum Minorum Capuccinorum* 2000 (3), pp. 831-834.

[67] Barry Bearak, "Why People Still Starve: The Real Crisis of Hunger in Africa," *The New York Times Magazine* (July 13, 2003), p. 32-35, 52, 60-61; cf. "Attacking Poverty: Opportunity, Empowerment and Security," *World Development Report 2000/2001* accessed: www.worldbank.org/poverty/wrdpoverty/report/overview.pdf.; also, FAWE Secretariat, *Girls' Education and Poverty Eradication: FAWE's Response* (May 10-20, 2001). Accessed at: www.fawe.org.

[68] For poverty, cf. *The Constitutions of the Capuchin Friars Minor* (1990), "Chapter Four: Our Life in Poverty," n. 59-74, For minority, cf. *ibid*, n. 33:1, 33:2.

[69] "Our Prophetic Presence in the World," *The Fifth Plenary Council of the Order*, in *The Path of Renewal* (Rome: OFMCap.), n. 34.

With the cries of today's victims in our midst- millions of abortions every year, the exploitation of women in so many countries, inhuman working conditions, worldwide abuse of freedom in various forms, systematic unemployment justified in the name of economic growth, increasing disparity between rich and poor within and among nations, terrorism and torture – one can ask whether we too have become hardened, whether we too have not developed ways of ignoring the forms of death that surround us.[70]

In a later section of the document, the delegates stretch beyond a moral analysis focused on obligations, responsibilities and the "tendency to become closed in on its past, in its attitudes and complicity with the problems."[71] They focus, instead, on a more elusive psychological (rather than moral) condition that they render as "psychic numbing":

We Capuchins are not free from the limitations of the Church. When he was General Minister, Brother Paschal Rywalksi said in his report to the General Chapter of 1982 that we Capuchins were behind the Roman Church in many matters regarding our presence in the world. The various inquiries made in the Order in recent years, evidence the fact that we suffer from "psychic numbing" about the problems of the world.[72]

The friars do not explain what kind of limitation they have found. They do not set out their reasoning here or, to my knowledge, take up this diagnosis anytime after the Plenary Council.

In the next section of this work, we would like to begin an application of the psychological theory of self-transcendent consistency to the development of the fraternal economy. We would like to understand the limitations and desires that are likely to arise in the formation of the "fraternal economy." We would like to address how (religious) communities with professed ideals of compassion, minority and poverty can, at times and without much advertence, lose touch with and drift from their obligations to the

[70] *Ibid.*, n. 70.
[71] *Ibid.*, n. 76.
[72] *Ibid.*, n. 79.

poor and suffering around them. We do so with the following understanding.

The central claim of the research provided by Rulla, Ridick and
Imoda is their discovery and confirmation through empirical tests
of a *structure of Christian vocation* and an *anthropology of formation* in
the Christian life. They have presented us with a structural framework of the psychosocial and intrapsychic dynamics that can lead
toward or away from the internalization of the self-transcendent
values of religion.[73] Their contribution does not rest solely or even
primarily on the exposition of certain values, attitudes and needs
(the *contents* of personality) or on how these variables interact in a
certain situation at a particular moment in history.[74]

Rulla and his colleagues have presented a broader theory and
a more radical claim, i.e., to have uncovered and confirmed con-
clusively a *structure of psychic life* (an anthropology of dialectics), as
it relates to the movement in each person to reach the core of his
or her vocation, to live out – with integrity and the totality of one's
life – the call to theocentric self-transcendence.

Because of this dramatic claim, one that proposes a structural
diagnosis and psychological analysis that is trans-situational and
trans-cultural, we are confident in the appropriateness and utility
of applying this theory to the "situation" of the development of
the fraternal economy in Capuchin life, as it has been described in
the first chapter. We turn our attention now to that application.

---

[73] For the critical distinction between the motivational configuration of compliance,
identification and internalization in Rulla's theory, cf. Rulla, *Depth Psychology and Vocation,
op. cit.,* pp. 150-151.

[74] A content analysis would accept that any value, attitude or need in individuals or
groups may be stronger or weaker, may be changed and interchanged, at various times
and under different circumstances.

Chapter Seven

The Belief in a Fraternal World:
A Fundamental Delusion?

The first one who, having enclosed a piece of land, took it upon himself to say, 'this is mine,' and found men foolish enough to believe it, was the true founder of civil society. What crimes, wars, murders, miseries and horrors would Mankind have been spared by one who, uprooting the stakes or filling in the ditch, had cried out to his fellows: Beware of listening to this impostor: you are lost, if you forget that the fruits belong to all and the land to no one!

Rousseau[1]

"Minority," "itinerancy," "solidarity," "participation," and "transparency" are engaging elements in the lexicon of John Corriveau's social teaching in the Capuchin-Franciscan Order in the years 1994-2004. But, they cohere around a central image, a controlling paradigm, and a fundamental metaphor of his soteriological insight for the Order and the pastoral plan he has initiated in the Capuchin community. That is the belief in a "fraternal economy."[2]

It is the "fraternal economy" that expresses how friars are to live the plan of redemption and the work of liberation in a world that abides by alternative principles of division and alienation. More than an economic plank for the redistribution of funds across the globe, Corriveau understands that he is challenging the central metaphor of our times, the "monopoly of imagination"

---

[1] J. Rousseau, *Discourse on the Origins of Inequality.* Harvard Classics, Vol. 34, Part 2 (New York: Bartleby.com, 2001).

[2] John Corriveau, "The Courage to Be Minors," *Circular Letter 22* (October 4, 2003), no. 7.3.

that dictates that *competition* is "the sole voice determining how things are experienced… the lens through which life is properly viewed or experienced."[3]

In his reflections on the results of the Sixth Plenary Council of the Order, John Corriveau noted that the Franciscan commitment to poverty called our first brothers to hard economic choices (and not simply to spiritual dispositions) that challenged the prevailing economy of their day:

> Those economic choices were also a conscious break with more obvious injustices of the growing market economy of their day, which was based on the appropriation of power and wealth by the few to the exclusion of the many. Their choice of poverty was a choice for discipleship, that is, to relate to one another and to their neighbors after the manner of Jesus. It was a conscious choice for a more fraternal world, a more human world.[4]

Corriveau states that it was Francis' intention (and that of his companions) to build a new security based on efforts of mutual dependence and actions of brotherly solidarity. Commenting on our Franciscan challenges today, he goes on to state that we are called to do nothing less than to establish a "fraternal economy" that challenges capitalism's reign on our social and religious imagination. For he notes, "capitalism proposes competition as the best response to protect and administer resources."[5] But, the Church proposes solidarity and mutual dependence as the more sure, lasting and just foundation for human security and well-being.

We note that Corriveau speaks of the turn of the early friars toward a more fraternal world as a "*conscious* break" and a "*conscious* choice," a deliberate decision on the part of these men to challenge the economic, social, political and ecclesial arrangements of their day in favor of a more compassionate and communal presence as "lesser brothers" (friars minor). In the light of Rulla's psychosocial theory of self-transcendent consistency and the anthropology of vocation developed by Rulla, Ridick and Imoda, the question ob-

---

[3] Walter Brueggemann, 'Welcoming the Stranger," *Interpretation and Obedience* (Minneapolis, MN: Fortress Press, 1991), pp. 290-310.

[4] John Corriveau, *Circular Letter 13* (May 31, 1998), no. 4.2.

[5] *Ibid.*, no. 5.2.

tains - how stable is the belief in a fraternal world? What kind of "conscious choice" can we depend on in the development of the fraternal economy? In the psychodynamic world of religious motivations, how secure is the desire for the "divinely inspired economy" likely to be?

We will now discuss the implications and consequences of employing the "anthropological structure" of Rulla, Ridick and Imoda in a congregation intent on the development of the fraternal economy. Because of this work's particular focus on "formation," we will necessarily limit our discussion to those aspects that are particularly relevant and could be most useful to the initial training and preparation of men who seek to enter the Capuchin-Franciscan Order in the 21st century. We will direct our attention to the following subjects:

- The Globalization of Desire and its Resistance in the Fraternal Economy;
- Sharing and Solidarity in the Fraternal Economy;
- Ethnic Identities and Humility as Alternative Social Practice in the Fraternal Economy.

We will conclude this chapter with an assessment of Rulla's psychosocial theory of self-transcendent consistency, as it applies to the development of an understanding of the dynamics of the fraternal economy in Capuchin life.

THE GLOBALIZATION OF DESIRE AND ITS RESISTANCE IN THE FRATERNAL ECONOMY

Nobel prize laureate, Joseph E. Stiglitz, has defined globalization as "the closer integration of the countries and peoples of the world which has been brought about by the enormous reduction of costs of transportation and communication, and the breaking down of artificial barriers to the flow of goods, services, capital, knowledge, and (to a lesser extent) people across borders."[6] It is associated with the creation of new institutions, international cor-

---

[6] Joseph E. Stiglitz, *Globalization and its Discontents* (New York: W.W. Norton, 2002), p. 9.

porations, which can move capital and goods, but also technology, across borders, thereby shrinking separation between nations and the isolation between peoples.

But, globalization is primarily an economically-driven movement propelled by market forces and financial concerns to provide greater opportunities for trade, to increase access to markets and technology, to widen the circle of those in the world able to receive advanced health care and to extend the principles of democracy and freedom. Its achievements are impressive; however, despite its economic successes, its cultural discontents are growing. One impact that is of concern is in the area of the proliferation of desire and its effect on religious and cultural consciousness.

As we have already seen, Marita Wesley-Clough, trend expert for the Hallmark Company, described the impact and velocity of social changes today:

> Trend cycles seem to be emerging more rapidly as a result of technology, accelerated social diffusion, instantaneous communication and more willingness to accept - or inability to escape - new ideas... When everything is accessible instantaneously, the ability to assimilate, to differentiate and to choose becomes more difficult.[7]

Globalization has been described as "the ideal of a New World with no shores." [8] It may also be a New World with fewer emotional boundaries. Globalization's emotional impact is only now being assessed. Wesley-Clough describes the cultural and emotional damage of globalization on consumers: "Under those circumstances, a culture can suffer from a feeling of mental and emotional paralysis, a kind of frozen framework – like kids in the candy store of the world. It becomes increasingly difficult to discern the truth – to sort out what's best."[9]

---

[7] Marita Wesley Clough, "Twelve Consumer Trends and Counter Trends for 2004 and Beyond," accessed: 11/15/04, www.retailindustry.about.com/cs/retailtrends/a/bl_trends2004.htm.

[8] Serge Sur, "The State Between Fragmentation and Globalization," *European Journal of Law* 8 (1997), 3.

[9] Wesley-Clough, *op.cit.*

Joe Holland has described developments in critical Catholic consciousness. He says that we have come to the end of the modern world as a coherent period in social history. That era ushered in the hope of an ever-expanding progress and brought forward the promise of liberating humanity from fate, through scientific prowess and technological mastery. Its root metaphor was the machine of Newtonian physics and its picture of the world was the efficient forward movement of autonomous mechanical parts acting as counter-weights on one another. "It focused on progress as evolution, freedom as competition, and a dualism of private religiosity and public secularism, all guided by technocratic pragmatism."[10]

Today, he says, we are moving away from the social world of Newtonian physics where we are nothing more than particles "dispersed in a competitive equilibrium or massified as a single force."[11] We are moving ahead with the root (social) metaphor and foundational structures that emphasize not the hierarchical biologism of classical antiquity nor the inevitable competition and privatization of classic economic liberalism (with its deep narrative themes of "emancipation" and "liberation"), but those that highlight the "circle of community" with core themes of creation. Postmodernism is described as "a vision of history as the creative power of living tradition, of structure as the creativity of community across nature and humanity, and of religion as human participation in the ongoing divine creation and recreation."[12]

Globalization as the simple (non-reformed) extension of classical economic liberalism produces, what we may call, *dangerous desires*, emotional wants and needs that are instantaneously accessed but which defy assimilation, differentiation, and epistemological assessment. We note five characteristics of desire in the global economy.

First, there is the *proliferation* of desire. Marketing and advertising collapse the distinction between necessity and superfluity.[13] The reach of need and want run to infinity. The consumer is trained to

---

[10] Joe Holland, "The Post-Modern Paradigm Implicit in the Church's Shift to the Left," in Mary Jo Leddy and Mary Ann Hinsdale, *Faith That Transforms* (New York: Paulist Press, 1987), p. 46.

[11] *Ibid.*, p. 56.

[12] *Ibid.*, p. 58.

[13] For a discussion of necessity and superfluity in the writings of St. Francis, cf. Michael Cusato, "Commercium: From the Profane to the Sacred," op.cit., p. 197-199.

exceed his/her satisfaction and to desire an infinite array of goods, products and services.

Second, there is the *materialization* and *commodification* of desire. In late antiquity, the end of desire (i.e., teleology) was the divine, since, as Scripture indicates, "we have no true and lasting abode here."[14] St. Augustine would give its classical enunciation in his phrase, "our hearts are restless until they rest in Thee, O God." In early twenty-first century economic thought, however, desire first becomes material and then becomes product. Secularization collapses or cancels out the incarnate view of the world, which once held that the divine and the material abide in a hypostatic union and *commercium* (without confusion, change, division, or separation).[15] Today, desire has extension but little reach, in that it is infinite in its expectations and demands but, according to commercial evangelism, must be satisfied in time and with product availability.

Desire also undergoes *segmentation* and *isolation*. In her catalogue of 12 retail trends for 2004 and beyond, Wesley-Clough predicts increased polarization:

> Look for increased polarization – whether political, economic, religious or philosophical. Regardless of age, ethnicity or affiliation, individuals long for the security of alignment with those 'like us.' Ethnic 'tribes' within countries and cities; elite social clubs; gatherings of loyal brand devotees, as well as group identities created via fashion, language or symbols. Increasing gravitation toward communities of like minds- people whose interests, worldviews or values reinforce our own.[16]

Desire in the global economy dissects the world into market shares where the unprofitable are increasingly replaced, marginalized or simply ignored, as the definition of common good collapses into simply common wealth, whatever can be exchanged, made

---

[14] For the contrast between desire in late antiquity and in modern social theories, cf. John Milbank, *Theology and Social Theory: Beyond Secular Reason* (Cambridge, MA: Blackwell, 1993), pp.430-434.

[15] The Council of Chalcedon (451), in *The Catechism of the Catholic Church*, n.467. For an understanding of "commercium" in the early Franciscan sources, cf. Cusato, *op.cit.*

[16] Wesley-Clough, *op. cit.*

transparent, expanded and proliferated for profit.[17] Culture, in the growing market economy, loses its currency except as commodity.

Our brief excursion into the philosophy of postmodern desire has been designed to explore the contrast between desire in the market economy and desire in the fraternal economy, between the *dangerous desires* of classical liberalism and the *fraternal desires* of evangelical brotherhood, as this has been developed in the social teachings of the Capuchin Order. We want to know what an anthropology of vocation, with its psychosocial theory of self-transcendent consistency, can teach us about desires in the fraternal economy. How are the *dangerous desires* of the market economy different from the *fraternal desires* of the "divinely inspired economy?"

As we have seen, the desires of the market economy are fundamentally insecure and unstable. Except for their "infinity" or, perhaps more accurately, because of their innumerability, the desires that emerge from the globalized society are reducible to commodities.

In the anthropological vision of Rulla, Ridick and Imoda, however, there is a single desire around which the whole psychological scheme revolves. It is the self-transcendent love of God and one's neighbor as oneself, in imitation of the Christ who gave his life for his friends (John 15:13). It is perhaps more accurate to say that desire in the fraternal economy is, first and foremost, God's primary and pre-existing desire and love for us, since our vocational call is a graced response to God's action toward us.[18] Whereas the "dangerous desires" of the market economy are rooted in the natural (social-philanthropic) reach for prosperity, success, notoriety and profit, the desires of the fraternal economy are rooted more deeply in the *dominion* of God, a recognition that all creation belongs by right to God and that, in Franciscan terms, we own nothing in this world.[19] We receive by grace; our desire is not to acquire anything of our own.

Fraternal desires, in the light of the theory of self-transcendent consistency, are embedded in the desire that God has for us,

---

[17] This is one of the "discontents" discussed by Stiglitz, *op. cit.*, pp. 214-252.

[18] Rulla, *ACVI*, p. 34.

[19] For the explanation of "sine prorio" (nothing of one's own), Cf. *Second Life of St. Francis by Thomas of Celano*, n. 56; *Constitutions of the Capuchin Friars Minor* (1990), Chapter 4, n. 62.

in the gracious call that God issues to humankind to be a "free communion of persons without domination or deprivation." The foundation of fraternal desire is not accumulation or achievement. It is fraternity and communion. Because it is rooted in the embrace of God for all humanity and, indeed for all creatures, fraternal desire encompasses a cosmic fraternity.

In order to be secure, motivations in the fraternal economy must be fundamentally theocentric.[20] But, using the insights from our study of Rulla's theory, we can now also speak of a fundamental *hierarchy of desires* in the fraternal economy. At the level of values, we can see that there are those desires that seek communion, solidarity, minority, transparency and participation originating in and for the true love of God and the self-less outreach to our neighbor. These desires are sincerely valued and publicly proclaimed as theocentrically ordered ideals for oneself and the community. We can also see, on the other hand, those fraternal desires that are consciously held and publicly advanced, not for God's glory but for one's own or for any other limited or partial good. We are repeating here the distinction Rulla and deFinance make between theocentric self-transcendent values and social-philanthropic natural values.[21] This is at the conscious level of personally valued and publicly proclaimed self-ideals.

Fraternal desires of the second type conceive of fraternity merely as socialization and companionship. Community is reduced to the useful and positive value assigned to a free and voluntary association for a common purpose and for a common good.

These two types of fraternal desire are at the level of contents of the Christian personality. They refer to two distinct elements or variables in the construction of a personal or institutional ideal.

We may also speak of a fundamental *dialectic of fraternal desire* that is possible in the fraternal economy. As we have seen, there

---

[20] Milbank contrasts the stability of the social practice of Christianity with the inevitable chaos of modernity, when it writes: *"Christianity, however, recognizes no original violence. It construes the infinite, not as chaos, but as a harmonic peace which is yet beyond the circumscribing power of any totalizing reason. Peace no longer depends upon the reduction to the self-identical, but is the sociality of harmonious difference... Such a Christian logic is not deconstructible by modern secular reason; rather, it is Christianity which exposes the non-necessity of supposing, like the Nietzcheans, that difference, non-totalization and indeterminancy of meaning necessarily imply arbitrariness and violence."* Cf. Milbank, *Social Theory, op. cit.*, p.5.

[21] Rulla, *ibid.*, pp. 160-162.

is in the vocational life a constant tension of two *structures* in the personality, between the *ideal self* and the *actual self*. The first dialectic of desire in the fraternal economy is a *conscious choice* between the ideal of the fraternal economy with its communion, solidarity, participation and transparency and its actual realization and embodiment in time and space, in the here and now. It is the tension between the *ideal community of gospel brotherhood* and the *actual community of gospel brotherhood*.

This *first dialectic of fraternal desire* is the realized and determined effort to break from all that destroys, denies, obstructs or hinders the realization of universal communion across borders and boundaries. To choose this ideal desire, often against tremendous odds, is to proclaim the kingdom of God in the world. To consciously deny or in freedom to forego this fraternal desire for immediate satisfaction or gratification is sin. The first dialectic of desire in the fraternal economy is between virtue and vice, conviction and convenience about communion. But, there is a second dialectic that is possible.

The second dialectic of desire in the fraternal economy is that which exists between the consciously proclaimed value of evangelical poverty and the (dissonant) emotional needs and/or attitudes, subsconsciously held by a friar. This is the situation of the friar who genuinely believes and honestly wishes to promote compassion and solidarity but who, at the very same time, is held back from a complete gift of himself in whatever area of social concern that is of value to him by dissonant emotional needs, like aggression and domination. Even if and, perhaps mostly, because the source of this tension is unconscious, the desire for the fraternal economy (the yearning for communion and the extension of brotherhood) can manifest itself (to public view) as somewhat ambivalent, sometimes hot and sometimes cold. The individual, for example, attends to the challenges and obligations required to further communion across the borders and boundaries of his local community, but he does so intermittently, inconsistently and only occasionally, depending, to some degree and in various intensities, on the mood of the moment or the degree of personal interest or need interpreted as necessary.

There is a fundamental ambiguity in the globalization of desire that is possible and, if the statistics from the studies of Rulla, Ridick and Imoda are correct, highly likely in the development of the fraternal economy. While Corriveau has indicated that the decision for evangelical poverty is a "conscious choice" and a "conscious break" with one's social inheritance, our analysis of Rulla's theory would indicate that the situation involves more than a simple disposition of the will.[22] There is an unconscious dimension to the fraternal economy that is not reflected in Corriveau's exposition. It might be argued that such is the meaning and the force behind his statement that formation in the fraternal economy will take effort and demand a profound conversion. But, as we have seen from our previous chapters, definitions of conversion may not include and may actually reject a consideration of the "psychological complexities of faith."[23]

We have spoken of the globalization of desire in the market economy as accelerating in social and cultural influence because of the proliferation, commodification, materialization, segmentation and isolation of human want and need. Clearly, the Capuchin who honestly proclaims and genuinely lives (in the first dimension) will have to choose (on a regular basis and with considerable courage) between the *dangerous desires* of the market and the *fraternal desires* of evangelical poverty. They are not the same. The former, by definition, promotes competition, greed, avarice and self-interest. The latter seeks compassion, generosity, solidarity and self-transcendence.

The Capuchin who lives primarily in the third dimension, in the theoretical frame of Rulla, would find himself unable to construct the fundamentals of a fraternal world. Limited by intense emotional conflict and consistently plagued by the force of primitive needs and their defenses, this friar would interpret the development of the fraternal economy as an assault against his safety and a threat to his trust in the comforting world he has constructed around him. This is not to impugn his holiness, for grace is able to work on the most meager of gifts we have to offer in response

---

[22] We refer the reader to Bernard Lonergan's important distinction between three understandings of "will": will (the capacity to will), willing (the act of willing) and willingness (... "the state in which persuasion is not needed to bring one to a decision."). We are speaking here, at this point, of "willingness." Cf. B. Lonergan, *Insight: A Study of Human Understanding* (Revised Students' Edition) (London: Longmans: Green, 1958), p. 598ff.

[23] cf. our discussion at the beginning of Chapter Six p. 109ff.

to God's call. It points to the apostolic or evangelical effectiveness of his actions and the clarity with which his deeds will be seen by others as promoting or hindering the mission of Christ in the world today.[24]

The Capuchin who operates from the horizon of the second dimension of his personality will experience, what we might call, a "consistently inconsistent" tug of war between his dangerous desires and his fraternal desires. Because of the complex of emotional needs (both conscious and unconscious, consonant and dissonant) and the values that have become a structure of his vocation, the friar will proclaim and sincerely believe the importance of establishing a fraternal economy. But, this same friar will also be inconsistent in advancing it. He will resist its implementation and do so without full knowledge, consent or choice of this very resistance.

This friar will defend himself against the construction of the fraternal economy at those times and to the measure that his personal stake in the matter is threatened. On the other hand, there will also be times when he will promote it. He will do so, however, for conflicting and largely ulterior motives, that is, to advance a personal cause or to propel an individual agenda, even if this cause or agenda is objectively unnecessary or even potentially detrimental to the construction of the fraternal economy.

It is clear, therefore, that the desire to promote the fraternal economy in the Capuchin Order cannot be taken at face value. Valuing and proclaiming the fraternal economy is not enough. Enunciation of the fraternal economy is not enough; there must be integration and internalization. And this means the integration of the dissonant needs that co-exist with the proclaimed values.

While the dynamics of the fraternal economy may be complicated, they are also largely intelligible. Our analysis indicates that promoting and building the fraternal economy is more than simply a matter of a "conscious choice" and it is something other than a "conscious break" with one's social history and inherited past. The total complex of fraternal desires can be read. In fact, they must be

---

[24] For the distinction between apostolic effectiveness and efficiency and how the psychological dynamics of the various dimensions influence effectiveness, cf. Rulla, *ACVI*, *op.cit.*, 287-302.

read, since one does not break so easily from one's psychological heritage, especially that part which is unconscious.[25]

It is critical, therefore, that any further attempts to clarify the dynamics or conversion process involved in the development of the fraternal economy include not only the conscious core of evangelical poverty (the ideal of brotherhood for the love of God). It must also pursue, in some manner, the potentially destructive force of the unconscious and attend to the appropriation and integration of dissonant needs. Only then can we understand just how radical a conversion process is being proposed.

SHARING AND THE PSYCHODYNAMICS OF ECONOMIC SOLIDARITY

We remember the pivotal moment in the Circular Letters of John Corriveau when certain "troubling questions" arose regarding the communal, social and structural dimensions of evangelical poverty in the Capuchin Order.[26] There are provinces (mostly in the northern hemisphere), he reveals, that regularly experience a modest surplus of income, while there are jurisdictions (largely in the southern hemisphere) that, just as regularly, face habitual, large deficits. Beyond this, there is a significant and growing discrepancy between the health care provided to friars in the North and that which is available to friars in the South. It is, as it were, the case of two young friars traveling down the road together who come to a crossroad. One travels north and the other travels south. Along the path that leads north, the friar can expect adequate medical coverage, reasonable insurance protection and social security. Along the path that leads south, however, the friar will face an unstable and dangerous lack of medical services and social protection. A disease easily treated and nominally taken care of in the North can claim the life of the friar from the South. Friars who claim to be brothers in a universal fraternity, *sine proprio* - without anything of their own - evidence an economic and social disparity that mirrors rath-

---

[25] As confirmation of this point, Rulla, Ridick and Imoda have found that upwards of approximately 69% of religious develop a transferential relationship with their formation directors that is rooted, at least in part, on their unresolved conflicts with their parents. Cf., *Entering and Leaving*, pp. 151-160.

[26] See our discussion of these issues of *Circular Letter 9* in Chapter One, pp. 19-23.

er than challenges the inequitable distribution of resources in the modern world. Corriveau's extended meditations arise out of this realization of, what we might justifiably call, a "structure of sin."[27]

The world's unfair and unequal distribution of its resources has become embedded in the conventions, customs, and systems of economic life not only in the marketplace of contemporary society, but also in the monasteries and friaries of religious communities. Like all "structures of sin," the asymmetrical distribution may be lamented and vociferously denounced and yet the benefits that bend to the favor of one group (or certain groups) over another remain securely in place and are defended as normal or "just the way things are."

The complicity may be unconscious but it is also real. There may even be denial that such a discrepancy exists or that it is significant. More often than not, the pattern is one of silence and omission, as Gustavo Gutierrez reveals:

> One type of connivance (complicidades), which is clearer today now that we have a better knowledge of our social reality, takes the form of *sins of omission:* "We regard ourselves as guilty for keeping silence in the face of the events agitating our country. In the face of repression, detentions, the economic crisis, the loss of jobs by so many workers, murders and tortures, *we have kept silent* as though we did not belong to that world.' The *cowardice* that keeps silent in the face of the sufferings of the poor and that offers any number of adroit justifications represents an especially serious failure of Latin American Christians.[28]

The publication of Corriveau's circular letters after 1996 reveals a growing awareness, acknowledgement and confrontation of this social and religious problem in the Capuchin Order. One structural resolution of this problem was the foundation of the Office of Economic Solidarity in March 1999. Its stated goal is

---

[27] For a definition of "structure of sin," cf. Massingale, *Social Sin and Social Reconciliation, op. cit.,* pp. 110-113. Massingale writes of the distinction between "guilt" that arises from the recognition of personal sin and "responsibility" that is the appropriate response to the awareness of complicity in structural sin.

[28] Gustavo Gutierrez, *We Drink from our own Wells,* Translated by Matthew J. O'Connell. (Maryknoll, NY: Orbis Books, 1984) [emphasis added]. For an extended treatment of these manifestations and dynamics of social sin, cf. Massingale, *op. cit.*

"to implement the vision of economic solidarity as elaborated and proposed by VI Plenary Council of the Order (Prop. 21-28)."[29] We turn to a brief analysis of the statutes that structure the Office of Economic Solidarity, so that we can analyze (and perhaps propose) the formative requirements appropriate for the programs and practices of economic solidarity in the Capuchin Order, from the viewpoint of the psychosocial dynamics of self-transcendent consistency and the anthropology of vocation.

According to the "Statute for International Economic Solidarity," approved by the Minister General and his definitory on March 23, 1999, the need for renewal in the area of economic solidarity emerges out of an awareness that the structures of fraternal and juridic relationships in the Order have changed dramatically since 1980. The increase in large circumscriptions in regions of the Order in Asia, Africa and Latin America, along with the collapse of communism in Eastern Europe, have created an inequitable situation whereby there "now exists a sizable part of the Order with considerably less ability to respond to the needs of the brothers and its ministries than in other parts of the Order."[30] The Statute outlines the rules and procedures for new mechanisms and structures of economic solidarity that are designed for three purposes. First, they are to "create deeper awareness of our international brotherhood." Then, they are to develop "stronger bonds of Capuchin unity throughout the world." And, finally, they are to be a "model of just and equitable sharing within the Church and society."[31]

The document repeats the fundamental intention of economic solidarity. Economic solidarity is not to be seen as an expression of law or juridical obligation, although it has moral dimensions.[32] Economic solidarity in the Capuchin Order flows more deeply "from the generosity of love" and builds mutual confidence and requires transparency on the part of those who give and those who receive.[33]

---

[29] Cf. The Capuchin website for this goal, www.ofmcap.org.

[30] *Statute for International Economic Solidarity* (Curia Generalizia dei Frati Minori Cappuccini, March 1999), www.ofmcap.org, n. 1.2.

[31] *Ibid.,* n. 2.1

[32] See the requirement for "transparency" and "equity" in n.2.3. of the "Statute," *op.cit.*

[33] *Ibid.,* n. 2.3 (e) and (f).

If economic solidarity in the Capuchin Order is to be a model of "just and equitable sharing" within the Church and society, we can pose the question: "How and under what conditions are those who presently benefit from the *status quo* of economic arrangements and financial configurations in the Order likely to give and to share from their surplus? Under what circumstances, are they likely to "hear the cry of the poor" and respond effectively (as the African brothers requested), when they hold the advantage in an inherited and sustained asymmetrical relationship?

We know that the requirements of "economic solidarity" are more stringent than the simple redistribution of surplus assets. After the Sixth Plenary Council of the Order, the whole terrain of economic relationships in the Capuchin Order shifts dramatically and is transformed. The Plenary Council speaks about the development of a *"culture* of solidarity." As Proposition 22 indicates:

> Solidarity is not primarily about giving things to others. It is mutual dependence and brotherhood. The culture of solidarity creates new ways of understanding and living relationships with others. By going among the lepers, Francis changed his way of relating to them. To be in solidarity means taking care of each brother and sister, especially of those who are excluded from sharing in the benefits of society. Listening to the cry of the poor, we must work to ensure that global solidarity becomes a new social order.[34]

The question obtains, "will belief in a fraternal world translate into greater empathy for those (brothers) who are suffering in other parts of the world?" Will the belief in a fraternal world (as a *conscious* break from the social conditions of the day, in Corriveau's terms) necessarily lead to stronger bonds in the fraternity? Or might they actually grow weaker?

It is axiomatic to assume that growth in the belief in a fraternal world (by friars around the world) will lead inevitably and inexorably to a greater sense of connection, a deeper level of mutual understanding and a tighter bond of commitment. But, psychological research in a parallel question would give us pause.

---

[34] Proposition 22, *Sixth Plenary Council of the Order,* quoted in "Statute," *op.cit.,* n.2.1.

Melvin J. Lerner, a social psychologist, has conducted a series of experiments to test whether those who believe in a just world develop stronger or weaker bonds with those who are suffering.[35] According to his hypothesis, people have a strong desire or need to believe that the world is an orderly, predictable, and just place, where people get what they deserve. The theory maintains that the belief in a just world provides coherence and assures us that the plans for our lives, the goals we set and the actions we perform will have predictable results. When we encounter evidence that the world is not fair (or just), we have a need to restore justice in two ways: (1) by helping the victim or (2) persuading ourselves that no (real) injustice has occurred. In short, we either help the victim or derogate the victim.

In a 1967 study, Lerner and his colleague videotaped a simulated "learning" experiment in which it appeared as if participants were given electric shocks. When it seemed that participants (victims) were unable to extricate themselves from the situation, or when the victims took on the role of "martyr" by voluntarily remaining in the experiment despite the painful experience, they tended to be re-interpreted by observers as "more deserving" of their fate and their suffering.[36]

When the subjects of the experiment had the opportunity to intervene and rescue the innocent party from the unjust suffering, they did so. They stepped in, helped and saw the victim in an objective light. But, when the experimental conditions were such that subjects could not intervene, when they could not stop the injustice and rescue the victims from their suffering, the subjects began to re-evaluate the personal worth of the victim. The more unjust the suffering, Lerner found, "the greater the tendency to find negative attributes in her (the victim's) personality to denigrate her."[37]

---

[35] M.J. Lerner and L. Montada, "An overview: Advances in belief in a just world theory and methods," in L. Montada and M.J. Lerner (eds.) *Responses to Victimization and Belief in a Just World* (New York: Plenum, 1998).

[36] M.J. Lerner and G. Matthews, "Reactions to the Sufferings of Others Under Conditions of Indirect Responsibility," *Journal of Personality and Social Psychology* 5 (1967), pp. 319-325; also, Melvin J. Lerner, *Belief in a Just World: A Fundamental Delusion* (New York: Plenum, 1980); Melvin J. Lerner, "'Normative' and 'Intuitive' Senses of Justice," *International Society for Justice Research* (June, 2001) at www.isjr.org/Newsletter-Issue1-01.html.;

[37] Lerner, *Belief in a Just World, op.cit.*, p. 48.

Research has shown that objectively innocent victims do not always elicit the sympathy of others or their helping behavior. To the contrary, very often objectively innocent victims are blamed, devalued, or have their sufferings discounted or minimized.[38] According to the "belief in a just world" (BJW) theory, decent people sometimes increase the suffering of victims because they need to hold onto the belief that they live in a fair and balanced world. It is a way of retaining in the face of contradictory evidence, a belief in a world in which people get what they deserve and only what they deserve. It is a way that people have of convincing themselves that suffering in the world is controlled and relatively constant. If the subjects (of the experiment) can attribute to the victims some negative characteristics that "deserve" to be punished, then the sufferings of the person can be justified and a primordial sense of justice (order and right) in the world can be maintained.

Lerner describes the ambiguity in the conviction surrounding the belief in a just world:

> We have seen persuasive evidence that people are strongly motivated by the desire to eliminate the suffering of innocent victims, and that the main barrier in the way of this motivation's appearing in social action is people's fear of losing their place in a just world. The desire to maximize one's own outcomes is a relatively trivial motive in people's lives, that gains its importance only as it enters into the person's concerns with deserving and justice... At times, people feel that justice is served when people's needs are most effectively met; at other times, people's deserving is seen as relative to their effort, their contributions to a task, their station in life, what they can win in a fair competition. And both of these sets of problems are inextricably bound up with the way people decide who is in their "world," and what place they have in that world.[39]

---

[38] W. Ryan, *Blaming the Victim* (New York: Pantheon, 1971); L. Montada and M.J. Lerner, *Responses to Victimization and Belief in a Just World* (New York: Plenum, 1998); M.J. Lerner and C.H. Simmons, "The observer's reaction to the 'innocent victim': Compassion or Rejection?" *Journal of Personality and Social Psychology* 4 (1966) 203-210.

[39] Lerner, *Belief in a Just World, op. cit.*, p. 194.

In a most recent piece, after years of experiments, Lerner concludes that people walk around with "two remarkably different senses of justice." He describes them as "normative" and "intuitive."[40] He describes the "normative" sense of justice as consisting in the "publicly available societal norms that define people's entitlements and the more or less rational deliberations people employ, individually or collectively, to arrive at moral judgments."[41] It is the rational norm-based product of moral reasoning.

He contrasts this normative sense of justice with an "intuitive" form that is "based upon people's *immediate* sense of right and wrong, that takes the form of *automatic* judgments of blame, with attempts to restore justice."[42] He says that these intuitive reactions are spontaneous and accompanied by strong emotions such as anger, outrage and sadness. They can contradict, over-rule and, curiously, stand side by side with a rational and objective assessment of an unfair or unjust situation or interpretation of suffering. They appear, he says, to be expressions of "primitive scripts" and beliefs that 'bad things are caused by bad people' and 'bad things happen to bad people.' The normative and the intuitive, then, appear to be two forms of justice that abide, side by side. In the end, it is important to note that the "intuitive" sense of justice defies rational correction and, although primitive, has a powerful and personally costly impact on a person's self-esteem and their understanding of and behavior in their world.

The "belief in a just world" theory maintains that "victims of undeserved suffering" do not always win the sympathy of others. It is not inevitable that those who suffer will garner support and invite solidarity, even when their suffering is recognized and acknowledged as inappropriate, unfair and undeserved.[43] Sometimes good and decent people will increase the sufferings of victims whom they know to be victims (*normative justice*) because, powerless to reduce or change the condition of those victims, they prefer to

---

[40] Lerner, "Normative," *op.cit.*, p.2

[41] *Ibid.*

[42] *Ibid.*, p. 3 [emphasis added].

[43] Cf. Gouranga P. Chattopadhyay, 'The Other' in the Politics of Relatedness between Developing and Developed Nations," *Melbourne Symposium of the International Society for the Psychoanalytic Study of Organizations* (2003), accessed: www.ispso.org/Symposia/Melbourne/Chattopadhyay.htm.

maintain their prior convictions about the state of the world as being fair and just (*intuitive justice*).

There is in the end, one might say, no undeserved suffering in the world. When injustice appears inevitable and a solution intractable, victims become more vulnerable to attributions of blame, even by those not directly responsible for the unjust situation and who admit that the conditions under which the victims suffer are indeed unjust. Victims are especially vulnerable the greater the belief in a just world.[44]

Will friars inevitably share with one another and strengthen their solidarity with brothers who are unjustly suffering on the strength of their common belief in a fraternal world? Will the proclamation and acceptance of the belief in a "fraternal economy" enhance their commitment and bond to their brothers suffering around the world? The research of Rulla and Lerner gives us pause.

As stated above, Corriveau's conceptualization of the fraternal economy is decidedly deliberative, willful and intentional. He conceives of it, as we have seen, as a "conscious choice" and a "conscious break" from one's inherited structures. Lerner's research indicates that matters of fairness, justice and right operate at two levels: the normative and the intuitive. The normative is a type of rational assessment that can objectively evaluate the sufferings of others, come to the proper conclusion that they have been treated unfairly, and seek to overturn or ameliorate their pain and the conditions which originated it. But, Lerner has also uncovered the "intuitive" sense of (in)justice that is both primitive and emotive. It is doggedly resistant to rational correction. This "intuitive" sense of justice will cast archaic interpretations of blame and guilt onto situations of apparent and objective innocence, when it is needed to maintain a primordial belief in a just world. Victims are *more* vulnerable, not less, when the belief in a just world is strongest.

Will the Capuchin Order resort to a similar mechanism? Given that the "fraternal economy" is spoken of in its largely idealized or normative form, have we not set up, perhaps, the conditions that increase the vulnerability of those already suffering from an

---

[44] Isabel Correia, Jorge Vala, and Patricia Aguiar, "The Effects of Belief in a Just World and Victim's Innocence on Second Victimization, Judgements of Justice and Deservingness," *Social Justice Research* 14:3 (September 2001), pp. 327-342.

asymmetrical relationship in the Order? As long as the belief in a fraternal world remains a largely idealized (contained) goal of the evangelical life, it appears that friars in the South will be more vulnerable, not less, to the misunderstanding and insensitivity of friars in the North.

Rulla's research on the second dimension may confirm this possibility. As we have seen, it is in the first dimension that religious are most free to choose between the dictates of their ideal self (self-ideals and institutional ideals) and their actual self (predominantly their manifest self or present behavior). Here religious have the opportunity to make a conscious choice between good and evil, virtue and vice, because they are aware of the choices before them and largely free structurally to pursue their self-transcendent options.

Given the example above, friars would be aware of two realities. The first would be their understanding and acceptance of the goal of the "fraternal economy" and the demands of economic solidarity. The self-transcendent aspects of the fraternal world, described so well in the Plenary Councils and Circular Letters of the Capuchin Order, would be personally accepted and publicly proclaimed as a primary value of the fraternity (e.g., the SI-II or self-ideal in situation of Rulla's theory).

But, in the first dimension, there is also a second awareness. Friars are also consciously aware and accepting of the emotional needs which directly or indirectly contradict the value in question. This *dialectic of desire*, as we have seen, is a conscious choice between communion and convenience. In our example, it is the conscious choice for the fraternal economy over against any and all hardships, resistances, personal preferences, individual accommodations or satisfactions. In the first dimension, the actual conditions of fraternal life (the "self-transcended" dimensions of community, if you will) are integrated into the ideal of the fraternal economy. It is a conscious and deliberative process.

In the third dimension, the idealized form of the fraternal economy is split off from its actual form (in the real world). Here a friar can seesaw tragically between his (all-good) belief that he has arrived fully and blamelessly in the fraternal economy (a magical belief) and his (all-bad) belief that the fraternal economy in which he lives is hell.[45]

But, it is in the second dimension that we find the most vulnerability. We recall that the *dialectic of fraternal desire* manifested in

---

[45] Cf. the splitting mechanism in psychotic and borderline states in O. Kernberg, "Neurosis, Psychosis and Borderline States," in Harold I. Kaplan and Benjamin J. Sadock, *Comprehensive Textbook of Psychiatry*, Vol. IV (Baltimore: Williams and Wilkins, 1985), pp. 621-630.

the second dimension is between the ideal self (of one's theocentric self-transcendent values) and the actual self of one's unconsciously held (and vulnerable) self-concept or latent self. This is the arena where dissonant needs accumulate and attach themselves to one's publicly professed ideals. The two can co-exist in a state of chronic ambivalence and inconsistency because of the power of the defenses that keep the vocational tension unresolved and out of awareness.

Note that we have indicated that individuals are an integrated unity of all three dimensions. The first dimension of conscious choices can and does co-exist with the second dimension of unconscious and inconsistent accommodations. Every individual has some level of conflict, though most are not to the degree of a pathological condition.

We recall that Lerner spoke of two "notions of justice" that co-exist in every person: a normative sense that evaluates the conditions of injustice objectively (according to norms) and an intuitive sense that also assesses but from "primitive" scripts, based on people's "immediate sense of right and wrong" which take the form of "automatic judgments of blame." We also recall that he said that these spontaneous judgments were accompanied by powerful, though not fully integrated, emotions (such as anger and outrage).

In a similar way, Rulla speaks of the operations of "rational wanting" and "emotional wanting" in his psychodynamic theory.[46] The former is a reflective judgment or appraisal based on one's values. The latter is an immediate emotional appraisal, in the here and now, that draws us toward or away from an object or situation.[47] In Rulla's scheme, it is the first dimension that is characterized primarily by rational wanting and the third dimension that is characterized by the pressures of emotional wanting. It is in the second dimension where the normative and the intuitive co-exist in a troubling vocational mix.

We can then hypothesize and recommend for further reflection that the situation of friars who are already suffering from an unjust situation may become *more vulnerable* (not less vulnerable) to misunderstanding, misinterpretation and derogation, as the values of the fraternal economy are amplified *and* there is a prevalence of friars with mixed (albeit unconscious) motives and inconsistent desires (i.e., in the second dimension). We remind the reader that,

---

[46] Rulla, *Depth Psychology and Vocation, op.cit.,* pp. 30-34.
[47] Rulla, *Depth Psychology and Vocation, op.cit.,* p. 31-34.

in the theory of self-transcendent consistency, that pertains to 60 to 80% of those in religious life.[48]

Because of the *dialectic of fraternal desire,* shaped by the unconscious force of dissonant needs and attitudes in the second dimension, proposing the fraternal economy simply as a conscious choice and evangelical ideal may have the unintended consequence of *increasing* the vulnerability of brothers already suffering as the innocent victims of poverty.

To overcome this tendency to derogate the victims of undeserved suffering and an inequitable distribution of resources in the Order, religious leaders must attend more directly to the unrecognized emotional needs and their defenses that are at large in the fraternity, the dynamic that keeps the asymmetrical relationships in place, at an intuitive and immediate level of cognition and appraisal.

ETHNIC CONFLICT AND HUMILITY AS SOCIAL PRACTICE IN THE FRATERNAL ECONOMY

On February 2, 2004, delegates from around the Capuchin world gathered in Addis Ababa, Ethiopia, for an historic International Capuchin Assembly on the theme of "Gospel Brotherhood in a Multi-Ethnic World." [49] They had been called together by the Minister General and his Definitory, with the assistance of the General Office for Justice, Peace and Ecology in Rome, to consider how a multi-ethnic brotherhood could become an instrument of gospel peace in the world today.

The tragic shadow of the Rwandan genocide ten years earlier loomed large in the background as this conference opened, as did the various manifestations of ethnic divisions, cultural conflicts

---

[48] This work is not a statistical research of particular component variables, which are, in and of themselves, worthy of further attention. Our aim is to provide an introduction to the concept of the "fraternal economy" and, in these introductory chapters, tease out some *possible* conclusions and implications that derive from a careful reading and application of Rulla's theory and research on this evolving concept. Clearly, a statistical study could and should be done to confirm or deny this hypothesis.

[49] Cf. *Gospel Brotherhood in a Multi-Ethnic World, A Capuchin Letter to Friars around the World,"* (February 17, 2004) in *Bulletin* XLI, No. 3 (Summer, 2004), pp. 94-103.

and caste differences in the Order itself.[50] The power of the Franciscan vision of a universal gospel brotherhood gave the delegates the confidence to write:

> As Capuchin-Franciscans and as men living and ministering virtually everywhere in the world, we have a unique opportunity to be "instruments of peace," particularly in those situations of conflict that are driven by ethnic tensions, religious intolerance, and economic and social injustice.[51]

Reflecting on the cultural and ethnic conflicts erupting in the world, divisions exacerbated by the uncontrolled spreads of HIV/AIDS and the escalation of intra-national violence in society, the delegates concluded that "the Franciscan charism is ideally suited for helping to promote a culture of human rights in the world and to assure respect for those rights, beginning with our own communities and then in the institutions and structures of the wider society."[52] They located the particular force of the Franciscan insight about social harmony in the face of growing ethnic polarization to be in reconciliation "rooted in relationship and a spirit of humility":

> Reconciliation, whether it involves transcending the boundaries of ethnicity and culture or those of religion or nation, is part of our Franciscan witness. It is rooted in relationship and a spirit of humility. We were challenged to recall that our humility must be more than a pious ideal. Our Constitutions admonish us "not be fraudulent minors but those who are sincere in heart, word and deed, and they further warn that, 'the signs of humility that the brothers wear outwardly contribute little to the salvation of souls unless they are animated by a spirit of humility.'[53]

---

[50] In a personal interview, the Minister General related incidents of dangerous ethnic divisions in various parts of the Order, including Nigeria, and confided a fear that "another Rwanda" could flare up at any time in various parts of the Capuchin world. The hope of the Assembly was to provide a base of reflection and solidarity that could engage the underlying tensions and fears "below the surface" of the fraternal economy.

[51] *Ibid.*, p. 95.

[52] *Ibid.*, p. 97.

[53] *Ibid.*, p. 97-98.

They went on to consider this spirit of humility as a new *social practice* of leadership and fraternal economics, which addresses intercultural and inter-ethnic rivalries and administers the material resources of the Order in a new way, without domination or deprivation.[54] Without clarifying precisely how it functions as a new social practice of peace, the delegates offered that humility benefits both the vertical and horizontal dimensions of relationships by providing a non-dominating alternative to human exchange.

How might humility function as an alternative social practice for peace in the Capuchin Order? What insights might we derive from the theory of self-transcendent consistency? We turn to a brief analysis of these dynamics.

In his magisterial study of ancient and contemporary social theories, John Milbank argues convincingly that both modern and pre-modern understandings of social relationships are inevitably rooted in an ontology of violence, aggression and competition.[55] Tracing Augustine's description of the fundamental "ontological antagonism" that lies at the root of Roman law and practice, he states that the Roman notion of virtue could not be other than the pursuit of glory that comes from an attainment of self-control and victory over one's passion, because -

> The Romans, like all pagans, think there can only be virtue when there is something to be defeated, and virtue therefore consists for them, not only in the attainment and pursuit of a goal desirable in itself, but also in a 'conquest' of less desirable forces, which is always an exercise of strength supplementary to, although supporting, a 'right desire.'[56]

In his further analysis of modern social theories, including contemporary notions of politics and economics, Milbank finds a "hidden thread of continuity between antique reason and modern, secular reason." The hidden thread that connects the two worlds is the theme of an "original violence." He writes:

---

[54] *Ibid.,* p. 98.
[55] John Milbank, *Theology and Social Theory, op. cit.*
[56] *Ibid.,* p. 390-391.

Antique thought and politics assumes some naturally given element of chaotic conflict which must be tamed by the stability and self-identity of reason. Modern thought and politics (most clearly articulated by Nietzsche) assumes that there is *only* this chaos, which cannot be tamed by an opposing transcendent principle, but can be immanently controlled by subjecting it to rules and giving irresistible power to those rules in the form of market economies and sovereign politics.[57]

Milbank contends that it is the Church, and only the Church, that today publicly and authoritatively stands as an alternative social practice to the nihilistic and inevitably competitive economic construct of modernity and post-modernity. The Church is a social space, unlike all others, that admits of no original violence.

> It construes the infinite not as chaos, but as a harmonic peace which is yet beyond the circumscribing power of any totalizing reason. Peace no longer depends upon the reduction to the self-identical, but in the sociality of harmonious difference.[58]

Milbank contends that the Church is the social practice of peace in a lapsed (not originally) chaotic and violent world. It is a non-antagonistic social practice that refuses to make current or to take as normative the nihilistic inevitability of chaos, competition, avarice and greed found in modern theories of economics and politics. The Church is rooted in the mystery of peaceful relations between Father, Son and Spirit. The Trinity exists as a free communion of persons without the need for domination (a diversity of non-competition) and with a difference that does not end up in deprivation.

How does Milbank suggest that imagining a state of total (and original) peace might help communities that are locked in a world of deep-seated conflict that only fantasy or folly would encourage us to minimize or avoid?

---

[57] *Ibid.*, p. 5.
[58] *Ibid.*, p.5.

It helps, because it allows us to unthink the necessity of violence, and exposes the manner in which the assumption of an
inhibition of an always prior violence helps to preserve violence
in motion. But, it helps more, because it indicates that there is a
way to act in a non-violent world which assumes the ontological
priority of non-violence.[59]

Milbank argues that the one practice that differentiates the
Christian community from all other social entities is its generous
offer (to all) of *the forgiveness of sins*. Antique reason and modern
secular reason offer no such relief or escape from inevitable competition, which Hobbes once referred to as the "war of all against
all." The heroic ideals of ancient and modern life are similarly
founded on an ineradicable ontological violence of domination or
deprivation in the pursuit of personal glory and the fear of death.
But, the Christian ideal is different, in that "mutual forgiveness and
bearing one another's burdens becomes the *modus vivendi* of the
Church: an 'atoning' way of life."[60] Milbank provides the originating image that defines the social practice of Christianity:

> Instead of Jove, the stayer of a preceding battle, Christians wor-
> ship the one true God who originates all finite reality in an act
> of peaceful donation, willing a new fellowship with himself and
> amongst the beings he has created. In 'the heavenly city', be-
> yond the possibility of alteration, the angels and saints abide in
> such a fellowship; their virtue is not the virtue of resistance and
> domination, but simply of remaining in a state of self-forgetting
> conviviality.[61]

Salvation in Milbank's theory is eminently social, because the
Church provides an alternative "city," a refuge constituted by the
practice of protection offered by 'friends,' even to their 'enemies':

> Instead of a peace 'achieved' through the abandonment of the
> losers, the subordination of potential rivals and resistance to en-
> emies, the Church provides a genuine peace by its memory of

---

[59] *Ibid.*, p. 111.
[60] *Ibid.*, p. 397.
[61] *Ibid.*, p. 391.

all the victims, its equal concern for all its citizens and its self-exposed offering of reconciliation to enemies. [62]

In the social teachings of the Capuchin Order, the alternative city is constructed by humility and the practice of *misericodia* (mercy), as Francis writes in his "Letter to a Minister":

> I wish to know in this way if you love the Lord and me, His servant and yours: that there is not any brother in the world who has sinned – however much he could have sinned- who, after he has looked in your eyes, would ever depart without your mercy, if he is looking for mercy. And if he were not looking for mercy, you would ask him if he wants mercy. And if he would sin a thousand times before your eyes, love him more than me so that you may draw him to the Lord; and always be merciful with brothers such as these.[63]

This is the reason why Corriveau rightly attends to the practice of humility in *Circular Letter 21*, after exploring (for several years) the theological and spiritual dynamics of the fraternal economy.[64] He calls humility the chief characteristic of our gospel brotherhood, because humility characterizes the self-revelation of God, in the Franciscan vision.[65]

What does the theory of self-transcendent consistency and its anthropology of vocation add to our understanding of humility as an alternative social practice of peace in situations of ethnic conflict and over against the ontology of violence that surrounds us? Perhaps, it helps us in clarifying the origins and the proper forms of conflict in vocational life.

Humility in Franciscan thought is fundamentally a radical repositioning of oneself, away from an arrogant possession of creation and toward a grace-filled receptivity of goodness originating in God. It is a public abandonment of one's social position of

---

[62] *Ibid.,* p. 392.

[63] "Letter to a Minister," in Regis J. Armstrong, J.A. Wayne Hellmann, and William J. Short, *The Saint: Francis of Assisi-Early Documents, Vol. I* (Hyde Park, New York: New City Press, 1999), pp. 97-98.

[64] *"That Excessive Love," Circular Letter 21* (April 18, 2003).

[65] *Ibid.,* n.2.1.

superiority and unearned privilege, in imitation of the Christ who emptied himself (kenosis) and became obedient to the point of death – death on the cross. (Phil. 2:8). It is not the abandonment of conflict, but the embrace of the cross.

In the theory of self-transcendent consistency, we can distinguish three levels of conflict that emerge in vocational life. They are qualitatively, and not just quantitatively, different.

The first level of conflict is that which emerges in the *first dimension*. This is the struggle between consciously held, publicly proclaimed values and the consciously owned emotional needs of the individual. In the multi-ethnic environments in which we exist, this first level of inter-cultural conflict may be understood as the personal and conscious appropriation (or conscious negation) of the value of gospel brotherhood across the boundaries of culture, etc. It implies the acceptance or rejection of the "courageous and passionate confidence to move forward and beyond the frontiers of language, class, culture, ideology, gender, orientation and caste that separate the poor from the rich in the illusory world of the *majores* and *minores*."[66]

This is the level of inter-cultural conflict that is open to ordinary and accepted forms of education and diversity training. Because the arc of tension is between the *ideal self* (with its personal and social ideals) and the part of the *actual self* that is related to present behavior and one's dominant self-concept, educators can promote cross-cultural learning by (1) highlighting the institutional self-transcendent ideal of peace, harmony, fraternity and communion; (2) underlining and accentuating the positive dimensions of one's personal commitment to evangelical brotherhood and the establishment of the fraternal economy across boundaries and borders; and (3) demonstrating how emotional fears and attitudes around achievement, dependency, nurturance, and autonomy, for example, can be integrated with the publicly proclaimed values of fraternity.

Another level of inter-cultural conflict is that which erupts from the highly primitive emotional needs and defensive narrative (social) scripts or interpretations of fraternal living. These are the intuitive and spontaneous appraisals that are uprooted from

---

[66] David B. Couturier, "Communities of International Compassion: Post-Novitiate Formation in Capuchin Life," Post-Novitiate Congress (Assisi: September 2004).

and unattached to the gospel ideals of communion, gospel brotherhood and the fraternal economy. These are the immediate impressions, images, interpretations and assessments that erupt from the dominating emotional needs of individuals (and groups). They are the intuitive sense appraisals that divide communities and split congregations into segments that are alternatively "all good" or "all bad." Only therapeutic intervention can heal the ruptures that this form of inter-cultural conflict constructs.

But, there is a third level of inter-cultural conflict that lies midway between a conscious understanding and acceptance of pluralism and a largely primitive and defensive negation of differences.

This is the experience of diversity, which is, at one and the same time, an acceptance of the ideal of difference *and* its defensive manipulation or minimalization. This is the case of an individual who accepts in principle and as a consciously held value that a friar should "move forward and beyond the frontiers of language, class, culture, ideology, gender, orientation and caste that separate the poor from the rich," *and also*, at the same time, defends himself against the courage and passionate confidence it takes to accomplish it. The friar holds this inconsistency without awareness of his manipulation or minimalization of diversity.

The difference that difference makes touches and threatens, in some way, an emotional need within the individual (e.g., abasement, dependency, succorance or harm avoidance). Because of the structural horizon of expectations and desires built up in this second dimension of his personality, the friar is aware of the value he places on diversity and cultural differences but is largely *unaware* of the fears he has about diversity and ignorant of the defenses he uses to avoid its implementation.

We turn now to an assessment of the theory of self-transcendent consistency.

THE THEORY OF SELF-TRANSCENDENT CONSISTENCY AND ITS APPLICATION TO THE DEVELOPMENT OF THE FRATERNAL ECONOMY: AN ASSESSMENT

In the last chapter, we sketched the general lines of the system and research involved in the theory of self-transcendent consistency and the anthropology of vocation developed by Luigi Rulla and his colleagues, Joyce Ridick and Franco Imoda. In this chapter, we offered a substantive, though necessarily incomplete, application of the theory to elements of the fraternal economy, as these have been discussed in the Plenary Councils of the Capuchin Order and in the Circular Letters of its Minister General, John Corriveau. We wish to conclude this chapter with a brief assessment of the contributions that Rulla's theory makes to the development of the fraternal and demonstrate a potential deficit in that same theory.

As we have seen and pointed out several times in this chapter, the fraternal economy is presented in the Circular Letters of John Corriveau as a largely conscious and deliberate enterprise of the will. In his presentation at the 2004 Congress on the Post-Novitiate, Corriveau wrote,

> Francis withdrew his brothers from a world of competition and greed by conscious and clear economic choices. The Plenary Council began a process of delineating equally concrete economic choices in order to create among the brothers and the peoples they serve a "fraternal economy" whose purpose is the enhancement of communion rather than the protection and increase of wealth.[67]

Corriveau continued, "Economic structures are the single most oppressive aspect of our world. Economic structures are the underlying motive of most conflict in our world."[68] One need not quibble with Corriveau's major insight, since he is focusing on the fraternal economy as a fundamental *value* of the Capuchin Order and is using his circular letters in a compact way to clarify the meaning of evangelical poverty and situate it securely within the constellation of Capuchin-Franciscan values. However, our application of Rulla's anthropology of vocation might supplement his frame with an attention to the whole range of dynamics, motivations and desires, both conscious and unconscious, that go into the construction of "economic structures" and the fraternal economy. Too often, the world of finances and economics is portrayed as an

---

[67] John Corriveau, "Formation to Franciscan Capuchin Values in Post-Novitiate," (Assisi, September 14, 2004), p.4.

[68] *Ibid.*, n. 5.1.

intensely objective and scientific domain of (only) facts and figures that are somehow impervious to emotions and impenetrable to the desire for the transcendent. Our analysis indicates the importance and the utility of evaluating the psychological underpinnings of the fraternal economy.

We have distinguished the dialectics of fraternal desire that can emerge in the fraternal economy. In our discussion of the belief in a fraternal world and the psychodynamics of economic solidarity, we laid out some warning signs. We noted that friars who are already suffering from an unjust situation may become more, not less, vulnerable to misunderstanding, misinterpretation and derogation, under certain conditions. These insights register the importance of further analysis of the psychological dimensions of the fraternal economy.

By way of critique of Rulla's contribution, we can offer the following. Rulla's theory of self-transcendent consistency and the research that supports it are an elaborate and intricate analysis of the intrapsychic dynamics that attend the construction, maintenance and development of self-transcendent values in vocational life. Rulla's attention is drawn to two areas of conversion in religious life, the personal and the interpersonal. The methods of formation he provides for growth in vocational life are those which attend these two areas of conversion. Vocational growth sessions, along with proportionate and supported pastoral experiences, have been shown to be powerful and, indeed, essential mechanisms for increasing the capacity to internalize the self-transcendent values of religion.[69]

But, they are insufficient. Rulla leaves largely unexamined the social and organizational dynamics of contemporary institutions. What is missing from Rulla's theory and the research of Rulla, Ridick and Imoda is a concentration on the "workplace within" and the "psychodynamics of organizational life."[70]

Rulla himself admits that his theory is best applied to internal rather than external structures, when he writes:

---

[69] Rulla, Ridick and Imoda, *ACVII*, pp. 177-225.

[70] Larry Hirschhorn, *The Workplace Within: Psychodynamics of Organizational Life* (Cambridge, MA: MIT Press, 1993).

The anthropology here proposed as a Christian personalism concentrates on structures inside the person rather than on structures outside the person; that is, on structures which help one become what one is: a being which is by nature called to theocentric self-transcendence so as to be able to love the Divine You and the human you in a responsible way, with the help of grace. Moreover, this anthropology takes account of the existential situation of the person as a being who must overcome conscious and subconscious limitations on freedom (limitations which, nevertheless, do not diminish the person's basic responsibility). The helps to formation suggested in this tenth section, both for the intrapersonal and interpersonal areas, are meant as a modest contribution to assist the human person in his dialogue with the indispensable and primary communication of God's grace.[71]

Rulla offers the rationale for why he limited himself to the intrapersonal and interpersonal dimensions of religious life. He writes tellingly:

> It is the divisions, inconsistencies, and disharmonies, conscious and unconscious, lying within the individual human heart, which provoke and sustain the external injustices, disunities, and fractures of society.[72]

Left largely untreated in Rulla's work is how these personal divisions are transformed into structural inconsistencies and, indeed, how they become social or structural sin "embedded or expressed in the institutions, structures, and conventions of social, political, economic and cultural life."[73]

It is as if Rulla is unaware of how *structures of sin* are created and maintained not only by individuals but also by groups. Massingale, however, demonstrates how social or structural sins arise in a group or culture, how they affect us and how they double back as (reinforcing) inducements to personal (and social) sin.[74] In

---

[71] Rulla, *ACVI*, p. 452.

[72] *Ibid.*, p. 455.

[73] Massingale, *op.cit.*, p. 333.

[74] *Ibid.*, p. 330.

fact, injustice often hides in the conventions, customs, and systems of organizations, including religious ones. Having morphed into structures of sin or, as we shall see in the next chapter, "social defenses," the conventions appear normal and "just the way things are," when, in fact, they carry group biases and cultural discrimination.

Today, religious communities face a world of increasing diversity and an ever more dangerous disparity.[1] It seems clear that *international* issues will take up more and more of our moral imagination as religious leaders in the 21st century. Religious communities are undergoing a profound process of organizational challenge and transformation. A chronic vocational shortage now threatens the institutional viability and structural integrity of many religious congregations in the United States.[2]

Given the power of organizational forces both within and without religious congregations, it appears that the tools and methods of an intrapersonal and interpersonal psychological approach are a necessary but insufficient foundation for an understanding of the fraternal economy.

The fraternal economy is not only an intrapsychic reality; it is also a structural one. It is a system of fraternal relationships, as well as economic and political ones, within a religious congregation that spans a hundred countries and several hundred cultures. As the initial "Statute of Economic Solidarity" in the Capuchin Order indicates, it has rules and regulations, conventions and procedures to guide its operations. In order to provide a more complete picture of the psychological dynamics of the fraternal economy, we must expand our skills and widen our attention to the distinctively *organizational* dimensions of evangelical poverty, as it is being developed in the Capuchin Order. We must do this, without ever losing sight of what we have gained from our profound education into the intrapsychic dynamics of the fraternal economy.

---

[1] David B. Couturier, "From Diversity to Disparity: The Structural Conversion of Religious Life," *Horizon* 14:4 (Fall, 1989) pp. 23-28.

[2] D.J. Nygren and M.D. Ukeritis, *The Future of Religious Orders in the United States* (Westport, CT: Praeger, 1993).

CHAPTER EIGHT

THE FRATERNAL ECONOMY AND THE DEVELOPMENT OF THE CORPORATE IMAGINATION: A SOCIO-ANALYTIC PERSPECTIVE

In this chapter we turn our attention from an intrapsychic to an organizational analysis of developments in religious congregations. It is clear that religious life in the West has undergone and continues to undergo a profound transformation.[3] The decision of the Capuchin-Franciscan community to transition from an economic philosophy and structure framed in the juridic relationships of the nineteenth and twentieth centuries to one adapted to principles of solidarity in the twenty-first is set within the organizational context, or deep narratives, of renewal and refounding.[4]

It is important that we understand clearly and accurately enough this organizational context. Therefore, we will study the social, cultural and ecclesial forces that are now conditioning the renewal and restructuring efforts of religious communities. We will look specifically at the ways that these forces are shaping the "corporate imagination" of members, since it is from the "deep narratives" or shared "interpretive schemes"[5] of that corporate imagination that religious understand their mission and make sense of their action in the world. We will do this from a specific socio-analytic perspec-

---

[3] David J. Nygren and Miriam D. Ukeritis, *The Future of Religious Orders in the United States: Transformation and Commitment* (Westport, CT: Praeger Press, 1993); Patricia Wittberg, "Ties that No Longer Bind," *America* 179 (September 26, 1998), pp. 10-14.

[4] Gerald A. Arbuckle, *Strategies for Growth in Religious Life,* (Hyperion Books, 1988); *Out of Chaos: The Refounding of Religious Life* (New York: Paulist Press, 1988;*From Chaos to Mission: Refounding Religious Life Formation* (New York: Continuum International Books, 1996).

[5] J.M. Bartunek and C.A. Lacey, "The roles of narrative in understanding work group dynamics associated with a dramatic event," in J.A. Wagner (ed.) *Advances in Qualitative Organizational Research.* Vol. I (Greenwich, CT: JAI Press, 1998), pp. 33-66; J.M. Bartunek, *Organizational and Educational Change: The Life and Role of a Change Agent Group* (New York: Erlbaum, 2003).

tive, the field of study that analyzes the "psychodynamics of organizational life," in the tradition of interpersonal psychoanalysis.[6]

In this way, we hope to supplement the study of the *intrapsychic* dynamics of the fraternal economy already discussed in previous chapters with a presentation of its *organizational* dynamics. We hope to offer the reader a fuller and more complete understanding of the challenges and opportunities facing religious formators responsible for the education of the next generation of friars in the fraternal economy of Franciscan life.

We will address ourselves to three specific questions:

1. What are the major social, cultural and ecclesial forces now impacting religious life, in general, and the development of the "fraternal economy" in Capuchin life, in particular, especially in the West?

2. What are the institutional "narrative frames" or organizational "interpretive schemes" that religious bring with them to understand these social, cultural and ecclesial forces? What are their contributions to the development of a shared "corporate imagination" and what are their deficits?

3. How does a socio-analytic reading of these conditions inform the formative challenges implied in the transition from a "market global economy" to a "fraternal economy," especially in Capuchin communities in the West?

---

[6] For an introduction to the psychoanalytic or socio-analytic approach, cf. William M. Czander, "Understanding Work and the Organization from the Psychoanalytic Perspective," in W. Czander, *The Psychodynamics of Work and Organizations* (New York: Guilford Press, 1993), pp. 123-143; Kenn Rogers, "The Socio-Analytic Approach to Organizational Consulting," (Newark, NJ: The College of Medicine and Dentistry, 1974); Laurence J. Gould, "Psychoanalytic and Non-Psychoanalytic Approaches to Work Group and Organizational Consultation: An Overview and Appraisal of Theory and Practice," (Second Cornell Symposium on Psychoanalytic Studies in Organizational Behavior," March 8-10, 1985); James Hunt and Marion McCollom, "Using Psychoanalytic Approaches in Organizational Consulting," *Consulting Psychology Journal* (Spring, 1994), pp. 1-11; Laurence Gould, "Using Psychoanalytic Frameworks for Organizational Analysis," in M. Kets de Vries et al. (eds.) *Organizations on the Couch* (San Francisco: Jossey Bass, 1991); L. Hirschhorn and C. Barnett (eds.) *The Psychodynamics of Organizations* (Philadelphia: Temple University Press, 1993); David Armstrong, "Names, Thoughts and Lies: The Relevance of Bion's Later Writings for Understanding Experiences in Groups," *Free Associations* 3:2 (1992), pp. 261-282.

We begin with a brief overview of the forces impacting religious congregations and the organizational features of renewal and refounding in late twentieth and early twenty-first century religious life in the West.

THE PERFECT STORM: THE TRANSFORMATION OF RELIGIOUS LIFE IN THE LATE TWENTIETH CENTURY

A few years ago, the novelist Sebastian Junger, wrote a semi-fictionalized account of an astounding tempest that battered a small fishing boat off the coast of Gloucester, Massachusetts.[7] He called his novel and the event, "the perfect storm," because several powerful meteorological forces had to coalesce at the right time, in the precise manner and at the same place to produce the fury and the calamity that unfolded over the course of several treacherous days. It was a once-in-a-century event. Junger called it "the perfect storm" because it brought out from those who lived through it the highest qualities of courage and stamina. Even for those who succumbed to the extraordinary convergence of forces, it was an unparalleled event of the highest drama and tragedy.

Religious in the West are living through a "perfect storm" of organizational dynamics. They are witnessing the convergence of a remarkable and, indeed, unparalleled set of social, cultural and ecclesial forces that are coming together, reinforcing one another, and building momentum in unison. They are in the middle of conditions they could not have predicted and for which they are, in many ways, ill prepared. Let us highlight four of these forces. Each one would be challenging enough on its own. Taken together, they present a daunting challenge for the development of the "fraternal economy" in Capuchin-Franciscan life.

The first force is the new reality of terrorism that now grips the context of their vowing. Religious now live in a new world order shaped by the specter and threat of terrorist attacks and the extreme measures governments resort to in order to secure their cities and protect their people from state and extra-state sponsored

---

[7] Sebastian Junger, *The Perfect Storm*, (New York: W.W. Norton, 1997).

madness.[8] The unchecked and unrelenting spread of HIV/AIDS and famine in Africa, the dangerous rise in religious intolerance and violent religious fundamentalisms, the brazen violation of human rights, the trafficking of women and children for commercial and religious purposes are becoming, in some cases and in various parts of the world, sponsored enterprises and political tools.[9]

Bryan Massingale cautions against the rise of a national security ethos that stands in stark contrast and, indeed, is challenged by the narrative and foundations of biblical security.[10] The Franciscan historian, Joseph Chinnici, spoke recently of two competing social narratives in the animation of justice, peace and the integrity of creation within American Franciscan communities.[11] The first interprets social conditions, political challenges and religious issues out of the deep narrative of emancipation and liberation. This "interpretive scheme" arose largely from the civil rights struggles and liberation movements of the 1960s as a power to effect social change. It is a conceptual frame that is informed by the rejection of oppressive structures and entrenched authority. It rides on the hope of "a new day" and the necessity of ushering in radical change.

The second narrative scheme is quite different. It interprets the same social, political and religious conditions out of an alternative conceptual frame, that of security and defense. What people seek are safety not liberation, integrity not incitement, and the enforcement of values and rules that will reinforce security and stability in the world.

From this vantage point, religious communities debate, as do other communities in America, the significance of terrorism in international relations and progress in domestic policies. The issues surrounding tolerance, vigilance, accountability and transparency in organizations are heightened with every disclosure of corporate

---

[8] Michael Brown et. Al. (eds.) *New Global Dangers: Changing Dimensions of International Security* (Cambridge, MA: MIT Press, 2004); Philip B. Hymann, *Terrorism, Freedom and Security* (Cambridge, MA: MIT Press, 2004).

[9] Princeton N. Lyman and J. Stephen Morison, "The Terrorist Threat in Africa," *Foreign Affairs* 83:1 (2004), pp. 75-86.

[10] Bryan N. Massingale, "From Homeland to Biblical Security," *Origins* 32:6 (February 20, 2003), pp. 598-602.

[11] Joseph Chinnici, Presentation to Franciscan Animators of JPIC, (Detroit, MI, November 14, 2004).

fraud. This conceptual frame holds that we now live in a world that requires greater assurances, tighter regulations, stiffer penalties, higher walls and zero tolerance.

This leads us to the second force facing religious organizations in America – that which comes from the sexual abuse scandal and the impact of the writing, reception and revision of the Charter for the Protection of Children.

Clearly, it is too early to offer an accurate prediction about the lasting impact of what has been described as the worst crisis ever to hit the American Catholic Church. Initial reactions to the publication of the Charter, however, have not always been positive. There is some evidence that it has deepened the crisis of morale in religion and the mistrust of bishops and other religious leaders.[12] The crisis has evoked concerns over trust and credibility in the Church and has been exacerbated by the decisions of bishops to seek bankruptcy protection, in some cases, and to close, merge and yoke parishes on a wide scale, in others.[13]

Peter Steinfels reads these times in the American Catholic Church as one of angry polarization.[14] He characterizes the Catholic population as a "people adrift," struggling to make sense of their contrary theological intepretations. On the one side there are those who interpret the issues facing the Church in a liberal mode. On the other side are those who read the same concerns from a decidedly conservative reflection. The present discourse of the Church, he notes, is a continual and irresolvable stalemate between these two contrary (and, he would say, contrarian) narratives.

The sexual abuse scandal and its aftermath have required of religious communities of men greater efforts at institutional vigilance and transparency and have led them to construct new systems of accountability and oversight with lay members of the Church.[15]

---

[12] David France, Our Fathers: The Secret Life of the Catholic Church in an Age of Scandal (New York: Broadway, 2004); Jason Berry, *Vows of Silence: The Abuse of Power in the Papacy of John Paul II* (New York: Free Press, 2004).

[13] Mark D. Jordan, *Telling Truths in Church: Scandal, Flesh and Christian Speech* (New York: Beacon Press, 2003).

[14] Peter Steinfels, *A People Adrift,* (New York: Simon and Schuster, 2003).

[15] The majority of religious congregations of men in the United States has now contracted with an outside accreditation agency that will monitor their compliance and risk management in the area of the sexual abuse of minors.

The third force to impact religious congregations is the chronic, multi-generational and largely unresolved vocational shortage in priesthood and religious life. Despite a growing Catholic population, fed mostly by the influx of new (and largely, Hispanic,) immigrants, priestly ordinations in the American Catholic Church have dropped by 40% since 1971.[16] There are 50% fewer religious women and men than a generation ago.[17] The median age of religious continues to climb, cresting today at an average of 70 years for women religious and 63 for male religious.[18]

Seventy-eight percent of religious women are over the age of 60 and only 7% of religious women are under the age of 40.[19] Nearly one out of every three priests is retired.[20] Twenty-seven percent of parishes in the United States are without a priest. Fifty percent of all parishes worldwide are without a resident priest.[21] Today, there are 2.8 ordinations per year per diocese in America.[22] The American Catholic Church is not at zero growth, that is, it is not replacing priests and religious who are retiring and dying, even as the needs of the Church (and American society) continue to change in complexion and complexity.

The final force impacting American religious life can be termed the reinvention of work in male religious communities.[23] This area concerns us directly since it affects how religious men work, where they serve, and how effective their mission can be in the modern world. By the term "reinvention of work," we signal the dramatically different ways that religious men are expected to serve and

---

[16] Accessed at: www.cara.georgetown.edu/bulletin/religioustatistics.html., 2004.

[17] The statistics are from "Frequently requested church statistics," www.cara.georgetown.edu/bulletin (2004).

[18] Accessed: www.usccb.org/consecratedlife/research.html. (2004).

[19] Nearly 60% of religious men are over 60 and 21% under 40. These statistics are from "Information:Research, 2004", accessed: www.usccb:consecratedlife/research.htm. (2004).

[20] Joseph Claude Harris, "The Shrinking Supply of Priests," *America* 183:14 (2000), at www.americanmagazine.org/gettext.cfm?article/TypeID=1&textID=2298&issueID=387.

[21] www.futurechurch.org (2004).

[22] William Ciezlak, OFM Cap., developed the statistic on ordinations for a research project at the Franciscan School of Theology in Berkeley, CA (private conversation, October 2001).

[23] This next section is treated extensively in the article, David B. Couturier, "The Reinvention of Work in Religious Communities of Men," *New Theology Review* 11:3 (August 1998), pp. 22-35.

minister than was required even just a generation ago. Let us briefly explore this issue.

Ministry has become more complex and stressful, for greater numbers of religious men. According to a recent study by priest-sociologist John H. Morgan, the average Catholic priest works between 60 to 70 hours per week on ministry.[24] Without structural changes and as fewer men enter priesthood and greater numbers retire, that number is sure to climb dramatically. Beyond this, religious men who do serve in ministry are expected to exhibit a greater range of competencies across a wider plain of ministerial cultures than at any previous period of religious service.

Religious men are working differently than they were just forty or fifty years ago, because American society is working differently. There has been a fundamental culture-wide re-organization and re-imagining of what it means to labor and to serve in Western culture. Religious men are caught in the wake of this profound sociological transformation.

One way to describe this change is to note that we have moved as a society from a relational (family) culture to a global work culture.[25] It was not that long ago that Americans, in general, and Catholics, in particular, identified themselves by the neighborhoods they belonged to, the churches they attended, and the people who were significant in their lives. We were a "relational culture" bound to our families for identity, meaning and affirmation. We are now a mobile society and have become a "global work culture" that gets its meaning and affirmation from the incentives of a globalized competitive, capitalistic system.[26] We are more and more beholden to the exigencies of the stock market and the dynamic forces of trade policies. The average middle class laborer is working longer and harder, for less and less. We are defined by what we do, not whose we are.

---

[24] John H. Morgan, *Scholar, Priest and Pastor: Priorities among Clergy Today* (South Bend, Ind: Graduate Theological Foundation Books, 1998).

[25] Amitai Etzioni, *The New Golden Rule: Community and Morality in a Democratic Society* (New York: Basic Books, 1996).

[26] For a theological analysis of the social atomism of contemporary cities, cf. Graham Ward, *Cities of God* (New York: Routledge, 2000). For an insightful rendering of St. Augustine's theology of cities, cf. "Between the Cities," in E.M. Atkins and R.J. Dodaro, (eds.), *Augustine's Political Writings* (Cambridge: Cambridge University Press, 2001).

Even as American families are more dependent on and tied to their work, the fundamental relationship between the American worker and business has changed dramatically.[27] Gone is the time that businesses and corporations were loyal to their workforce. Gone is the company that promises security for hard work and competency. The bottom line of business today is profit for the anonymous stakeholder. Workers are caught in the almost never-ending cycle of mergers and acquisitions that provide immediate returns for investors in an increasingly volatile market system. In this turbulence, the American worker has learned to rely on himself/herself, instead of the company and its leadership. The loyal and secure American worker has been replaced by the entrepreneurial knowledge worker who relies on her/his own ingenuity and foresight.[28] The American worker appears more insecure and the toll on families is enormous.

A recent study from the Economic Policy Institute showed that the average middle class mother and father are working an extra 6 weeks per year (an extra 246 hours per year) since 1989.[29] This means less time with children and less time with parents, friends and neighbors in need. It suggests less time available for volunteerism, charity work, and religion.

Religious themselves are working differently because they have vastly different relationships with their own religious organizations.[30] One way of describing the change is to say that religious have moved from institutions of single interest to institutions of multiple interests.

A generation ago, religious provinces coalesced around a limited set of ministerial interests. Teaching orders taught in schools; clerical orders ran parishes and congregations that ran hospitals staffed them at almost every level of the operation. This coherence

---

[27] H.S. Baum, *Organizational Membership: Personal Development in the Workplace* (Albany, NY: State University of New York Press, 1990).

[28] Herman E. Daly and John B. Cobb Jr., *For the Common Good, op.cit.*

[29] Lawrence Mishel, Jared Bernstein and Heather Boushey, "The State of Working America 2002-2003," (Economic Policy Institute: www.epinet.org., 2002). The text indicates that the average American two-parent family now works 660 more hours per year, a full 16 more weeks, than it did in 1979.

[30] W. Gordon Lawrence, "Salient Dynamics in Religious Life," in Seth Allcorn, *Psychoanalytic Interpretations of Organizational Cultures* (Chicago: International Society for the Psychoanalytic Study of Organizations, 1994), pp. 137-154.

gave religious congregations a clear mission and a limited set of objectives. In fact, the primary (organizational) task of the Catholic Church for over a hundred years was relatively direct: (1) to defend the faith in an alien land, and (2) to move a generation of immigrant Catholics up and out of disadvantage.

Now religious Orders have diverse missions, multiple tasks, varied systems of ministries and competing cultures of service.[31] It is not uncommon for a single province to run vastly different kinds of operations that demand complex but exclusive sets of skills. It is no longer possible to train for a limited range of ministries and it is increasingly difficult to transfer religious from one culture of service to another. Those in a social service culture of ministry, for example, are not immediately assignable to an educational culture. Those trained in a parochial culture are not often equipped to service in an educational or social service culture. The competencies of one are not easily translatable to the others.

To complicate matters even more, there is no longer a shared lexicon of terms that can even describe what religious do when they serve.[32] In fact, religious men and women are often working under three divergent views of their labor. These differences impact attitudes toward authority, decision-making, benefits, retirement, compensation and formation.

For example, some religious are secure in a theology of priesthood as the guiding model of authority, order and work in the Church. This theology divides the world of service into those ordained for leadership and decision-making and the laity who only advise priests on ecclesial matters.[33]

There are others, however, who see their role and their activities under the rubric of a theology of ministry (not orders) where the operative working principle is one of collaboration, not

---

[31] Beyond these "cultures of service" is an important but unrecognized dimension of contemporary religious life – the operation of seven competing cultures of religious life. There are, in essence, seven interpretative schemes regarding beliefs, emotions, rituals and resources in religious life itself. Cf. David B. Couturier, "The Learning Cultures of Religious Life," *InFormation* 6:3 (November/December 1998), pp. 1-10.

[32] John H. Collins, *Diakonia: Re-Interpreting the Ancient Sources* (New York: Oxford University Press, 1990) provides a look into the theological complications of the New Testament texts for service.

[33] Susan K. Wood, *Ordering the Baptismal Priesthood: Theologies of Lay and Ordained Ministry:* (Collegeville: Liturgical Press, 2003).

advisement. In this light, all church is ministerial. Some service is presbyteral ministry and some is lay ministry. All ministries share a common fundamental base of action.

The complications arise when religious trained in one "culture of service" (i.e. "orders") try to cross the boundary of another culture of service (i.e. "ministry"). Imagine for a moment a religious trained in an organizational culture that highlights mature collaboration, mutual action and shared decision-making. Now imagine that same religious moving into a service culture that reminds him/her that his/her contributions are only advice; they are not authoritative decisions.

There is a third term that is also being used in some parts of the Church: "work." Influenced by John Paul II's theology of work, it views all human labor as flowing from the work that God does in the world.[34] In this theological light, labor does not have to be located in the church or in a religious setting for it to be redemptive. All workers are called to co-create with the Father, co-redeem with the Son and co-sanctify with the Spirit in the labor of the day. Applying this theology to church service, the once sharp distinctions between ministry and work break down as do the lines of authority and decision-making. If all work is potentially a co-creative, co-redemptive and co-sanctifying Trinitarian experience, one may not need the category of "ministry" (or "ordination") as the only or strict parameter of religious service. Religious are thereby drawn more deeply into settings that are not strictly church-related.

One need not claim theological clarity here, since theologians have yet to tease out the differences and make sense of the tensions. We need only highlight the confusion that is emerging in religious organizational language. The formative and organizational implications are significant. We are unclear about how to answer the direct question – "do religious do ministry or do they work?"

Another aspect of the reinvention of work that needs to be pointed out is the "de-institutionalization" and "re-institutionalization" of corporate works in religious communities.[35]

---

[34] John Paul II, Encyclical Letter, *Laborem Exercens* (September 14, 1981).

[35] Dennis Holtchneider and Melanie Morey treat the serious complications emerging in the trend toward sponsorship models of governance in religious institutions. Cf. "Relationship Revisited: Catholic Institutions and their Founding Congregations," Occa-

Partly because of the vocation shortage and partly because of religious frustration with bureaucracies that were failing to meet the needs of the poor, many religious in the 1970s and 1980s called for the dismantling of the corporate works of their Provinces. Institutions were closed, properties were sold and religious became more comfortable with province-endorsed personal ministries instead of province-owned institutions.

During this time period, more and more religious hired themselves out (or were assigned) to third-party agencies, organizations other than their own religious congregations. They found jobs with dioceses in a host of diocesan-sponsored/owned ministries. They became diocesan directors and religious education coordinators, among other things. Rather than service in the organizational culture of their own religious congregations, many religious became employees of diocesan bishops. Time and experience have shown that the dismantling of the corporate work of religious congregations did not mean the de-institutionalization of religious life and the lowering of organizational bureaucracy, as some had predicted. In some cases, it simply became the re-institutionalization of religious congregations under an increasingly diocesan mode of thinking and operating. A good number of religious simply transferred their cultural loyalties to the diocesan bishop (or some other institutional entity), because of their ability to hire and provide "ministerial" employment. This diocesanization has had a profound impact on religious life culture and living.[36]

One final aspect of the reinvention of work has to do with the pluricultural context of contemporary pastoral service. Until the 1950s and 1960s, religious served in mostly ethnically-private settings, churches and communities characterized by a single ethnic culture (i.e., French, German, Polish or Irish). It was not uncommon to see several Catholic Churches just blocks away from one another. One church was Polish; another served the Irish community; and still another served the French-Canadian Catholic immi-

---

sional Paper 47: Association of Governing Boards of Universities and Colleges (Washington, DC, 2000).

[36] Paul K. Hennessy, CFC, treats these issues in greater detail in "The Parochialization of the Church and Consecrated Life," in Paul K. Hennessy, CFC (ed.), *A Concert of Charism: Ordained Ministry in Religious Life* (New York: Paulist Press, 1997).

grants. God was being worshipped in the multiple languages of America but in different houses of worship.

Sometime in the 1970s, it became current to bring the multiple cultures of American society into one church to share a single sacred space. Now priests and religious are expected to minister daily in more than one language and to be adaptable in upwards of ten cultures simultaneously. This is a dramatic shift in ministerial responsibility and it has been attempted with little foresight and pastoral planning. Few ministers (presbyteral or lay) have the capacity to do this with confidence. Fewer yet have the paradigm by which to lead this pluri-cultural form of ministry effectively into the future.[37]

We turn now to the "narrative schemes" that religious have used to interpret these organizational challenges.

THE NARRATIVE FRAMES AND INTERPRETIVE SCHEMES OF RELIGIOUS COMMUNITIES

Religious communities have inherited two kinds of pastoral planning strategies, two mindsets or narrative frames, to help them address the organizational challenges emerging in religious life. We will analyze them and ask ourselves whether they are adequate for our purposes in the development of the fraternal economy in Capuchin-Franciscan life today.

The first "interpretive scheme," one that still operates in some dioceses today, is that from the era of religious expansion. This was the time period of the great builders of Catholic life in America, the men and women who constructed the great monasteries, motherhouses, schools, hospitals and universities that dot the American landscape. This was a time when American Catholics wanted to influence every aspect and touch every part of American life with the Gospel message. It was a time of tremendous zeal and unified purpose.

James Hennessy, in his history of American Catholicism, offers a powerful example of that period. He introduces us to the

---

[37] This topic was treated at an important national consultation conducted by Rev. Clarence Williams (October 7-9, 2002).

achievements of Cardinal Dennis Dougherty of Philadelphia. He writes:

> Cardinal Dennis Dougherty opened 92 parishes, 89 parish schools, three diocesan high schools, 15 academies, a woman's college, and a preparatory seminary. Other ventures included a diocesan retreat house, orphanages, a school for the deaf, and other special institutions and hospitals.[38]

And Dougherty accomplished this, all within the space of his first two years as Archbishop of Philadelphia!

This was a period of intense enthusiasm and singular devotion. America was a great frontier. Religious saw America as a land of open and seemingly endless ministerial possibilities.[39] The American landscape was ripe for evangelization and religious were going to pick it- enthusiastically. The mood of this era was expansive, confident, zealous, focused, optimistic and unified. The era of expansion began in the 1820s and reached its peak in the 1950s.

Beginning in the 1960s, the American Catholic Church followed its European counterparts into a new organizational period of diminishment. Even with the increase of the Catholic population, this period is characterized by a precipitous, unprecedented and chronic loss of vocations that affects how pastoral ministry and community life are experienced at every level of church life.

The period of diminishment is characterized by several features:

1. The structures of Catholic life adjust to the unprecedented and chronic loss of vocations;
2. Creative ministries develop in a more focused and limited way, as congregations move from province-owned institutions to province-endorsed personal ministries;
3. There is a large-scale relinquishment of grand institutions (i.e., hospitals, orphanages, schools, seminaries and motherhouses).

---

[38] James Hennessy, *American Catholics: A History of the Roman Catholic Community in the United States* (New York: Oxford Press, 1981).

[39] Theologian, Mary Jo Leddy, contrasts this distinctively "frontier" mentality of American theology with Canadian models of theology in "Exercising Theology in the Canadian Context," in Mary Jo Leddy and Mary Ann Hinsdale, *Faith that Transforms* (New York: Paulist Press, 1987), pp.127-134.

This leads to a re-institutionalization of some religious communities and to "privatization of ministries," in others.
4. The language of the period becomes one of "downsizing,"
letting go, handing back, yoking, twinning and merging.

The general attitude of this period is one of hanging on, survival and maintenance. Religious do their best to hold onto good
ministries, important pastoral programs, and even the possibility of weekly Eucharist for growing numbers of communities of
faith. The emphasis in religious congregations turns from vitality
to one of viability, as religious begin to question the very surviv-
ability of their provinces or congregations.

In this period, religious and priests are now expected to do
more with less. During a period when work is being reinvented
in American society, religious now are expected to demonstrate
their competency and credentials in religious service. This comes
as a surprise and with some distress for religious who have worked
unencumbered in fields of pastoral service for many years. In the
past, good will and the strength (and historical weight) of their
founding charism were enough evidence for their credibility as
providers of religious services. Up until now, they had conducted
their pastoral tasks as a religious endeavor without intrusion from
"outside" agents of supervision and accountability for many generations. That was beginning to change dramatically.

Several dynamics come to light as the social impact of the loss
of vocations and traditional institutions takes hold. We can name
a few.

The first is the dynamic of forced choices. The recognition
of limits and the pressure for sheer survival and maintenance encourage religious to make difficult, even wrenching, choices for
the quality of their life and service. These choices seem imposed
by circumstances outside their control. These are the hard choices
between key values and important rituals of religious life. Religious
have the feeling of being forced to choose between community life
and ministry and between ministry and prayer.

With ministry requirements increasing (especially as religious
move into third-party agencies), religious find themselves choosing
between the needs of their community life and the requirements

of their ministry. In order to find appropriate work, some religious have to sacrifice living in common. With work drying up for an increasingly elder population of religious and health care costs rising dramatically, some religious women, for example, are forced to live in houses and communities of other congregations. This was not always their first choice. In some cases, these houses are the only religious convents available to them within a reasonable distance from their ministries.

The religious ministry market has become tight and limited, especially as parishes and church social service departments become more economically vulnerable. Unfortunately, religious men and women can be among the first to be let go from parochial assignments, in a favor of part-time lay volunteers.

This diminishment mentality can also lead to a forced choice between ministry and prayer. The increased pressures to find or maintain suitable work force some religious to sacrifice the experience of shared prayer.

Another dynamic is that of institutional insecurity. The confidence of the previous period of expansion is replaced by a sense of constant change, disruption and instability. A clear strategy to defend the faith and move a generation up and out of disadvantage becomes diffused and is replaced by cycles of experimentation and entrepreneurship. Religious do become more realistic, as they recognize their limitations and try to adapt their organizational structures to the new environment of institutional transparency. This is realized in more focused educational programs, the adoption of pastoral planning methods, the application of strategic discernment in decision-making and the implementation of budgetary controls and accountability throughout religious life.

Diminishment encourages religious to try to do more than they are able. Religious will force themselves to make up for what is lost or missing in their social or ecclesial world. In the psychology or strategy of diminishment, nothing is ever enough. There is no end to the needs and requirements piling up. No effort, process or strategy ever gets religious beyond the impression that they are merely "surviving" and "maintaining" religious life for "something" or "some time" in the future.

As we have noted, in this environment priests and religious are expected to work longer and harder. Retirement ages are increased in order to hold onto a generation of ministerial workers who have been the base of church work for over forty years. Seminarians are prepared to pastor upwards of four churches simultaneously. They expect to serve as priest alone. They are not told how and the models and attitudes they are provided oftentimes only increase the polarization in the clergy and their isolation from lay ministers.[40] Diminishment thinking offers little institutional relief.

Several years ago, Ukeritis and Couturier conducted workshops across the United States studying the role that the corporate religious imagination of leaders has on the dynamics of leadership in religious congregations.[41] Using a variety of organizational diagnostic tools and case study analyses, they have found a particular set of vulnerabilities emerging in congregations, particularly those cast in a "diminishment" interpretive scheme. The results of their research indicate the following tentative conclusions:

1. The ten-year window of opportunity for significant structural change or irreversible institutional decline has passed with little notice or appreciable adjustments on the part of a large number of religious congregations.[42]

2. Religious congregations that moved from "maintenance to mission" may be moving back to maintenance once again.

3. The vocation shortage is now chronic and destabilizing the ministerial identity of increasing numbers of religious congregations.

4. Religious communities continue to interpret their renewal problems in terms of an identity confusion among members rather than as a fundamental shift in patterns of work and economics that negatively impact their religious congregations.

---

[40] Such is the research findings of Dr. Dean Hoge in a piece, "Recent Research Findings Pertaining to the Formation of Religious Priests," (Presentation at the *Formation for Celibacy Conference,* Jacksonville, FL, December 2002).

[41] These workshops, "Inside the Faith/Outside the Box: Enlivening the Theological Imagination of Religious Leaders," were sponsored by The Center for the Study of Religious Life, Chicago. (2003-2004).

[42] Cf. Miriam D. Ukeritis, "What has happened since the FORUS study gave religious life 10 years to make life-saving changes?" *Horizons* 27:1 (Fall, 2001), pp. 9-14.

5. It appears that the restructuring and reorganizing of governance may be in the service of maintenance more than mission.

6. Religious leaders are more adept at responding to the personality difficulties of individuals than to the structural disorders of their communities.

7. The balance has shifted toward a greater number of retired members over active and fully employed members.

8. There appears to be a growing number of unemployed and severely-under employed religious.

9. Religious are experiencing greater difficulty finding and maintaining employment in church-sponsored institutions. Religious are moving from province/congregational-owned institutions to province/congregational-endorsed personal religious ministries and to province/congregational-endorsed personal non-ecclesial jobs. Much of this may be due to the increasingly vulnerable financial status of dioceses and parishes.[43]

The narrative frames and interpretive schemes of religious congregations in the United States have shifted from the "icon" of expansion to that of "diminishment."[44] Although a new organizational frame of reference may be emerging (i.e. "enlivening"), the majority of religious communities appear resigned to a continuous state of diminishment. This should be of some concern to Capuchin-Franciscan communities, since the transition from a global market economy to a fraternal economy must take place within this particularly difficult organizational context.

While the institutional ideal may be set as a conscious choice to embrace solidarity across the frontiers of class, ideology, culture (etc.), the organizational dynamics are limited by several, important institutional factors. First, the vocational crisis has not stabilized. Religious congregations in the West are not replacing or keeping

---

[43] Notes from the "Inside the Faith/Outside the Box" Workshop (2004).

[44] Reed and Bazalgette define organizational icons as "symbolic markers that help organize complex, sometimes contradictory events in ways that orient us to reality," "Reframing Reality in Human Experience; The Relevance of the Grubb Institute's Contributions as a Christian Foundation to Group Relations in the Post- 9/11 World, (The Grubb Institute of Behavioral Studies, 2004), p. 1.

pace with the numbers of religious men and women who are retiring from active service or dying. Second, the economies of religious congregations in the West (or Northern Hemisphere) are
still exceedingly vulnerable.[45] The higher percentage of religious
in retirement (>60%), the loss of salaried and stipended income
due to fewer vocations, the dramatic rise in health care costs, and
the changing attitudes towards charitable giving and philanthropy
in the Catholic lay community[46] all signal a vulnerable institutional climate for the proposed change in economic philosophy and
theology. Third, the "reinvention of work" in male religious communities has made some congregations or provinces unsure of or
unsteady with regard to their primary task as a religious institution.
The functional privatization or individualization of ministries in
some congregations or provinces might make the conceptualization of or a move to a provincial or congregational fraternal economy nothing more than a pious fiction.

How then do we help congregations and provinces attend to
these institutional dynamics and the "interpretive schemes" that
help them make sense of their identity and action as an organization? How do we help the Capuchin-Franciscan community understand (some of) the organizational dynamics at play as it moves
from one economic structure to another? The field of socio-analytic organizational development has emerged as an important font
of action research on institutions in transition. We will now introduce the main lines of its thought and begin an application to the
needs of the Capuchin-Franciscan community.

---

[45] The Conference of Major Superiors of Men has recently polled its membership
regarding the proposed termination of the bishops' annual collection for retired religious. The recommendation of members indicates that the financial situation of religious
communities will grow worse in the next seven to ten years because of the aging of
religious congregations.

[46] Arthur C. Brooks, "Religious Faith and Charitable Giving," *Policy Review Online*
121, accessed: www.policyreview.org/oct03/brooks.html.

THE FRATERNAL ECONOMY: A SOCIO-ANALYTIC READING

In 1923 Freud defined psychoanalysis as three things: "the name (1) of a procedure for the investigation of mental processes which are almost inaccessible in any other way, (2) of a method (based on that investigation) for the treatment of neurotic disorders and (3) of a collection of psychological information obtained along those lines, which is gradually being accumulated into a new scientific discipline."[47] Today, as Eisold has indicated, psychoanalysis has expanded into "an array of procedures, a range and variety of techniques and methods that have been developed for exploring the puzzling and irrational aspects of human experiences."[48] It includes traditional psychoanalysis, applied psychoanalysis, psychoanalytic psychotherapy, group therapy and socio-analysis or the psychoanalytic study of organizations.[49]

They cohere around a central task of "exploring the unknown aspects of human experience – what has been disavowed, obscured, repressed, forgotten, displaced, dissociated, avoided, reframed, etc. etc. etc.—the work of helping patients and clients to regain their capacity to think about parts of their experience with which they are not in touch."[50]

When applied to organizations, socio-analysis refers to an interpersonal method of applied psychoanalysis used to uncover and treat the anxiety and irrational processes that develop between individuals, groups and organizations as they attempt to work toward a common goal or achieve a common purpose.[51]

---

[47] S. Freud, "Two encyclopaedia articles," *Standard Edition* XVIII (1923), p, 235.

[48] Kenneth Eisold, "A Clinical Theory of Psychoanalysis: The Common Ground of Psychoanalytic Practice," accessed: www.ispso.org/Symposia/Toronto/1999eisold. htm, 1999.

[49] There is as yet no standard lexicon for this application of psychoanalysis to organizational development and consultation work. In the United States, it has been spoken of as the psychoanalytic study of organizations (cf. "The International Society for the Psychoanalytic Study of Organizations" at www.ispso.org.) and in Australia, it has been referred to as "socio-analysis." The roots are the same and are found in the interpersonal wing of psychonanalysis founded by Fromm, Sullivan and Thompson at the William Alanson White Institute in New York City.

[50] Eisold, *op. cit.,* p.. 2.

[51] Larry Hirschhorn, *The Workplace Within: The Psychodynamics of Organizational Life* (Cambridge, MA; MIT Press, 1993).

Fundamental to the theory and practice of socio-analysis is the argument that all organizations face uncertainties as they try to accomplish difficult tasks in the world.[52] In order to achieve their goals, meet deadlines, turn resources into products and get individuals to cooperate with one another on shared tasks, organizations develop routines and structures, practices and procedures, that are meant to "get the job done" as efficiently as possible. They also function to contain anxiety and to channel fear in a way that is meant to reduce the anxiety impacting the group.

Isabel Menzies originated the concept of "social defenses" in her study of nursing practices in a British hospital.[53] In a review of nursing procedures, she catalogued a series of actions that defied an ordinary logic of treatment and attention to the good of the patient. She noticed nurses waking up patients to give them drugs even when it would have been more beneficial to let them sleep. Menzies also found nurses rotating shifts and wards in a mechanism and a ritualization that helped nurses de-personalize their patients and contain the anxiety they experienced in performing tasks that were "by ordinary standards… distasteful, disgusting and frightening." By using standardized rituals and procedures, the nurses could split off their own feelings, follow orders, avoid their anxious feelings and implement "impersonal rules" in a way that allowed them to continue working in a setting fraught with danger and risk.

The social defenses employed by nurses provided a container for their anxiety, but also distorted the true relationship with patients and real risks in the workplace. Hirschhorn has identified several fundamental principles of the socio-analytic practice in organizations:

First, every organization has primary operational and developmental tasks to accomplish. These are difficult to achieve and thus create (normal) feelings of anxiety throughout the institution.

---

[52] Leroy Wells, Jr., "The Group as a Whole: A Systemic Socioanalytic Perspective on Interpersonal and Group Relations," in A.D. Coleman and M.H. Geller, *Group Relations Reader Two* (Washington, DC: AK Rice Institute, 1985), pp. 49-85.

[53] Isabel Menzies, "A Case Study in the Functioning of Social Systems as a Defense Against Anxiety," in Arthur Coleman and W. Harold Bexton, (eds.) *Group Relations Reader* (Sausalito, CA: GREX, 1975), pp. 281-312.

Second, groups within the organization manage their anxiety by developing and using a set of social defenses together. In fact, one can say that individuals and groups in an organization collude with one another, at an unconscious level, to avoid the work of the organization. That is, there are two sets of group behavior acting at cross-purposes in every institution. On the one hand, there is the assigned work of the institution (the conscious goals and objectives of the organization). On the other hand, there is the basic assumption behavior of the group. This is the set of behaviors, unconsciously agreed to by the group, to minimize injury to the emotional needs of the group and avoid the challenges of the task at hand.

There are three basic types of social defenses. Using the work of Bion and Melanie Klein, Hirschhorn identifies the three modes of social defenses operating in organizations: (1) "basic assumption behavior," (2) the "covert coalition" and (3) the "organizational ritual."[54]

The "basic assumption behavior" is a defense employed by a group (at the nonrational level) that holds that a "cohesive group mind exists and can be sustained without work or development." That is, the group believes that its hard work can be done without work. Clearly, this is a fantasy shared by members of a team or a group within an organization trying to limit the feelings of isolation and depersonalization that erupt as difficult tasks emerge in group life. [55]

Two basic assumption behaviors identified by Bion are: the dependency assumption (in which groups 'dumb down' to increase its reliance on all powerful leader) and the fight/fight assumption (in which groups unconsciously agree to fight the task before them or flee from it as a way of avoiding the demands of their work.) [56]

The "covert coalition" social defense allows a group to hide behind an all-powerful team that has been invested with the imaginary powers of the group to redeem the situation and fix the prob-

---

[54] W.R. Bion, *Experiences in Group* (New York: Basic Books, 1961); M. Klein, *Contributions to Psychoanalysis 1921-1945* (London: Hogarth Press, 1948); Hirschhorn, *The Workplace Within, op.cit.*

[55] Elliott Jaques, " Social Systems as a Defense Against Persecutory and Depressive Anxiety," in M. Klein et al., *New Directions in Psychoanalysis* (London: Tavistock Publications, 1955), pp. 478-498.

[56] David Armstrong, *op.cit.*, pp. 275ff.

lems facing the group. The "organizational ritual" defense emerges when groups develop a host of practices and procedures that are meant to avoid or defer action rather than accomplish it, so as to reduce the tension that comes from achieving something difficult.

The third principle that Hirschhorn provides is that a group dominated by its social defenses has a difficult time reading its challenges accurately and its options correctly. Over time, the organization misses important clues about pressures in the environment. In a normal planning schedule, institutions go through four steps in their analysis and discernment. First, the group identifies and evaluates what is changed or changing in the environment that may impact their "product." Second, the group tests its assumptions, or shared meanings, about the importance or relevance of these changes. Third, the group develops new options or scenarios that more accurately fit the changed environment and new assumptions of the group. Finally, the group chooses a preferred scenario and makes the necessary changes in policies, practices and procedures that will get the group to its desired results. In a situation where social defenses predominate and where basic assumption behavior trumps the primary task of the group, members of the organization misread changes in the environment. Their analysis is obscured by the prevailing emotional needs circulating in the institution. Members are likely to use one another to contain and manage their shared anxiety, but, in the process, learn how to distort task, roles and authority. All of this is done at the non-rational level of the institution.

There are three things that a psychoanalytically trained organizational consultant does to help an organization trapped in its social defenses. First, he or she helps identify or reminds the group of its primary task or mission. She or he also reveals the primary risks (or challenges to the work at hand). Second, the consultant exposes and engages the complexity of the work and uncovers the anxieties emerging in the group that are turning into distortions, defenses and evasions of the work in the institution. Then, the consultant provides a "reflective space" in which group members can take up their work again without the need for projection, splitting or denial.

The fundamental insight in the psychoanalytic or socio-analytic tradition is that individuals and groups experience anxiety in the workplace because of the difficulty (and specifically related to the difficulty) that ensues from (shared) work challenges. Just as individuals create personal defenses to ward off anxiety and to lower tension, so too do groups develop social defenses, at an unconscious level of operation. These social defenses distort relationships, minimize difficulties, and reorganize priorities in group life. It is the task of the organizational consultant to read these social defenses accurately and to apply reparative strategies that will steer the group back to its primary task or mission.

Let us apply these insights to the organizational challenge of moving the Capuchin-Franciscan community, especially in the West, from a global market economy to a fraternal economy. We can do this only in a general way. While the socio-analytic tradition would counsel that all organizations develop social defenses to ward off institutional anxiety, specifically how and when they emerge and in what form depends greatly on leadership styles and the particular features of the organizational culture with which we are working. With these limitations, we can offer the following comments.

These are particularly anxious times for religious congregations. The spectre of terrorism and the chronic intergenerational vocation crisis focus group attention on issues of survival. The American Catholic Church is increasingly polarized over various doctrinal issues (e.g., sexual morality, liturgical reforms, and the role of women in the Church).

The transition to a fraternal economy implies a profoundly new or, at the very least, a dramatically different emphasis with regard to the primary task or mission of Capuchins in the 21st century. As Corriveau has indicated and we have studied in a previous chapter, that mission can no longer be equated primarily with clerical ministries. The fraternal economy serves the understanding that Capuchins exist in the Church and in society to form a gospel brotherhood and to propose a vision of evangelical fraternity that extends to all creation under a good and loving God.

This re-described mission implies new roles in the Capuchin-Franciscan Order. The Seventh Plenary Council of the Order began to address the ways that leadership positions can be reconfigured so that they advance a non-dominating and non-depriving form of power and change in the world. There is as yet no full-blown analysis of the political philosophy and theology that undergird the fraternal economy but, clearly, it would be a useful extension and development in Franciscan understanding.

There will be no movement toward appropriate task and role development in the fraternal economy, unless and until there is a proper re-design of authority relationships. Individuals and groups must have authorization to effect the changes required for true solidarity. Difficulties are likely to erupt at the new boundaries being drawn on the map of the fraternal economy.[57] In the old juridic-dependency model of the nineteenth and twentieth centuries, there were "thick" boundaries between semi-autonomous provinces. Exchanges between provinces were tightly defined and ordered by Constitutional principles that gave provincial ministers great latitude of power within their jurisdictions. Exchanges between jurisdictions were relatively rare and largely circumscribed by the "mother province and daughter jurisdiction" dependencies that promoted the build-up of foreign mission territories in the Order.

The new exchange structures of the fraternal economy will require investment in the management of the new (non-colonial) boundaries between provinces and jurisdictions. It is in that area "in-between" and at those decision-making borders that a new host of psychological factors and social defenses are likely to erupt. Relationships, both those in law and those "in-the-mind', will have to be renegotiated, as all sides of the fraternal economy adjust to their new task, their new roles and their new authority to build solidarity in the Order and in society. The "conscious break" with old economic habits and structures will come with "unconscious mechanisms" and defenses that are designed to ward off anxiety in the Order and return the group to a more comfortable and satisfying experience of group life before the change.

As the old organizational consensus begins to unfreeze in the Order, it is likely that groups within (i.e. provinces) will go through significant periods of group doubt and disillusionment. This is apart from any personal adjustments that individuals might make to accommodate the change to a fraternal economy. We are speaking here of group and inter-group dynamics.

---

[57] J. Krantz, "Group Process Under Conditions of Organizational Decline," *Journal of Applied Behavioral Science* 21:1 (1985), pp. 1-17.

For the past thirty years, the Management Design Institute of Cincinnati, Ohio, has been helping religious organizations diagnose their stage of group development and disillusionment.[58] They have identified five stages in the cycle of group development and disillusionment.

The first is a stage of no doubt, where the group (as a group) experiences cohesion, shared agreement, and a fundamental attitude of group cooperation towards their institutional ideals and objectives. It is a time of teamwork and shared purpose.

The second is a stage of operational doubt, where the group begins to sense the presence of new organizational difficulties that need to be managed. While group cohesion remains a high priority and emotional experience for members, attention shifts to the resolution of the problem that has emerged. This is a "skill and mastery" phase in group life. While disillusionment is low, concern is growing in the organization. At this stage, however, the group believes that the problems can be solved and the difficulties managed with good leadership and group effort.

The third stage is a phase of ideological doubt. Problems in the institution have not been resolved to the group's satisfaction and doubts linger as one problem-solving technique after another fails to ameliorate the situation. Disillusionment is growing, having reached the stage wherein individuals and groups question the reasonableness of actions and the rationale for operations as they are. Confusion reigns in the institution, as more and more people begin to ask why things are developing as they are. If no trustworthy or satisfactory answers are forthcoming, the organization slides into its next phase.

The phase of ethical doubt is characterized by angry polarization. The organization has crossed an important divide in its institutional life, between the rational aspects of group life and the non-rational aspects. At this point, emotional needs and anxious concerns prevail as groups try to make sense of what has gone wrong and what is going on in the institution. Groups are now forming camps within the organization. Projection and splitting are organizational defenses used to protect important "pieces" of institutional life from being lost in the confusion of change. Im-

---

[58] Cf. www.managementdesign.homestead.com

posing reforms through rational fiat by management or leadership is a tempting but ultimately fruitless option. Exclusively rational measures, at this point, are likely to freeze camps in the organization in their projective identifications. The disillusionment is no longer over techniques (as in the period of ideological doubt). Disillusionment has settled into a shared emotional attitude, often circumscribed by social defenses meant to protect "images," "icons," or "interpretive schemes" of the organization.

If the emotional needs of the group are not addressed effectively during the period of ethical doubt, the organization slides further into what may be a protracted period of absolute doubt. If hot debates and angry exchanges characterized the previous period, this era is cold and isolated by comparison. Individuals and groups have settled into fixed positions but are unwilling to discuss or debate their underlying assumptions anymore. The hurt is too deep and the emotions in the group are too raw. The disillusionment in the institution is so profound that members settle into a "passion-less" stance of performance and maintenance operation. People will do their duty and little else. They no longer see or trust the vision that attracted them to the work in the organization. It has been obscured by experiences of doubt and disillusionment at the rational and non-rational levels of their group life.

These stages of group doubt and disillusionment are a normal cycle of development in institutions. It is reasonable, therefore, to expect them to be part of the transitional phases in the movement from a global market economy to the fraternal economy in the Capuchin-Franciscan Order.

SUMMARY

In this chapter, we have looked at the organizational dimensions of the transition to a fraternal economy in the Capuchin-Franciscan Order. We have outlined the various forces (both within the Order and those without) that are likely to condition and impact that transition. International terrorism, a chronic vocational shortage, a national institutional scandal and the reinvention of work in society and religious communities are the context of the move to the fraternal economy for Capuchin Provinces in the West. These are insecure times and these are anxious conditions.

We have studied how organizations respond to anxiety in the workplace by creating social defenses meant to ward off the noxious elements of group life. These various unconscious mechanisms provide momentary (emotional) cover for groups in the institution but ultimately distort tasks, limit roles, confuse power dynamics and constrain options for development throughout the organization.

The transition from the juridic dependency relationships of the 19th and 20th centuries to the fraternal economy of the 21st is a move that impacts organizational life at its most profound levels, at the point of primary task, roles and authority. Corriveau has rightly called it a "profound conversion" that will dramatically impact how friars live and relate with one another across the boundaries of language, class, culture, ideology, orientation and caste. We have identified the psychological challenges and defenses that are likely to emerge and hide in the systems, structures, conventions and customs of the Order's organizational life. We are reminded that these social defenses are group-sanctioned behaviors. Besides the individual needs and personal defenses that can erupt at the cross-section of self-transcendent values (those studied in previous chapters), we have identified another level of emotional defense. It is at the level of group life and fraternal living.

The fraternal economy is a system and network of relationships with specific codes, rules and regulations. After our survey of organizational literature, it should be clear that this system and network function at two levels, the rational and the non-rational. The fraternal economy is a conscious break and a conscious choice for relationships built on evangelical principles of fraternity and solidarity. But, the fraternal economy is also, at the very same time, an institutional structure conditioned and affected by the same principles of organizational development and regression as all other systems. It is not exempt from the psychological dynamics that play out at the institutional level.

We are speaking here of something more than individual (psychological) games played out by individuals in institutional settings. There are those. But, we are addressing another level of analysis and another dimension of complexity. We are speaking here of individual behaviors and group (collusive) processes that hide within the systems, conventions, codes and customs of institutions. They are the practices and procedures that become normative and function as "cultural artifacts." They are the routines and rituals that are the mechanisms by which tasks are accomplished or objectives are avoided. Some of these are conscious and open to interpretation by groups so inclined to self analysis and group assessment. But, some of these are not conscious; they evade detection by ordinary (rational) means of strategic planning and organizational development.

It is clear, then, that any development of the fraternal economy in the Capuchin-Franciscan Order must attend to two separate but inter-related fields of psychological analysis. The first is at the level of the individual. Rulla is correct when he says,

> It is the divisions, inconsistencies, and disharmonies, conscious and unconscious, lying within the individual human heart, which provoke and sustain the external injustices, disunities, and fractures of society.[59]

The fraternal economy must be built from the conscious, self-transcendent ideal of God's goodness and the fraternal relationship God wants for all creation. It must pay attention to the divisions, inconsistencies and fractures that exist, consciously and unconsciously, within the human heart.

But, as we have seen, these inconsistencies become unfair structures and unjust systems through social mechanisms of defense, for which individuals are only indirectly responsible and often largely unaware. Groups can develop anxieties in their institutions and members can collude with one another to reduce tension and avoid responsibility for change in the organization. They can do this through elaborate mechanisms and intricate conventions, with little or no awareness that their actions are defensive. These social defenses can double back and reinforce the inconsistencies that Rulla finds so troubling in the personal life of religious.

---

[59] Rulla, *ACVII*, p. 452.

A more complete understanding of the psychological dynamics of the fraternal economy must include both levels of analysis: the intrapsychic and the organizational.

We turn now to a first attempt at applying both levels to the question of forming Franciscans for the fraternal economy. We want to provide an initial outline of what it means to form religious for the fraternal economy, using the insights derived from Rulla's theory of self-transcendent consistency and from the practice of psycho-analytically informed organizational development.

CHAPTER NINE

THE ORGANIZATIONAL DYNAMICS OF THE FRATERNAL
ECONOMY AND THE DEVELOPMENT OF COMMUNITIES
OF INTERNATIONAL COMPASSION

Institutions are difficult to change and notoriously difficult to transform.[1] That is because organizations function in two dimensions and through two sets of conventions.[2] The first is the rational. These are the policies, procedures, rules and regulations that define the values and ideals, as well as the appropriate practices, of the institution. Here roles and rules are codified in manuals, statutes, constitutions and other official documents. These rational formulae prescribe ideal behavior and demonstrate the public and approved face of the organization to its desired constituencies. Limits are defined, infractions are determined and boundary behaviors are marked. The institution proclaims its mission, organizes its hierarchy, defines its objectives and describes the public limits and conditions of social change.

But, there is another side to organizations. More rarely analyzed but always confronting leaders is the non-rational dimension of the institution.[3] In it are the customs, conventions, informal roles and covert rules played out by all parties at all levels of the organization. Here individuals and groups act out "informal" scripts of personal hopes and communal expectations, individual fears and organizational anxieties about the meaning of work and

---

[1] W.W. Burke, *Organization Change: Theory and Practice* (Thousand Oaks, CA: Sage, 2002).

[2] Wilfred Bion, *Experiences in Groups* (New York: Basic Books, 1959).

[3] William M. Czander, *The Psychodynamics of Work and Organizations: Theory and Application* (New York: The Guilford Press, 1993).

one's place in the formal and informal structures of power and dependency.[4]

All institutions operate at these two levels. And every organization, including religious ones, go through cycles of development and disillusionment when environmental pressures, internal and external to the institution, push for change in the received wisdom of a group's organizational memory.[5]

Every organization develops a unique set of organizational defenses to protect its values and ideals. More powerful are the richly symbolized social defenses that organizations use to hide the non-rational conventions, customs and biases protecting institutional privilege and prestige.[6]

Organizational anxiety develops in an institution whenever there is a threat to the performative behavior of the group.[7] A healthy group will manage this anxiety with a process of strategic discernment, i.e. by analyzing the emerging changes in its experience, testing core assumptions, evaluating changes in direction and making appropriate decisions for the good of the group.[8] Healthy leaders accept their institution's primary task, recognize their group's organizational anxiety, and are not afraid to challenge the organizational defenses that mimic change but are little more than the protection of obsolete privileges.[9]

---

[4] Deborah M. Kolb and Jean M. Bartunek, (eds.) *Hidden Conflict in Organizations: Uncovering Behind the Scenes Disputes* (Newbury Park, CA: Sage Publications, 1992).

[5] Cf. The stages of group doubt used by *MDI (Management Design Institute), Cincinnati, Ohio.*

[6] We are treating here the social defenses or group biases that are the normal fare of institutional development and regression. One ought not forget the critical part that social sin plays in the failures of group life and the promotion of injustice in social and religious institutions. For the concept of "group bias," see B. Lonergan, *Insight: A Study of Human Understanding* (San Francisco: Harper and Row, 1978) 191-206; 218-242. For the concept of social sin, cf. B. Massingale, *The Social Dimensions of Sin and Reconciliation in the Theologies of James H. Cone and Gustavo Gutierrez* (doctoral dissertation, Rome: Academia Alphonsiana, 1991), 332-333.

[7] Larry Hirschhorn, *The Workplace Wihtin: Psychodynamics of Organizational Life* (Cambridge, MA: MIT Press, 1993.

[8] Isabel Menzies," A Case Study in the Functioning of Social Systems as a Defense Against Anxiety," in Arthur Coleman and W. Harold Bexton, (eds.) *Group Relations Reader* (Sausalito, CA: GREX, 1975), pp. 281-312.

[9] Larry Hirschhorn, *Reworking Authority: Leading and Following in the PostModern Organization* (Cambridge, MA: MIT Press, 1997).

Organizational development specialists order their thoughts about institutions around the concept of "culture."[10] Therefore, they read communities, groups, corporations and churches in that fashion – seeing organized beliefs, emotions, rituals and tools operating formally and informally and, as we have noted, at the rational and non-rational level.[11]

In this chapter, we will read religious communities today as distinct organizational cultural forms and try to understand the shifting organizational dynamics at play as new pressures are brought to bear on them as they transition from market economies to the fraternal economy, as this has been outlined in our first chapter. We will focus primarily on religious communities in the American context as a concrete and available example of this significant transitional dynamic.

My operating theses are these. Religious communities in the United States were organized primarily and performed well for the development of the American *parochial culture*, that loosely-knit network of neighborhood parishes that defended the faith at the local level and sought to move generations of immigrant Catholics up and out of disadvantage with telling speed and devotion.[12] What we see on the horizon, however, is the challenge to move from a parochial to an international mission culture, as we witness the increasing globalization of the world's economy and its technology and services. We are in a world rapidly changing from the parochial to the global.[13]

The challenge facing religious communities is not simply the accommodation to a new set of demographics, both within and outside our religious congregations. We need a dramatically new perspective on the challenges we place before religious men and

---

[10] Eric Eisenberg and Patricia Riley, "Organizational Culture," in Fredric M. Jablin and Linda L. Putnam, *The New Handbook of Organizational Communication* (Thousand Oaks, CA: Sage Publications, 2001), pp. 291-322; E. Schien, *Organizational Culture and Leadership* (San Francisco: Jossey Bass, 1985); M. Alvesson, *Cultural Perspectives on Organizations* (Cambridge: Cambridge University Press, 1993).

[11] Frank A. Dubinskas, "Culture and Conflict: The Cultural Roots of Discord," in Kolb and Bartunek, *op.cit.*, pp. 187-208.

[12] Paul K. Hennessy, "The Parochialization of the Church and Consecrated Life," in Paul K. Hennessy, (ed.) *A Concert of Charisms: Ordained Ministry in Religious Life* (New York: Paulist Press, 1997).

[13] David Hollenback, SJ, *The Global Face of Public Faith: Politics, Human Rights and Christian Ethics* (Washington, DC: Georgetown University Press, 2003).

women. As members of the new fraternal economy, they must not only see themselves as religious working at the local or provincial level, they must also begin to see themselves as *international actors* in a world where the twin dynamics of global poverty and trans-national violence are dramatically changing the social and spiritual context of ecclesial (and religious) life across the globe. We must help our men and women develop the social virtue of international compassion and grow in the courageous and passionate confidence to move forward and beyond the frontiers of language, class, culture, ideology, gender, orientation and caste that separate the poor from the rich in the illusory world of today's *majores* and *minores*.[14]

The focus of this chapter, then, is on the development of religious communities in the fraternal economy as communities of international compassion and the systemic implications of the cultural shift from the parochial to the international and pluricultural.

From the Parochial to the International

We are a land of immigrants; we are the children of refugees and the sons and daughters of slaves. We are a people of diverse cultures and multiple languages. On any given weekend, God is worshipped in the 120 languages of the city of New York alone.

For us multicultural diversity is not new. We have always been a land of ethnic, cultural and racial differences. What is different today, however, is the recognized challenge of *intercultural and inter-racial* living, owning up front and working through the often-uncomfortable differences that rub up against one another as cultural groups live, work and pray in common space together.

Up until recently, Catholics in America lived and worshipped in relative ethnic and racial privacy, in separate religious ghettoes, that segregated Catholics according to their nation or culture of origin. Catholics grew up, worked, married and prayed in the exclusively Irish, German, Polish, French, Lithuanian, or African-American parishes of their upbringing. Rarely did Catholics enter the parish-

---

[14] For this definition of religious "itinerancy," cf. David B. Couturier, "Itinerarium in Extremis: Franciscan Formation and the Anthropology of the Fraternal Economy," Plenary Council VII (March 2004) at www.capuchin.net.

es of another culture, even when these churches stood across the block from one another, so strong was the religious affiliation with their culture of origin.

But, that religious segregation has changed. Now, Catholics in America are bound to their experience as a people of God across cultural, ethnic, racial, gender and sexual barriers. Catholic segregation today is likely to be more economic than cultural. Behind the diversity that draws considerable attention lies the more trenchant and less recognized disparity that divides our people. Behind almost every case of immigration and cultural displacement is the untold story of privation and misery at the point of international or cultural origin.

What we are seeing is the development of two worlds where the chasm between the wealthy few and the destitute many grows wider and the world in which each segment lives becomes increasingly unimaginable and incommunicable one to the other.[15] They are two worlds, separate and invisible, one of enormous and widening privilege, the other of escalating and largely unremitting privation. The latter is maintained by unparalleled technological mastery and military might and the other is sustained by a crushing and unserviceable global debt structure.

One of these worlds sees the other; the other often does not. Increasingly the poorer segments recognize the division between the two worlds. They see the yawning disparity between their sacrifices for the affluent and the meager services that are provided back to them. The poor can see the affluent easily enough – largely because of the ubiquitous reach of television. However, the affluent rarely see or, if they do see, rarely understand what they are seeing when they come across the conditions of the poor.

In a recent study of the situation of the working poor, Barbara Ehrenreich reports on their sacrifices, "They neglect their own children so that the children of others will be cared for; they live in substandard housing so that other homes will be shiny and perfect; they endure privation so that inflation will be low and stock

---

[15] I research the changes in global poverty and poverty eradication measures in my paper, David B. Couturier, "Minorité et élimination de la pauvreté: Les dimensions internationales de la compassion du Christ au 21ièsme siècle dans les communautés franciscaines," (Quebec, 2003). www.capuchin.net.

prices will be high. To be a member of the working poor is to be an anonymous donor, a nameless benefactor, to everyone else."[16]

But, the other world, the world of expected privilege and prestige, is losing touch and consciousness of its neighbors as it increasingly shields and isolates itself from the demanding consequences of compassion. In a 2000 article on the "disappearing poor," James Fallow gives a reason for this optical refraction on the part of the privileged – they are less and less likely to share common spaces and services with the poor.[17] Walks in public parks and along the town square are replaced by high-priced memberships in private health clubs and exclusive access to resorts. Mixed neighborhoods and parishes where rich and poor once congregated and worshiped together give way to gated communities and "market segmented" suburbs, on the one hand, and deteriorating public schools and services, on the other. Not only are the victims of poverty and privation largely permissible, they are increasingly invisible to those who have the means to respond effectively. Nowhere is this permissibility and invisibility more acute than in the international arena.

During the last twenty years, more than 65 million people have become infected with HIV, the virus that causes AIDS.[18] Twenty-five million people have succumbed to the disease, more deaths than those killed in all the battles and wars of the twentieth-century combined.[19] More than forty million people are now infected, two and a half million of them are children.[20] Eleven million children in sub-Sahara Africa try to survive as orphans of AIDS.[21]

Since the time of Jesus, it is estimated that the worlds' wars have claimed 149 million deaths.[22] At current rates, it is projected that, by the year 2010, more than 100 million people will have been infected with the HIV virus. By the year 2020, that number

---

[16] Barbara Ehrenreich, *Nickle and Dimed: On (Not) Getting By in America* (New York: Henry Holt and Co., 2001), p. 221.

[17] James Fallow, "The Invisible Poor," *New York Times Magazine,* March 19, 2000.

[18] Greg Behrman, *The Invisible People* (New York: Free Press, 2004), pp. xi-xiv.

[19] UNAIDS. *2004 Report on the Global AIDS Epidemic,* July 2004.

[20] *Global Summary of the AIDS Epidemic: December 2004.* accessed: www.unaids.org/ wad2004/ EPI_1204_pdf_en/Chapter0-1_intro_en.pdf.

[21] Carol Bellamy, "The State of the World's Children-2004," UNICEF REPORT (New York: Unicef, 2003), p. 50.

[22] The following statistics are from Behrman, *op.cit.,* p.xi.

will climb to 250 million and, if nothing dramatically changes, less than 5% of those infected will have any access to anti-retroviral treatment.[23]

Nowhere is the crisis more ominous today than in Sub-Sahara Africa, now the site of 70% of the AIDS cases worldwide.[24] About 40% of the adult population of Botswana is HIV positive; more than 20% of adults in South Africa are infected. Life expectancies, already low, are plunging rapidly, with several African countries projected to have life expectancies reach thirty years or less by the year 2010.[25]

But, it is not just Africa that is at severe risk. Nicholas Eberstadt recently calculated the level of new infections that were likely in the three most prominent "next wave" countries, Russia, China and India.[26] Under three different scenarios – mild, intermediate or severe epidemics – Eberstadt estimates that, between the years 2000 and 2025, these three Eurasian countries are likely to experience an epidemic to the size of 66 million, 193 million or 259 million new infections, respectively.

He projects the economic impact of an "intermediate epidemic" on these countries. He forecasts 110 million new infections for India, a situation that would cut India's economic growth by 40%. China would find itself with 70 million new infections, driving its economy downward by 33%. Russia, already reeling from an economy that saw the Russian ruble drop 99% in value to the US dollar between 1991 and 2001,[27] would find itself with 13 million new infections and a 40% decline in its already faltering economy.

Clearly, AIDS is a global catastrophe that is at the point of eviscerating national economies and dramatically destabilizing national militaries in Africa. Some estimates project the infection rates in African armies as high as 50%. This combined with the creation of a whole new generation of HIV orphans, some eleven

---

[23] "WHO: AIDS Epidemic Update 2003,) accessed: www.who.int.hiv/ pub/epidemiology /imagefile/en/index11.html.

[24] Behrman, *op.cit.*, p. xi.

[25] Greg Behrman, *op.cit*, p. xii.

[26] Nicholas Eberstadt, "The Future of AIDS: Grim Toll in China, Russia and India," *Foreign Affairs* 81:6 (November/December, 2002).

[27] Andrei Schliefer and Daniel Treisman, "A Normal Country," *Foreign Affairs* 83:2 (March/April 2004) 20-38.

million strong, now positions whole countries in Africa and Asia for economic collapse.[28]

Internationally, as a Washington Post editorial indicated, the global AIDS pandemic has been "probably the most underestimated enemy of all time."[29] It is also among the most under-funded, as well. On June 30, 2004, the Board of the Global Fund to Fight AIDS, Tuberculosis and Malaria approved a total of $968 million for new grants over two years.[30] However, Dr. Peter Piot, the executive director of UNAIDS, has spoken of a "minimum $10 billion needed annually to mount an effective, comprehensive response in low and middle-income countries." [31]The money allocated by the Global Fund this year for AIDS relief falls far short of the bare minimum needed; it is only 9.6% of the total required. Because of lagging contributions from donor nations, the Fund may not be able to offer any new grants in 2005 or 2006, according to a recent report.[32]

The US administration has proposed a $200 million dollar contribution to the Global Fund in 2005, which is about 2% of what is needed to reach even minimum standards of care.[33] When compared to the actual expenditures for the war in Iraq, the allocation to combat AIDS over two years is approximately .1% of what was spent in one year by the US government on the war in Iraq.[34] With this one year military expenditure alone, the US government could have funded all worldwide AIDS programs for the next twelve years.

Two worlds, separate and invisible to one another, are emerging as the social and political context of the fraternal economy.

---

[28] National Intelligence Council, *The Next Wave of HIV/AIDS: Nigeria, Ethiopia, Russia, India and China (September 2002)*, accessed: www.odci.gov/nic.

[29] "Denial at Home," *Washington Post*, December 23, 2002.

[30] Press Release, "US $968 Million Committed for New Global Funds Grants," The Global Fund, June 30, 2004.

[31] Peter Piot, "AIDS: The Need for an Exceptional Response to an Unprecedented Crisis," 11/20/2003, accessed: www.worldbank.org/etools.

[32] *The Newshour with Jim Lehrer*, PBS, (July 15, 2004).

[33] In fairness to the US government, it now contributes 1/3 of all money in the Global Fund. In the three years since the Fund's inception, Japan has contributed a total of 269 million, Germany a total of 210 million and Saudi Arabia a total of 10 million. (*The Newshour with Jim Lehrer, July 15, 2004*).

[34] Tallied at $135,794,600,433.00 at 09/15/04 at 2:50 p.m., at www.costofwar.com.

RELIGIOUS CONGREGATIONS AS COMMUNITIES OF INTERNATIONAL
COMPASSION

Religious communities are now reflecting what has become increasingly true of Catholic congregations across the country – people of diverse cultures are beginning to live, work and pray in common space together. Their different concerns, hopes and expectations in this new intercultural and inter-racial living situation are rubbing up against one another and the friction is sometimes irritating and the outcomes often confusing. Cultural groups have vastly different understandings of time, relationships, authority, family, ritual, worship, devotions, the sacred and the profane. We are only now understanding and appreciating the difference that difference makes in faith.

Diversity training programs across the country have helped businesses and corporations widen their circle of understanding with regard to cultural differences at both the rational and non-rational levels. But, they have not managed to break through the ways that social groups use cultural differences to keep class differences in place.[35] Too often diversity training is a comfortable but unsatisfactory alternative to the more difficult and threatening disparity training needed in groups.[36]

Therefore, it is imperative that religious communities find a paradigm that allows them to access and assess both their levels of diversity and disparity. It is not enough to expose the wide spectrum of cultural differences emerging in the community and unconsciously hide the economic inequities that keep some groups in positions of privilege and others in positions of privation.

We have already spoken of the two worlds, separate and invisible, emerging as the dangerous context of international relations and ecclesial life in the 21st century. We need a picture of the reli-

---

[35] I. Huygens, *Journeys away from Dominance: Dissonance, Struggle and Right Relationships-the Journey to Accepting Indigenous Authority*. Paper presented at the 8th Biennial Conference of the Society for Community Research and Action, Atlanta, Georgia (June 2001).

[36] A. Mukherjee makes the distinction between multicultural and anti-racist approaches to diversity training in his article, "Education and Race Relations: The education of South Asian youth," in R. Ghosh and R. Kanungo (eds), *South Asian Canadians: Current Issues in the Politics of Culture.* (Montreal: Shastri Indo-Canadian Institute, 1992; see also, R.J. Watts, et al., "Sociopolitical Development as an Antidote for Oppression- Theory and Action," *American Journal of Community Psychology,* 27, 1999, p. 255-271.

gious community that is adequate to that social context. I believe the formation of religious congregations as communities of international compassion may be that picture. Let's fill this out.

At the end of his massive study of theology and social theory, John Milbank contrasts the ontological antagonism and violence inherent in contemporary theories of politics and international relations with the ontological peace that is at the heart of the Christian vision of God's desire for the world.[37] In contrast to the Hobbesian view that sublates all modern theories of economics, that of the inevitable and ever-present "war of all against all," Milbank argues that Christianity offers a distinct and revealed social alternative, a dogmatic narrative and practice that places an ontological priority of peace over conflict. Here is how Milbank writes it,

> Christians worship the one true God who originates all finite reality in an act of peaceful donation, willing a new fellowship with himself and amongst the beings he has created. In the 'heavenly city,' beyond the possibility of alteration, the angels and saints abide in such a fellowship; their virtue is not the virtue of resistance and domination, but simply of remaining in a state of self-forgetting conviviality. Here there is nothing but the 'vision of peace,' a condition that originally pertained also for the temporal creation, before the sinful assertion of pride and domination introduced a pervasive presence of conflict leading to death in both society and nature.

> But God and the heavenly Jerusalem – our 'true mother'- reach down in compassion for the salvation of the world. Salvation from sin must mean 'liberation' from political, economic and psychic dominium... This salvation takes the form of a different inauguration of a different kind of community.

> Instead of a peace 'achieved' through the abandonment of the losers, the subordination of potential rivals and resistance to enemies, the Church provides a genuine peace by its memory of

---

[37] John Milbank, *Theology and Social Theory: Beyond Secular Reason* (Oxford: Blackwell Publishers, 1990).

all the victims, of its equal concern for all its citizens and its self-exposed offering of reconciliation to enemies.[38]

Christian communities, therefore, are the social places or "experiments" where creative differentiation is accepted, domination and deprivation are rejected, and salvation is achieved in common by those who refuse to give violence any ontological purchase. Catholic communities exist as an interruption of history by those who practice charity and the forgiveness of sins. Evil, on the other hand, is nothing other than the "denial of the hope for, and the present reality of, community."[39]

This means a foundational and shared belief in the goodness of God, that God is good, all good, supremely good, all the time and to everyone. The goodness of God is the identity of God understood as the free communion of persons without domination or deprivation. It is that Trinitarian identity that is the social practice of the Church and the foundation of our international compassion.

In that sense, one of the key purposes of religious formation is nothing other than the social practice of peace, the rejection of domination and deprivation everywhere, and the experience of the free communion of persons that can only be achieved by the forgiveness of sin and hope in the life of the world to come.

We become communities of international compassion to manifest the fundamental goodness of God, in whom there are no boundaries, borders or perimeters. We create a more relational economy in our Christian communities at all levels to testify to our rejection of the nihilistic logic of self-promotion and isolation that under-girds almost all contemporary politics and economic arrangements. They hold that we inevitably must be antagonistic and violent with one another to protect our private property and promote our self-interests. Church communities exist, on the other hand, as the prophetic reminder to all other societies that we are the practice of peace by the forgiveness of sins, until He comes again.

The distancing of the political from the formational is therefore a gross misunderstanding of ecclesiology. Religious formation can never be a separation from or an avoidance of the political

---

[38] *Ibid.,* p.391-392.
[39] *Ibid.,* p. 432.

aspects of life, if we truly understand that the Church is meant
to be the social practice of God's Shalom through difference and
forgiveness. International compassion is the contemporary form
of that social practice in the fraternal economy, as postmodern
expressions of globalization weaken difference and entice groups
towards ethno-religious hatred.

RELIGIOUS FORMATION AND THE DYNAMICS OF INTERNATIONAL COMPASSION

A community of international compassion is one that makes
visible and tells the truth about the plight of the poor and the
condition of those who oppress them. It is a community that, first
and foremost, tells the truth about itself, its own tragic experiences
of pride and glory, and understands how to move forward and beyond the restrictive frontiers of language, class, culture, ideology,
gender, orientation and caste that separate the poor from the rich
in the illusory modern world of the *majores* and *minores*.[40]

A community of international compassion encourages religious to tell the truth about themselves, the whole truth about
themselves to themselves. It creates opportunities for dialogue and
faith sharing so as to examine and develop its own relational styles
of authority, agency and service as it seeks to conform itself to the
Christian social ideal of being a free communion of persons without domination or deprivation. Finally, it develops mechanisms for
religious (and formation directors) to participate individually and
corporately in social transformation so that the structures of political and economic living respond to and do not obstruct God's
desire for the priority of peace over conflict in the world. There are
then three levels of truth telling and three phases of development
in the process of forming the social virtue of international compassion in religious formation.

---

[40] For an analysis of the connection between pride, glory and truth-telling in Christian communities, cf. Robert Dodaro, OSA, *Christ and the Just Society in the Thought of St.
Augustine* (Cambridge: Cambridge University Press, 2004).

TABLE 1
THE LEVELS OF TRUTH-TELLING FOR INTERNATIONAL COMPASSION
IN RELIGIOUS FORMATION

Level of Truth-Telling	Dynamics	Phase of Formation
Personal Religious begin to tell the truth about themselves, the whole truth about themselves, in the redeeming love of Christ	Increasing levels of self-realization, honesty; Greater capacity for theocentric self-transcendence; review of life leads to ownership of economic, spiritual and social horizon. Personal bias/unconscious	**Postulancy**
Interpersonal The religious community tells the truth about itself and its own tragic experiences of pride and glory	Opportunities for dialogue and faith sharing across cultures and class; Examination of relational styles of authority, agency and service. Group bias; social defenses.	**Novitiate**
Structural Religious communities tell the truth about the world. Participation in individual and corporate acts of social transformation	Advocacy Solidarity Structural conversion Media and institutional refraction and distortion	**Post-Novitiate**

In postulancy, the earliest period of formation, a religious is helped to tell the truth, the whole truth, about himself in the redeeming and liberating love of Christ.[41] Here an individual comes to understand and own his personal and cultural history. He reads his story in the light of faith. This often means a confrontation with inconsistent needs and desires that run counter to one's professed values of compassion and the ideals of justice. A direct and personal experience with the poor, when combined with a comprehensive review of life, will help an individual take stock of his inherited economic, social and spiritual horizon and expand his capacity for caring and compassion.

In novitiate, an individual is inserted into the fraternal economy of brothers and attends to the implications of his confession of God's absolute goodness to all, across all languages, cultures and classes. It is an insertion into a fraternal community that has committed itself to tell the truth, the whole truth, about itself as a community of believers already but not yet fully a free communion of persons without domination or deprivation. By virtue of its actions as an evangelical fraternity and gospel brotherhood, the community has committed itself to becoming a distinct social experiment of peace over conflict, a peace achieved by the forgiveness of sins. A religious at this level begins to see how a community formed for peace (and not for aggressive acquisition) accepts differences and rejects domination. This second phase of religious formation is then an insertion into dialogue and faith sharing. It is the community's fearless exploration of its own tragic experiences of pride and glory that keep it from becoming a more transparent expression of God's abiding love for people, across the boundaries of culture, class, race, gender, orientation and caste. At this level, religious learn how to tell the truth about the community in the community.

In the later moments of religious formation (i.e., post-novitiate), religious are invited into a third level of truth telling about the world and its social arrangements. Having acquired some rudimentary skills in confessing the truth about themselves and their

---

[41] We rely here on the insights developed in our study of Luigi M. Rulla in chapters two and three of this work. By the "whole truth" about oneself we mean an honest, critical and complete awareness of one's central vocational inconsistency, since this, above all, the predictor of internalization.

own personal and social history, religious are encouraged to take another look at the world and its operations.

Here religious begin to apply their vision of God's absolute goodness and the ontological priority of peace over conflict to the structures and systems of contemporary society. Here they learn the theological methods of advocacy and the practice of solidarity. They also learn to decipher the institutional refractions and media distortions that every (power) group utilizes to obscure its efforts at empire-building at the expense of the poor.[42] At this level, religious become equipped to tell the truth, the social and religious truth, about churches, corporations, businesses, congregations and governments.[43]

Forming a religious congregation into a community of international compassion requires a new theoretical framework for religious formation, one that is ample enough to include all the dimensions of a religious' well being. Too often we circumscribe formational growth in largely personal and interpersonal terms. We often forget the impact that oppressive social conditions and deteriorating communal structures have on personal and interpersonal well-being. We make matters worse when we pathologize or re-interpret oppressive social conditions in intra-psychic or interpersonal terms. We induce passivity when power differentials in relationships and society are ignored.

The work of critical psychologist, Isaac Prilleltensky, has been helpful in pointing to the need to keep all three levels of well-being foremost in one's practice of formation for international compassion in the fraternal economy. We set out the values and the guidelines that attend each distinct but inter-related level of well-being of the individual.

The following table provides a picture of those three levels.[44]

---

[42] W. Bruggemann, "Truth-Telling and Peacemaking: A Reflection on Ezekiel," *Christian Century* (November 30, 1998), p. 1096-1098.

[43] Mark D. Jordan looks at the dynamics of truth-telling in churches in his work, *Telling Truths in Church: Scandal, Flesh and Christian Speech* (New York: Beacon Press, 2003).

[44] The table is adapted from the work of I. Prilleltensky and G. Nelson, *Doing Psychology Critically: Making a Difference in Diverse Settings* (New York: MacMillan Press, 2002).

TABLE 2
THREE LEVELS OF WELL-BEING

Psychological Well-Being	Values	Guidelines
Personal	Self-determination, personal growth, health. Caring and Compassion	Promote the physical and emotional well-being of individuals; personal empowerment; personal psychological, spiritual, emotional, physical health.
Relational	Respect for diversity, collaboration, and participation.	Promote respect and appreciation for diverse social identities in consideration of the need for solidarity. Promote peaceful, respectful and equitable processes of dialogue.
Collective	Social justice, Support for community	Promote fair allocation of powers, resources and obligations in community, given the differentials in needs, powers and abilities. Promote vital structures that meet the needs of individuals and disadvantaged communities.

Religious formators intent on the education for international compassion must develop three distinct sets of skills. The formator must first have the capacity to help the religious come to know himself, accept himself and change in the direction of his self-proclaimed values of charity, compassion and justice. Then, the formator must have the ability to invite the local religious (formation) community to understand and examine its own various relational (cultural) styles of authority, leadership and service. This is more than a matter of increasing socialization, tolerance and a naïve unity in diversity among the religious. At this stage, the religious community learns to model its own corporate behavior on the non-dominating and non-depriving example of Christ. And, finally, the community reaches beyond its borders to accept its responsibility as a "social experiment of peace and reconciliation" in the world today. It recognizes that its compassion is both personal and communal.

The following table outlines some of the skills that would be helpful to the formator interested in developing the social virtue of international compassion.

TABLE 3
THE ZONES OF CONVERSION

Zones of Conversion	Elements	Dynamics	Skills
Personal	Values Attitudes Needs (Charity, compassion, solidarity and justice> aggression, domination, harm avoidance	The movement to theocentric self-transcendence and the working through of the intrapsychic obstacles and ambivalence to international compassion	Psychological and spiritual skills for conducting formational growth sessions to help religious change in the direction of values.
Interpersonal	Diversity, collaboration, dialogue, participation	Family systems, social systems, secure relational styles	Facilitation of cross-cultural dialogue and international faith sharing
Structural	Intercultural living, solidarity, social justice	'Crossing the road' to the neglected other; negotiating the multiple cultures of formation	Advocacy Social reconciliation Conflict transformation

RELIGIOUS AND THE PLURICULTURAL

Thus far, we have been positing that the pluricultural dimension of religious life will be misunderstood and undervalued if
the *international* aspects of the fraternal economy (i.e., economic)
are bracketed out of the equation. We, therefore, have encouraged
a model of international compassion that relies on cross-cultural
formation advising, faith sharing and dialogue, and methods of
social reconciliation that will stimulate understanding, respect and
a love that crosses borders and frontiers of language, class, culture,
ideology, gender, orientation and caste. We need to focus more
directly on the pluricultural challenges implied in this transition.

We speak of the pluricultural (rather than simply the "multicultural") to indicate our recognition that the "white culture" of
privilege and prestige is often factored out a priori from the analysis of social dynamics in cross-cultural settings.[45] If religious communities truly wish to form their men and women for the world
church of the twenty-first century, they must invite all cultures
to the conversation, especially the dominant and normative ones
against which all others are rated.

Bringing diverse cultures to the common table is a new and
highly complex enterprise for religious congregations used to the
security and coherence found in single-culture endeavors. In a pluricultural environment, all rituals and procedures are called into
question, since the rituals and resources of every institution contain codes of expectation and evaluation on the social history and
cultural standing of individuals and groups.

In a pluricultural environment, religious rightly belong to various groups and experience multiple identities and several "religious belongings."[46] They inhabit manifold expressions of faith
and devotion and learn to live in the paradoxical and mysterious
intersection where cultural expressions cross paths.

There is no easy way to describe or define this intersection. For
religious communities that are used to order and certitude, this area

---

[45] Michelle Fine et al., *Off White: Readings on Race, Power, and Society* (New York:
Routledge, 1997).

[46] Edward Foley, Capuchin, "A Capuchin Contribution to the Church's Understanding of Priesthood: An Analogical Consideration of Biculturality and Double Religious
Belonging," (Seventh Plenary Council of the Order, Assisi, March, 2004).

"in-between" groups will be filled with paradox (and considerable confusion, initially) and will need patience to apprehend. Those in religious communities will constantly find themselves "on the border," both here and there, when they try to pray or make sense of their religious experiences. They will seek shelter in the familiar sounds of God and may find themselves annoyed by the "noise" of other voices. Only religious staff who have placed themselves in pluricultural situations of faith, who have learned how to divest themselves (especially of language) and cross over and into the religious language and cultures of others, will know how to accompany religious in the personal reflection, faith sharing and solidarity of international compassion.

When one participates and lives in a monocultural world, culture does not need to be explained or reflected upon. Cultural beliefs, emotions, rituals and tools are obvious and self-evident. They are the backdrop and the normative code for self-esteem and social standing. This is especially true of the white, male, middle-class (often Irish) American clerical culture that has dominated our religious and seminary systems in the United States. [47]

The introduction of a pluricultural dynamic will threaten the inherited system and call into question routines that have been, up until now, standard and obvious. The first ones to question these cultural codes may be victimized and are sure to be misunderstood and misinterpreted.[48] Therefore, it would be helpful for religious formators to clarify the difference between cultural questions and personality dynamics, so that structural issues are not easily pathologized.

What are some of these cultural codes that are likely to express themselves and diverge? The following list may be a helpful beginning:

- The place of the family in religious life.
- The experience of time.

---

[47] Nancy Zane, "Interrupting Historical Patterns: Bridging Race and Gender Gaps between Senior White Men and Other Organizational Groups," in *Off White, op. cit.,* pp. 343-353.

[48] I. Prilleltensky and G. Nelson, *Doing Psychology Critically: Making a Difference in Diverse Settings* (NY: Palgrace MacMillan, 2002).

- The understanding of friendship and the expression of intimacy.
- The place of devotion in the spiritual life.
- The attitude toward authority and obedience.
- The rate, pace and rhythm of self-disclosure.
- Expressions of status and competency.
- Appropriate rituals and expressions of forgiveness and displeasure.

THE SOCIAL DEFENSES AGAINST THE PLURICULTURAL

As we have been discussing, religious congregations are in the midst of a significant and dynamic change process as they transition from the parochial culture of immigrant Catholic life to the global and multi-centered Catholic world of the twenty-first century. We have been arguing that the first step in accepting the pluricultural aspects of this change is the recognition of the international dimensions of this transition. That is, while the diversity challenges of religious life are significant, they will be misunderstood and largely undervalued if they are not put into dialogue with the more noteworthy dynamics of cultural interaction and international relations at play in the world today – escalating global poverty and trans-national violence. As noted above, behind almost every case of immigration and cultural displacement are the untold stories of privation and misery at the point of international or cultural origin. Our international religious bear within themselves the stories of peoples enslaved, women and children trafficked, young people *desparacidos* and whole countries overwhelmed by a crushing and unserviceable global debt structure. These are the narratives that can dramatically change congregations rooted in the parochial culture of the 19th and 20th centuries into communities of international compassion.

But, this transition will not come about without a struggle. Every organization faced with significant pressures for change will develop a corporate anxiety and will display social defenses (often unconsciously) that are designed to forestall adjustments and avoid transformation.[49] Religious congregations are no different, in this regard.

As systems religious communities develop distinct beliefs, emotions, rituals and tools around a particular mission or primary task.[50] These cultural elements operate, as indicated in the early part of this chapter, at the rational and non-rational dimensions of group life. Every religious community has a unique story or "script" and holds a picture (in its organizational memory) of how the group ought to function in the real world.[51] This script has roles and parts for every player and those parts (formal and informal) are often assigned from one generation to the next. There are overt rules codified in the charter, statutes or manual of the institution. And then there are the covert rules, written nowhere, that clearly indicate how individuals and groups within the institution are expected to perform.[52] These are passed down informally, often in the food rituals and relational disciplines of religious life.[53]

When congregations face a period of significant transition as they do today, one should expect institutional resistance and organizational defenses. These are the mutually held, largely unconscious, and somewhat convincing reasons groups give to avoid or minimize change in their group life.

What are some of these social defenses likely to emerge in communities moving from the parochial culture to the international mission culture? Three defenses come to mind.

The first social defense is simply **to do nothing**. This is the community that intends to ignore demographics, factor out racial differences, discount cultural diversity and make believe that the next wave of their preferred candidate-type is just around the next conclave. Religious members and leaders see no reason to abandon the *parochial culture* that formed the faith of immigrants in the 19th

---

[49] Larry Hirrschhorn, *The Workplace Within: The Psychodynamics of Organizational Life* (Cambridge, MA: MIT Press, 1993).

[50] In fact, I trace the development of seven learning cultures in contemporary seminaries in, "At Odds with Ourselves: Polarization and the Learning Cultures of Priesthood," *Seminary Journal* 9:3 (Winter 2003) 64-71.

[51] Cf. Karl E. Weick and Susan J. Ashford, "Learning in Organizations," in Jablin and Putnam, *op.cit.*, pp. 704-731.

[52] Cf. Dubinskas, *op.cit.*

[53] Cf. Patricia Curran, *Grace Before Meals: Food Ritual and Body Discipline in Convent Culture* (Urbana and Chicago: University of Illinois Press, 1989).

and 20th centuries. They don't see the big deal or understand the great fuss people are making about cultural differences. They will usually frame their unintended theological insensitivity in two high sounding cultural theories. The first is *cultural universalism*, which holds that all cultures are more or less the same. It is imagined that all cultures are pretty much like one's own, so there is no great need to understand differences or make adjustments for diversity. The second is *cultural developmentalism* that holds that cultures progress inevitably upward from the primitive to the civilized. Nine out of ten times, the do-nothings maintain that the culture of others is primitive and theirs is civilized. The burden of adjustment therefore is on people of other cultures to reach the high cultural norms or standards now embodied in the religious congregation.

The second social defense is **to get groups fighting.** As difficult as it may be to believe, organizational plans often flounder because administrators set up or sustain conflicts between groups in the institution. This is an especially effective (and often unconscious) organizational tool used by a leader who is him/herself ambivalent about a proposed or needed change in the system. Cultural infighting is set in motion by leaders (both formal and informal) who pit one cultural group against another by advertising that resources in the organization are tight. This promotes a competitive and aggressive scramble for the scarce goods available.

This social defense emerges in a group whose leaders fail to provide a guiding vision for their pluricultural and international congregational experience. These leaders misname the primary task of the formation program and mismanage the ordinary tensions that come when cultural groups live, work and pray in common space together. They unconsciously promote the false idea that the common good in a pluricultural and international environment is a zero-sum game with inevitable winners and unenviable losers. They do not provide cultural groups with the organizational resources needed to diagnose these institutional processes or the facilitation required to move diverse communities toward social reconciliation.

The final defense is found in the system's **organizational rituals** and procedures. Every system has practices and procedures that help the institution achieve its purpose and fulfill its mission. These rituals and procedures are not only functional but also symbolic, carrying meaning and messages about task, roles and author-ity in the organization.

A group that wishes to defend itself (unconsciously) against change will create structures and procedures so burdensome and complicated that groups become paralyzed in their efforts to work harmoniously together. Cooperation and collaboration are made so onerous and the issues are presented in such dire tones that groups despair of ever finding their way to common ground.

It is critical that every religious community read its organiza-tional rituals (its policies, procedures and practices) for their hid-den cultural codes and covert economic meaning. As we said at the beginning of this chapter, cultural groups think differently about time, relationships, authority, family, rituals, worship, devotions, the sacred and the profane. A religious community's own inherited cultural code about these areas is encrypted in the ordinary rituals and performative behaviors of religious life. Every organizational procedure – from registration to graduation, from food rituals to body disciplines, contain coded messages to the religious about how the community thinks about them and their social history. Cultural audits are a valuable new resource for seminaries in the process of change.[1]

SUMMARY

The development of communities of international compas-sion (within religious communities of faith) is one expression of the transition from religious institutions oriented to the market economies of the nineteenth and twentieth centuries and those oriented to the fraternal economy of the twenty-first century.

Thus far we have addressed the likely psychological and or-ganizational impact on religious life systems transitioning from a parochial to an international and pluricultural model. As we have demonstrated, this transition will require a significantly high order of skills on the part of the formation system and demand a sub-stantial adjustment on the part of religious candidates.

---

[1] The Center for the Study of Religious Life in Chicago provides cultural audit tools and resources.

As indicated, one cannot bracket out the question of economic disparity when opening up the issue of (cultural) diversity, without doing a grave injustice to the social history and solidarity required of religious in today's global world. The process of coming to the social virtue of international compassion involves three critical and difficult steps: (a) increasing the level of self-realization and capacity for theocentric self-transcendence; (b) faith sharing and dialogue across cultures and class; and (c) participation in individual and corporate acts of social transformation and structural conversion for the sake of the Gospel.

Religious communities today are systems in transition. Facing the increasing pluri-culturalization of their environment and the few but rising number of international applicants, religious communities are reflecting the growing global and international context of contemporary life. It is clear that all communities must prepare their members, in some way, for the development of international compassion.

These new factors call for an intense look at the formational dynamics employed. In this chapter, we have considered the specific challenges facing religious communities transitioning from the parochial culture of the 20th century to the international and pluricultural context of the 21st. They involve religious in high level skills of formation advising, faith sharing, and advocacy in the twin dynamics of diversity and disparity.

This will not be easy.

Prevailing social theories stress division and, in the face of the growing globalization of our social and ecclesial relations, they posit the inevitability of competition and violence. Such is the nature of aggressive consumerism that supports our politics, our economics and, sadly, sometimes even our religious practices.

But, Capuchin-Franciscan communities are choosing a different path. They are declaring the goodness of God and are trying to live it out in a fraternal economy that crosses the frontiers and borders of language, class, culture, ideology, gender, orientation, caste, national identity and economic standing.

Religious men and women have the opportunity to challenge global despair and prepare a generation that can make a difference in the lives of the poor across our tracks and beyond our borders. They do this when they testify that our God is good and when they see themselves as agents of a God whose love informs and transcends all times and seasons and whose mercy moves within and beyond all cultures and nations, in the fraternal economy of God and as ministers of the international compassion of Christ.

CHAPTER TEN
A WORLD IN EXTREMIS:
TOWARDS A PASTORAL PSYCHOLOGY OF
FRANCISCAN ECONOMICS

In the time it takes to read this chapter, fourteen hundred children will die from starvation and related causes.[2] Over the next few minutes, eighty children under the age of 15 will become newly infected with the virus that causes AIDS and, as we speak, seventy children will die from the dreaded disease.[3] Eleven million children in Sub-Sahara Africa will struggle to find food and hope as they survive as orphans of AIDS.[4] Two and a half million children will try to live with HIV/AIDS; less than 5% of them will have any access to anti-retroviral treatment.[5]

In the next few minutes, twenty-three children will become fatal targets in the ethnic and religious conflicts breaking out across the globe.[6] In the last decade alone, 6 million children have been made homeless and 12 million have been injured or maimed. Civilians, not combatants, have become the prime targets and comprise 90% of the casualties of today's ethnic and religious wars.[7]

As we speak, three hundred thousand children are now forcibly conscripted into armies and militias, used for suicide missions, the strategic gang rape of enemies and numerous terrorist activities. They are the ones their adult commanders and child officers

---

[2] "Statistics relating to the plight of children around the world," accessed: www.worldofchildren.org/Plight of children.htm. (March 2004).

[3] "WHO:AIDS Epidemic Update 2003," accessed: www.who.int/hiv/pub/epidemiology/imagefile/en/index11.html.

[4] Carol Bellamy, "The State of the World's Children-2004, (New York: UNICEF, 2003), p. 50.

[5] "WHO:AIDS Epidemic Update," op.cit.

[6] "Patterns in Conflict: Civilians are now the target," www.unicef.org/graca/patterns.htm., April 16, 2003.

[7] Nick Danzinger, "Children and War," accessed: www.redcross.int/EN/mag/magazine2003 3 / 4-9.html.

send out to the front lines of combat or into dangerous minefields ahead of other troops.[8]

Fifteen thousand people will flee their homelands today, trying to escape from the violence and the devastation in their country of origin; the majority of these refugees will be children.[9] Children will be the most emotionally traumatized and physically abused among the 5.5 million people uprooted and displaced this year alone by the rising tide of religious intolerance and ethnic antagonisms across the globe.[10] In the 1990s, one out of every 120 people on the planet, 50 million people, were forced to flee their homes because of war and civil strife.[11] Children will be the great percentage of the 3,000 people today (1.2 million children this year) who will be sold into slavery and forced prostitution,[12] sequestered in rape camps, victims of a new and deadly campaign to use sexual violence as a commodity and method of modern warfare.[13]

As we ponder the meaning of the fraternal economy in our world today, we know that over 600 million children worldwide live in absolute poverty, 50% of all children in developing countries are malnourished, 153 million children under the age of five will go to bed hungry tonight.[14]

Taken together these disparate facts trace a frightening pattern of powerlessness and a deafening challenge to our solidarity with the next generation. Before we lock onto any formative the-

---

[8] "Stolen Children: Abduction and Recruitment in Northern Uganda," Human Rights Watch 15:7A (March 2003); "How to Fight and Kill: Child Soldiers in Liberia," Human Rights Watch 16:2A (February 2004); John Donnelly, "Africa and its children," *Boston Globe* (November 21, 2004).

[9] "World Refugee Survey 2003," (USCR, 2003), accessed: www.uscr.org.

[10] *Ibid.*

[11] United Nations Development Program (UNDP), *Human Development Report 2000;* Annemarie Kelly, et al., *Champions of Peace; The Role of CRS in Times of Violent Conflict* (Baltimore, MD: Catholic Relief Services, 2000).

[12] Francis Bok, *Escape From Slavery* (New York: St. Martin's Press, 2003).

[13] International Labour Office, *A Future without Child Labour* (Geneva: International Labour Office, 2002), p. 32; Elizabeth Mary Knorr, " Sexual Violence as Weapon of War: Communities Confronting Rape," (Geneva: The School for International Training), December 1, 2003; LaShawn R. Jefferson, "In War as in Peace; Sexual Violence and Women's Status," *Human Rights Watch World Report 2004* (January 2004).

[14] "State of the Food Insecurity in the World 2002," *Food and Agriculture Organization of the United Nations.* Accessed: awww.fao.org/dpcre[/005/y735c/y7352e00.htm; "Attacking Poverty: Opportunity, Empowerment and Security," accessed: www.worldbank.org/poverty/wdrpoverty/report/overview.pdf.

ory that might help us navigate our religious journey through the twenty-first century, we must test our understanding of this "world in extremis" and ponder the psychological and organizational assumptions we bring to our theological challenge.

THE WORLD IN EXTREMIS:
THE FRATERNAL ECONOMY IN A TIME OF GLOBAL POVERTY AND INTRA-NATIONAL VIOLENCE

Even in its early moments, the 21st century reveals dramatically different priorities and challenges than those that characterized the larger part of the 20th century. Gone is the confident world of modernity. Its religious constructs of certitude, universality and uniformity have been replaced by the *discourses of concern* for traditions lost, claims ignored, rights denied, positions assumed, voices suppressed and histories resisted.

The twenty-first century is poised to take the sobering and competing claims to suffering seriously, even in the various and diverse frames of secular and fundamentalist paradigms. At the center of its attention is the *world in extremis* and it is there that God will be lovingly revealed and/or loudly denied, in the origins and trajectories of global suffering.

The sobering experiences of children cited above have a common base and a saddening trajectory. Each of them is rooted in an escalating and widening global poverty that is now exacerbated by the eruption of intra-national, religious and ethnic conflicts. While the nature and frequency of international crises have changed dramatically and been reduced, there has been a proliferation of local and regional conflicts based on ethnicity, nationality and religion that use highly de-centralized, often terrorist-like applications of violence.[15]

Societies and cultures, already debilitated by years of foreign domination, must now confront a new and deadly combination of social challenges: unstable political institutions, inadequate health and educational systems, crushing debt payments to the architects

---

[15] Monty G. Marshall and Ted Robert Gurr, *Peace ad Conflict 2003* (University of Maryland, College Park, MD: Center for International Development and Conflict Management, 2003). Clearly, the war in Iraq is an exception.

and prime beneficiaries of globalization, and the virulent strains of tactical violence now becoming popular in the ethno-religious confrontations of fundamentalisms.[16]

The world in extremis, the context and subject of our kingdom work of redemption and liberation, is a world precariously poised between the dynamics of global poverty and the dynamics of violent but locally embedded social struggles.

It is here that religious formation must claim a new interest and expertise, at the intersection where crushing economic disparity and competing cultural claims crash. It is a significant transition and a daunting challenge.

For the better part of the twentieth century, religious communities have supported and sustained the development of the church's "parochial culture," the highly stable web of local ecclesial interests, regional compassion and provincial pride.[17] The challenge of Franciscan communities in the 21st century is the development of a new "international mission culture" that will be characterized by a renewed focus on God's salvific love and gracious compassion for the world, an enlivening of the quality of prayer and communion, a renewed attentiveness to mission across borders and cultures, and a life-long formation that understands its role in the "ecology of disparity" in which we find ourselves.[18]

It has become evident to many religious communities that we now live in a complex and globally interdependent world. A formative cosmology that once highlighted cultural uniformity and ethnic privacy in religious life is giving way to one that celebrates a world of profound differences. Religious life today is more responsive to the fact that Catholics form a community of many rich and varied cultures, speaking one faith with many voices. This awareness has translated into an increase in language studies and the development of cross-cultural training programs in religious formation. Liturgies in parishes and religious communities seek

---

[16] Gabriel A. Almond, R. Scott Appleby and Emmanuel Sivan, " Wrestling with the World: Fundamentalist Movements as Emergent Systems," in *Strong Religions: The Rise of Fundamentalisms around the World* (Chicago: University of Chicago press, 2003), pp. 145-190.

[17] Cf. Paul Hennessy, *op.cit.*

[18] David B. Couturier, "Minority and Poverty Eradication," (May 2003), accessed: www.fi-na.org/prov.html.

new forms by which to celebrate the global church whenever the local church gathers.

But, religious formation remains uniquely challenged to develop a pedagogy that will help religious cross economic barriers as well as cultural ones. Whereas the crossing of cultural lines implies entering sympathetically into the language and customs of "the other," the crossing of class lines means a spiritual realignment of one's horizon of power and responsibility in society, community and church. Today, formation ministry must not only confront a candidate's sensitivity to and acceptance of cultural diversity but also his or her readiness to confront the growing economic disparity emerging at every level of society.

Many young religious can go through their entire religious formation without ever changing or confronting their underlying economic horizon. The economic structures on which their charitable activities and cultural sensitivities are developed are presumed just and beyond critique. Our proposed shift from a diversity to a disparity discourse in formation literature is meant to situate our discussion in an interdependent but unequal world and to link more carefully the spiritualities of transcendence and justice.

Unfortunately, this is a world often treated with individual indifference and institutional ambivalence by some religious leaders, as if poverty and violence were not human constructs and subject to the same grace that moves the human heart to personal conversion. As we extend our discussion of the challenges of the fraternal economy, we need to take another look at our assumptions about poverty in the world.

Poverty, as we know it today, is "the explicit outcome of conscious political and economic decisions made by some humans."[19] Poverty is a series of deprivations that accumulate in peoples' lives and then reinforce one another. We are speaking of poverty today as material want, physical deprivation, the lack of basic necessities, failed economic institutions, gender and political inequalities and the loss of personal voice and agency. With Peter Henriot, SJ, I too believe that poverty is not an inevitable state of being. It is a con-

---

[19] Peter Henriot, SJ, "Catholic Social Teaching and Poverty Eradication: Key Concepts and Issues," *CAFOD Policy Papers, Presentation at the Conference on Debt Relief and Poverty Eradication in Uganda* (November 8-10, 2001), www.cafod.org/uk/policy/henriot_prsps.html., p.2.

sequence of the human (not divine) design of our social, political, economic and relational structures.[20] Poverty is a reality that we structure and which we tolerate. Henriot says it well. When Jesus told his disciples that we would have the poor with us always, he was making "an empirical observation not... a policy mandate."[21]

Poverty, then, is a structural disorder of the opportunity, empowerment and security that humans require, a disorder that creates and compounds extreme vulnerability to the normal and sometimes uncontrollable events that people face, like natural disasters, illness, violence and economic crises. The structural disorder of severe poverty requires a structural conversion of our religious communities. We turn to an analysis of severe poverty and our assumptions about its eradication in the fraternal economy envisioned by Capuchin-Franciscans.

THE STRUCTURAL DISORDER OF ECONOMIC DISPARITY AND ITS ERADICATION

When we look at the structural composition of societies today, we notice that the world has immense poverty amid great wealth. Of the world's six billion people, it is estimated that almost half (2.8 billion) live on less than $2 dollars per day. Almost 20% of the world, 1.2 billion, live on less than $1 dollar per day. To put this into some context for us, it takes about $18,000 a year (15,000 Euro) to sustain a male religious in the West in his simple and ascetic life, when his food, medical, insurance, housing and other needs are tallied up.[22] That is by my estimation 25 times more than what half of the world gets to live on and 50 times more than what the poorest of the world, 20% of humankind, must get by on.

The effects of global poverty are enormous. In rich countries, fewer than 1 child per 100 dies before its fifth birthday. In the poorest countries, 20% of all children will succumb before they

---

[20] *Ibid.*

[21] *Ibid.*, p.3.

[22] Unofficial estimate, Finance Department, Capuchin-Franciscan Province of St. Mary (White Plains, NY).

reach the age of five.[23] As stated above, 600 million children world-wide live in absolute poverty- an estimated one in four.

In a recent study of world income distributions, it was found that inequality is growing deeper and the gap between the rich and the poor is growing wider, as the affluent of the world reap the benefits of globalization, while the poor stagger at or below the poverty line.[24] Between 1988 and 1993, for example, global per capita income actually rose by a respectable 5.7%. However, it was the top fifth of the world's population that realized all the gain. All other incomes declined, with the bottom 5% of the poor seeing their real incomes decrease by another 25%.

A review of the dynamics of global poverty reveals five trends. We can now say that poverty is:

1. *deepening* in that, despite great progress, unprecedented techno-logical advances and solid economic growth, the poor are still falling deeper into destitution and at a faster rate;
2. *widening* in that the gap between those who have and those who do not is growing larger as the rich gobble up all the benefits of globalization, while the income of the poorest of the world continues to decline precipitously;
3. *increasingly militarized* in that armed conflicts, especially the eruption of civil war and ethno-religious confrontations, ex-acerbate and attenuate the already alarming confluence of risk factors for deprivation;
4. *increasingly feminized and juvenilized* in that women and children fall into poverty more easily and more frequently than men;
5. *increasingly internationalized* in that the increasing volume and va-riety of transaction of goods, services and capital across bor-ders (in essence, globalization) leave so many heavily indebted countries at the mercy of a few very rich nations that write the rules and set the tariffs of trade.[25]

---

[23] Bellamy, *op.cit.*

[24] Branko Milanovic, "True World Income Distribution, 1988 and 1993: First Cal-culation Based on Household Surveys Alone," *The Economic Journal* 112 (2002), pp. 51-92.

[25] J. Bryan Hehir, "Making Globalization Work for the World's Poor," *Fifteenth Pope Paul VI Memorial Lecture,* November 16, 2001 *(CAFOD Occasional Papers).*

It is not uncommon among those involved in international justice and peace work to complain about how difficult it is to get and sustain a religious community's attention when the conversation turns to justice. During a meeting of the President of Franciscans International with the Ministers General of the major Franciscan Orders, one of the Ministers asked a question that is germane to our research. He wondered why it is that Franciscan men seem to be losing enthusiasm and energy for matters of justice, peace and the integrity of creation.[26]

No one at the table denied his thesis. It is one of the most confusing aspects of our work: why otherwise good, decent and dedicated religious seem at times so disinterested and sometimes even antagonistic toward efforts that might deepen their awareness, extend their understanding and call for their action about the plight of the poor around the world.

One reason may be that we surmise that global poverty is inevitable and that its alleviation is virtually impossible. The crushing poverty of half of humankind persists even in the face of amazing technological advances, stunning scientific breakthroughs, and a growing international consensus against slavery, child labor, and the trafficking of human persons. It endures because we cannot yet conclude that we have the motive to reform the ecology of disparity.

In his book, *World Poverty and Human Rights,* Thomas Pogge comes to the conclusion that what we face is a failure of moral conviction. He writes, "extensive, severe poverty can continue, because we do not find its eradication morally compelling."[27] He goes on to say that it will not be morally compelling to us until we find the relentless rise in global inequality worrisome enough to warrant serious moral reflection.

In essence, we just do not find the present condition of our sisters and brothers morally disturbing enough to change the course of our actions. This may be so because the poor across our tracks and beyond our borders are among those Bryan Massingale calls the world's "permissible victims." They are the ones "whose lives

---

[26] Private meeting with Ministers Generals and the President of Franciscans International (the Franciscan NGO at the United Nations), October 3, 2001, Assisi.

[27] Thomas Pogge, *World Poverty and Human Rights* (Malden, MA: Blackwell Publishers, 2002), p. 2.

and dignity can be – and are – violated with little social outrage, public notice or civic protest."[28] These are the ones whose crises, however intense, persistent or determined, are made inaudible or tuned out in the great discussions of our churches and institutions.

But, there is a deeper reason, one that challenges our efforts to develop a fraternal economy among us. It is an underlying psychological ambivalence and institutional defense against the structural conversion needed to move our communities towards the international compassion required of us.

THE PASTORAL PSYCHOLOGY OF FRANCISCAN ECONOMICS

Clearly, stemming the tide of severe poverty will not be accomplished without enormous international cooperation and global sacrifice. As we have noted, the poverty we see in the world today is a "structural disorder." It needs a structural conversion. And for Franciscans the virtue that will energize the structural conversion of the conditions of global poverty is minority in the fraternal economy. The fraternal economy, with its virtues of minority and itinerancy, is our liberation from the "monopoly of imagination" that restrains our emotions, our intellect, our spirits and our structures from the call we have to be a free communion of persons in the world today, without domination or deprivation.

The Sixth Plenary Council of the Order made the connection between the gospel ideal of poverty and the choice of minority:

> To be lowly is a genuine manifestation of interior poverty, which in the Franciscan life project also expresses itself externally, as humility of heart and lack of power, and as solidarity with the needy and deprived. Without minority, our poverty would have no meaning and would become a source of pride, just as without material poverty, interior poverty would be unreal.[29]

---

[28] Bryan Massingale, "The Deacon: An Evangelical Agenda for the New Millenium," *National Catholic Diaconate Conference*. Maranga California. (June 24, 2000) accessed: www.permanentdiaconate.org/ncdc6.htm.

[29] *Living Poverty in Brotherhood, VI PCO* (Assisi, 1998), n. 3.

John Corriveau, in his reflections on the results of this Plenary Council, noted that the Franciscan commitment to poverty called our first brothers to hard economic choices that challenged the prevailing economy of their day.

> Those economic choices were also a conscious break with more obvious injustices of the growing market economy of their day, which was based on the appropriation of power and wealth by the few to the exclusion of the many, Their choice of poverty was a choice for discipleship, that is, to relate to one another and to their neighbors after the manner of Jesus. It was a conscious choice for a more fraternal world, a more human world.[30]

Corriveau states that it was Francis' intention (and that of his companions) to build a new security based on mutual dependency and brotherly solidarity. Commenting on our Franciscan challenges today, he goes on to state that we are called to do nothing less than to establish a "fraternal economy" that challenges capitalism's reign on our social and religious imagination. For he notes, "capitalism proposes competition as the best response to protect and administer resources," (5.2) but the church proposes solidarity and mutual dependence as a more sure, lasting and just foundation for human security and well-being.

Given this, the virtues of Franciscan life (i.e., minority and itinerancy) can longer be reduced to a perspective that renders them as interior and highly privatized virtues of humility and imperceptibility. In the face of the global poverty as we have presented it here, perhaps the most appropriate description of Franciscan minority in the 21st century is as a social virtue of international compassion.

Franciscans are international actors with a guiding vision and a sophisticated (if often untapped) network of communications.[31] As religious in an international fraternity, they can support compassionate and just organizations and, if necessary, reorganize sinful institutions and unjust systems. They can bring ideas, institutions and relationships around the world in order to help people make sense of their lives, ameliorate suffering, expand generosity, forge new structures of cooperation, and build bridges across the

---

[30] John Corriveau, *Circular Letter 13* (May 31, 1998), n. 4.2.

[31] I thank J. Bryan Hehir for this insight, *op. cit.*, p. 12.

treacherous political, economic, cultural and ethnic barriers that divide them.

Itinerancy is the courageous and passionate confidence to move forward and beyond the frontiers of language, class, culture, ideology, gender, orientation and caste that separate the poor from the rich in the illusory world of today's *majores* and *minores*. [32]Itinerancy is rooted in the intellectual conviction, emotional maturity and organizational flexibility of a free communion of Gospel brother/sisterhood. It is founded on the spiritually sure and ever creative premise that our God is good, all good, supremely good, all the time and to everyone. Franciscan itinerancy is our individual and communal response to the eschatological promise of the Christ who, in a world of excess and barbarous suffering, makes all things new and asks us to live in the *adventum* of a good and gracious God.

As we have seen throughout this work, there are significant psychological challenges to the development of the fraternal economy. Our research of the intrapsychic and organizational dynamics of religious life suggests that, while the majority of religious men and women sincerely wish to reach out to their sisters and brothers in need, they may be constrained, at the same time, by an underlying psychological ambivalence and social defense with regard to the poverty and plight of the poor.

As we have seen, empirical research suggests that young religious hold onto high ideals of deferent service, obedience, self-sacrificing for a better world, poverty, self-discipline and responsibility. They value their eternal life as their ultimate concern and strive less than lay comparison groups for merely coping with life as it comes. They show a higher sense of poverty, piety, mortification and chastity in their repertoire of professed values. They shun competitive power and control over others. These are men whose values coalesce around compassion and concern for others.

And yet, studies have also shown that, while young religious express high values of self-sacrificing for others, they demonstrate significant trends for aggression, domination of others and the avoidance of harm and criticism. The research indicates that high vocational ideals for social concern and justice are not enough to

---

[32] Cf. our analysis in Chapter 1.

presume that individuals within religious life or entering religious life have an effective capacity for solidarity with the poor. We have learned that the social imaginations of those studied are often enough constructed out of a compromise between high vocational ideals and inconsistent and largely unconscious personal needs.

Research and experience continue to show that the sincere proclamation of the ideals for justice, compassion and solidarity is only half of the story of religious motivation. On the other side and at a deeper level are the emotional compromises and non-rational concessions religious make over time to keep affective needs satisfied, especially when they come up against the hard and painful choices that the self-transcendence of prophetic zeal requires.

Religious formation programs have come a long way in underlining the values of minority, justice, compassion, transparency, participation and solidarity in religious life. And yet, the formation literature will be incomplete if it fails to address the obstacles and resistances (both personal and organizational) to the development of the fraternal economy.

We must take a fresh and sobering look at the formation programs called to address the high ideals of the fraternal economy to see in what ways they address and treat the troubling and often hard to read emotional compromises against (international) compassion.

Formation for the fraternal economy is further challenged by the structural ambivalence inherent in contemporary formation itself. There are several reasons for this.

First, our formation systems are focused primarily and almost exclusively on the personal conversion of friars. We note again Rulla's insistence that the focus of formation work be directly on the internal structures that cause inconsistencies and disharmonies in the external world. Rarely are formation programs conversant with the literature and the skills of the structural conversion of religious communities. While religious have attended appropriately to the spiritual, affective, intellectual and interpersonal development of individual friars, the same cannot be said of the communities that form the matrix of this development. Rare are the communities conversant with the assumptions of their own organizational dynamics, aware of their shared social defenses, and able to confess their social sin as a group.[33] While we understand more clearly today the values surrounding the development of the fraternal economy, we have up until now failed to explicate the organizational dynamics that lead to the fraternal economy's development or regression. These last chapers may be the first attempt to bridge the two poles of formation for the fraternal economy (the intrapsychic and the organizational).

If Franciscans are to enter more forthrightly as a brotherhood into the arena of power and minority, itinerancy and international compassion, they must continue to articulate the structural aspects of formation for the fraternal economy. They can no longer take the systems and structures around us for granted, as if they were not suffused with social sin and social defenses.

The formation for the fraternal economy is hampered further by the fact that religious men and women share no comprehensive, coherent or mutually agreed upon theory of religious formation. Formation theory and practice is an "eclectic" mix of numerous disciplines, traditions, insights and strategies. They have yet to be put into a comprehensive and agreed upon program.

A recent survey of formation programs in the United States concludes that we have seven "cultures of formation," distinct and sometimes competing systems of beliefs, emotions, rituals and tools.[34] Each of them is expressing values derived from magisterial teaching; all of them are attempting to be faithful to critical aspects of the church's thought after Vatican II.

But, they are enclosed cultures of religious life, each with a distinct language and set of rituals that form and contain a horizon of expectations that serves to delineate one from the other. They are fast becoming the cultures of ecclesial life, defining the preferred rituals and practices of church life across the country.

For example, the essentialist culture with its strict adherence to the language and praxis of "objective truth," magisterial pronouncements and the apologetic defense of the faith is markedly different from the existentialist culture, with its emphasis on

---

[33] Joseph E. Capizzi, "For What Shall We Repent? Reflections on the American Bishops, Their Teaching, and Slavery in the United States, 1839-1861," *Theological Studies* 65 (2004), pp. 767-791.

[34] David B. Couturier, "At Odds with Ourselves: Polarization and the Learning Cultures of Priesthood," *Seminary Journal* 9:3 (Winter, 2003).

personal growth, self-reflection and authenticity. The socialization culture with its emphasis on community, brotherhood, faith sharing and the dynamics of communal discernment stands in marked contrast to the interiority of the existentialist culture that preceded it. Each of the other cultures of formation (behavioral, neo-essentialist, liberation and professional) expresses key values of action, leadership, justice and creativity but does so in a language and in styles that are largely incomprehensible outside the parameters of one's preferred culture of formation. These cultures of formation have become "social defenses" used unconsciously by some to thwart the enlivening of religious communities for the twenty-first century.

If we intend to build the fraternal economy and its communities of gospel brotherhood, with the organizational flexibility and courageous passion to move beyond the frontiers of their own class and culture for the sake of international compassion, then we must listen carefully and attend cogently to the competing cultures of formation within our congregations. If we learn how to pass over and into these cultures, without judgment and with spiritual respect, then we might also learn from within – the techniques and dynamics necessary for the passage across the frontiers of gender, class and caste.[35]

What then are the basic requirements of a pastoral psychology of Franciscan economics? As we conclude these chapters, we note two.

A pastoral psychology of Franciscan economics includes both an intrapsychic and an organizational dimension. In the former, we attend to the complex of values, attitudes and needs that can advance or hinder the free communion we are to share with one another, without domination or deprivation. We help friars build up their personal and interpersonal competencies to tell the truth about themselves and their communities of faith. It is a truth that first includes their self-transcendent ideals of gospel love. It is a truth that also offers an acknowledgment (and working through) of the inconsistencies that might block, hinder or obscure the development of compassion across the boundaries of class, culture, ideology, gender, orientation and caste.

---

[35] For an analysis of this method of "passing over" and into other cultures, cf. Ewert H. Cousins, *Christ of the Twenty-First Century* (Rockport, MA: Element, 1992), pp. 1-14.

A pastoral psychology of Franciscan economics helps friars recognize the relational structures that are built up within them over time. These structures or "dialectics" become distinct horizons of expectations and desires in their interpersonal worlds. They are the horizon, among other things, of the personal ideals for justice, compassion and social concern, as well as the personal fears and individual defenses that keep religious from promoting compassion with a full and enlivened passion.

Beyond the intrapsychic dimension, a pastoral psychology of Franciscan economics also attends to the (institutional) structures and systems that are designed and sustained by religious communities and groups to promote the Franciscan ideal of evangelical fraternity in the world today. It looks to the organizational dynamics, both the conscious institutional codes and the unconscious social defenses, which can either advance the promise of solidarity or stall it in a frozen state of structural ambivalence or group disillusionment.

The interpretive schemes or narrative frames that help religious make sense of their organizational arrangements and challenges are, in a sense, more complicated than the rules and ideals contained in a congregation's Constitutions and Statutes. They are complicated because they emerge and are often defended at an unconscious level of institutional life. Organizations, as we have seen, run on "rational" and "nonrational" levels. Their internalized "icons" and "deep metaphors" are the (shared) lenses that groups use to read and interpret the official texts and approved "meaning" of their institutional ideals. They help religious make sense of their identity and action in the world. They are often shared uncritically at an unconscious level, far from the benefit of communal reflection and mutual discernment. As we have seen, these narrative schemes can serve as social defenses, keeping sincere and well-intentioned religious communities from achieving their own gospel ideals.

Twenty-first century religious live in a "world in extremis," dangerously poised with growing levels of severe poverty and a dramatic escalation of religious intolerance and ethnic violence across the globe. This is the world and this is the context in which Franciscans must make the transition from a global market economy to a fraternal economy that is consistent with their identity as an evangelical fraternity.

A complete pastoral psychology of Franciscan economics must include, therefore, two mutually re-enforcing and correlated levels of psychological analysis, one at the intrapsychic and the other at the organizational level.

EPILOGUE
FRANCISCAN FINANCIAL SCANDALS:
A SOCIO-ANALYTICAL PERSPECTIVE

As we come to the end of this work, we have learned of a new scandal hitting the Church. This time it has to do with money and involves, surprisingly enough, Franciscans. The information at hand is sketchy. Arrests have been made and the details will surely come out in Italian courts in due time. But, this much is admitted and clear. A major Franciscan Order is undergoing a financial crisis caused by alleged illegal activity by friars within the Order and other individuals from outside the Order. And the crisis is deep.

A few months ago, the Huffington Post reported that the general administration of the Order of Friars Minor (OFM's) was on the verge of bankruptcy.[36] The cause of this financial collapse in the Franciscan Order seems to have been due to poor oversight and alleged criminal actions that may have included, according to Swiss sources, arms and drug trafficking. The General Minister of the Order, Michael Perry OFM, had to admit "The systems of financial oversight and control for the management of the patrimony of the order were either too weak or were compromised, thus limiting their effectiveness to guarantee responsible, transparent management. We have initiated steps to address these concerns."[37]

It is reasonable to ask – how does a community of men with vows of religious poverty and who serve the poor and vulnerable well in some of the most desperate places in the world get involved in financial wrongdoing that may include the illegal sale of weapons and drug trafficking? Where was the oversight, the systems of control, and the power of conscience?

---

[36]   http://www.huffingtonpost.com/2014/12/19/order-of-friars-minor-fraud_n_6355532.html.

[37] ibid.

243

The courts and the legal system are sure to get to the bottom of the Order's alleged wrong doing. Those who engaged in illegal activities are likely to be arrested, indicted and convicted. Those who may have covered-up criminal acts are also likely to be prosecuted and punished. The legal system is well-equipped (though not always perfect) at bringing those to court who have knowingly and willingly flouted the law for their advantage.

As we watch this sad tragedy play out, the great number of Franciscans around the world who are hard working and holy will join others in hoping that justice prevails. I am convinced that the majority of Franciscans are shocked and angry that some in the Order may have been involved in criminal activities with the common fund.

But, it would be wrong to read this entire situation involving money and greed simply from the angle of conscious criminal activities. At the end of the day, institutional scandals are rarely only the work of one individual, the institution's "bad apple." More often than not, institutional scandals require a certain "ecology of dysfunction" in which to operate, an entire set of operations, emotions and practices that in hindsight provide the unconscious collusion that gives cover to the deviancies before they erupt. What we are suggesting is that looking at any scandal simply with an eye to conscious criminal behavior severely misunderstands the nature of institutional dysfunction. To look only at the behavior of those who willfully engage in malfeasance misses a great deal of the elements needed to allow bad behavior to gain a foothold in otherwise good and decent institutions. The matrix for understanding scandals must include conscious and unconscious data, along with covert and overt operations.

A few years ago, I published an article that discussed these dynamics.[38] The question at hand was this – how is it possible for good organizations to get involved in bad things? How do institutions, like churches, synagogues and mosques, find themselves blindsided by organization-wide misbehavior that officials claim they "never saw" and of which they stated they were "unaware?"

Clearly some scandals are very much cut and dry; they are the product of criminal behavior, pure and simple. They are due to

---

[38] David B. Couturier, "When Religious Leadership Fails: The Psychology of Administrative Scandals," *Human Development* 28:1 (Spring2007), p 5-11.

really bad behavior by a select few. But, administrative scandals and organizational failures are rarely fully explained by the criminal behavior of a few select individuals. The field of socio-analysis, which studies the unconscious behavior of individuals and groups within an organization, suggests that, alongside the criminal behavior of the few, is the unconscious collusion of the many. In simple terms, we can say that, in many instances of institutional failure, there were things to be seen that were missed, hints of wrongdoing that were ignored, and signals of things amiss that went unheeded, all with the best of will and good intentions. In situations of institutional scandal and corporate malfeasance, we often learn that there were individuals and groups who "knew but did not know" what was happening. Essentially, groups have a distinct way of keeping from consciousness what they already know at a more unconscious level. It is the work of socio-analysts to ferret out these anxiety-causing sentiments that hold so much of the organization's uncomfortable truths. [39]

Researchers learned much from studying NASA's Challenger and Columbia Space Shuttle disasters. We learned the extent to which scientists understood the particular vulnerabilities of the infamous "O" rings that eventually came apart. We also know the precise protocols that were developed to contain the risks involved in these essential pieces of equipment. The risks were understood. Although the vulnerabilities were well-known, in an odd and paradoxical way, they were not well-expected. The elaborate protocols and procedures developed to avoid any failure of the "O" rings functioned in a very opposite way. The realization that "O" rings could fail, when combined with elaborate protocols to keep them from failing, actually lowered scientists' normally-high level of caution. Because they had become familiar with their knowledge of potential vulnerability and because they had also developed protocols that, time and time again, protected the project from failure, scientists developed an unconscious accommodation that proved deadly. Because the "O" rings had not failed, even though they could, the scientists believed that they wouldn't fail in the future. Protocols and procedures became their defense and, because this was a group expectation, it became a "social defense."

[39] Kenneth Eisold, *What you Don't Know, You Know: Our Hidden Motives in Life, Business and Everything Else* (New York: Other Press, 2010).

The same is true in every organization. As I indicated in my article, religious institutions have a comparable way of containing their fear of failure behind supposedly "fail-safe" procedures. They are fail-safe until one day they fail, because people had become comfortable with a risk with which they were familiar and for which they had defensive protocols and procedures. They worked time and time again, until they didn't. Here is how I stated the situation.

> Administrative scandals can emerge in church settings when anomalies and inappropriate behaviors find an organizational ritual and institutional routine to contain them. No one need declare these behaviors appropriate, ethical, legal or moral, in order to normalize or routinize their management and administration. We are talking here of unconscious social processes, devoid of ill-will but naïve, nonetheless, as to the long-term impact and consequences of such practices.[40]

When it comes to financial scandals, religious institutions often have procedures and processes that are meant to catch malfeasance and criminal behavior. No religious institution, worthy of the name, wants criminal behavior in its ranks. But, religious institutions need to know two important things about procedures that can go wrong. The first is that *routines* meant to catch inappropriate behavior and criminal activity have an unintended side-effect. They can lull us into a false belief that we are fully protected and safe, all of the time and in every way.

It is not that we, as leaders, are unaware of the risks. We know the vulnerabilities of our institutions. But, we say to ourselves, we have the risk management tools needed to avoid bad behavior. In that way, we contain our anxieties and our protocols become our social defenses against danger. The procedures meant to protect us against our risks become part of the system of blind spots that keep us from attending to what's changing in our situation in a negative way. This is called the "normalization of deviancy."

---

[40] David B. Couturier, "When Religious Leadership Fails: The Psychology of Administrative Scandals," Human Development 28:1 (Spring, 2007), 9.

It is because deviancy and anomalies are rare that they pale in comparison with the grand achievements and spectacular accomplishments of the organization. When, however, they find a niche in the organization's procedures and practices, are dealt with according to protocol and have not yet become a threat to institutional safety, they can become "routine anomalies." Having become routine anomalies in the management of the organization, negative feedback on such matters is unwelcome and deemed inappropriate.[41]

All organizations are susceptible to the "normalization of deviancy" in their procedures and practices. But, religious institutions are especially vulnerable because they tend to be run by very nice people who speak in positive tones and optimistic language. If they inadvertently and, more so, unconsciously send out the message that only "good news" is allowed, they set themselves up for a catastrophic failure.

Again, here is how I wrote about that phenomenon:

The situation is especially volatile in organizations that have learned how to "repress the negative." These are the groups whose corporate culture is characterized by a need for only positive feedback, optimistic projections, and good news. These institutions project an "avoidance of the blunt negative," sending out the signal that all news must be good news and all data contradicting present agenda is to be eliminated or recast. Needless to say, none of these dynamics finds its way onto the printed page or public address system. But, they do find their way covertly and informally into the board room and strategies sessions where decisions are made.[42]

The second thing religious institutions need to remember about procedures is the role that anxiety plays in their development and maintenance. One of the lasting takeaways from this book may be its focus on the anxiety that finances produce in all institutions, including religious ones. Money makes us anxious, whether we have it or we don't. If we have it, we are afraid we will lose it or

---

[41] *Ibid.*
[42] *Ibid.*

we are anxious because we want more. If we don't have it, we are anxious about ways of getting and maintaining it. This anxiety is felt not just individually, but collectively as well, sometimes without conscious awareness of the anxiety at all. Companies with too little cash create an enormous amount of anxiety on the work floor and in the board room. And companies flush with cash are anxious for ways to spend it wisely or to invest it well. The defenses we use to manage our group anxieties are conscious and unconscious. How we manifest them are either overt or covert.

This work has demonstrated why it is important for religious organizations to understand and manage their "unconscious" operations.

THE FIVE HABITS OF THE FRATERNAL ECONOMY

To avoid financial scandals in the future, Franciscan institutions need to develop the five habits of the fraternal economy: (1) transparency, (2) equity, (3) dialogue/participation, (4) solidarity and (5) austerity.

I would like to suggest that these habits are indivisible and holistic. These are not part-time habits of the heart. A community cannot build a fraternal economy with only one or two of them. These habits belong together.

A few years ago, I participated in an international discussion of the need for financial transparency between provinces of the Order. We were discussing the need for a verifiable economic transparency in each of our Provinces, when one of the Italian Provincials rose to voice his "agreement" but only to a point! He went on to suggest that full financial transparency was not needed and probably not possible. He offered that his Province would agree to "greater transparency." My remark to my colleagues was that "greater transparency" suggested a choice to be non-transparent. An organization is either transparent or not transparent. There is no in-between.

A fraternal economy organizes itself for communion. A fraternal economy begins with transparency and expects accountability at all levels of the Province. A fraternal economy is more than cooperative. Because of its belief in "solidarity," there is a place at the table for those who would normally be excluded or remain unheard because of normative codes of social or religious exclusion. In a fraternal economy, decisions and behaviors must adhere to a principle of "austerity," which involves a generous willingness to sacrifice for the good of the other. Financial malfeasance thrives in a climate where any of these five principles are weakened or ignored.

TRUTH-TELLING

As we have seen throughout this work, the psychodynamics of Gospel brotherhood lead to a triple form of truth-telling across all the major zones of life. It begins with the truth, the whole truth, we tell about ourselves. It leads to the truth-telling we speak about our communities and our relationships. This level of maturity is organized around intimacies ordered toward a generous and receptive transcendence. And, finally the psychodynamics of Gospel brotherhood begs for the truth about our social structures. Franciscans committed to the building of a fraternal economy cannot (metaphorically speaking) construct off-shore social relationships and institutional franchises by which they game their religious life. They must tell the truth (and act accordingly) about every social system that involves itself in unfair and unethical business practices. There must be a coherence between all levels of truth-telling in Franciscan life - individually, relationally and structurally. Falsity in one level usually leaks into the other levels. Coherence between the levels is what will give religious life its integrity well into the future.

In any scandal, including financial ones, it would be unwise simply to find a few culprits and be done with them. There is no doubt that it is usually the case that there are only a few in any organization that become involved in illegal or immoral behavior. But, that fact does not excuse the group. There is more going on when scandals hit. There is more known than most can immediately recall, because the knowledge of which we speak is contained in our anxieties and held in our defenses, well below the level of conscious awareness.

Finances cause anxiety and anxiety is protected and projected in our defenses, both individually and as groups. This book has argued that we are in a turbulent time when it comes to economic changes. We have just been through a devastating recession, from which we have yet to recover. There have been massive lay-offs and drastic reductions in wages, and young adults are very worried about their prospects for a satisfying career and a secure family life. To treat economics as simply a matter of bottom-lines and rational calculations would be a gross misreading of the way the mind works. It would defy the anthropological foundations of modern economics.

As this book has argued, there are issues of deep concern to the middle class. They include wage stagnation, global debt levels, rising income inequality and the growing phenomenon of under-employment and mal-employment, especially among young people. We need to develop economic structures and models that treat workers more fairly and provide a guarantee not for equal outcomes but for equal opportunity. The economic deck should not be stacked against the vast majority of Americans in favor of the privileged very few.

The early artisans of our economic liberalism took a dim view of God. They did not reject God outright, but it is clear that God was sent to the corner and told not to interfere in the country's public life, including all that comes under the rubric of "economics." The Market thereafter had a both a free and an invisible hand to conduct its affairs as it saw fit.

The artisans chose to see the work of wealth in private terms, as a matter for competing self-interests in, as Thomas Hobbes was wont to say, a "war of all against all." Economics was thus framed essentially as a series of collateral private acts.

This book has argued that this initial economic dogma based on privacy hides, as Milbank has stated and we have quoted often in several of these chapters, an "ontology of violence." Modern economics presumes a distant and stingy God. It depends on individuals armed with their self-interests competing in the public square for attention and ascendancy. Modern social theorists argue that this agonistic theory of choice and competition is the best guarantee for security and stability. Experience, however, suggests violence breeds violence and a growing chasm is building between those who "own" the system through a structured and predetermined accumulation of wealth (cf. Piketty) and those who are falling further and further behind.

The Church sees the situation quite differently. The freedom simply to choose whatever one wants may be the highest form of freedom in a free market system but it falls far short of freedom's lasting potential in human life. And the Church, after the Resurrection of Jesus, cannot conceive of the world only in terms of sin, threat, violence and aggression. The Church rejects the fecundity of evil. She conceives of the world not as a battle zone of competing economic self-interests devoid of objective adjudication. Because of her belief in the Trinity and its mission in and *pro nobis*, she is attuned to a world within the "donation of peace" that is the legacy of the Resurrected Christ. Our graced impulse now is for communion, not competition. In sidelining God at the time of the Enlightenment, modern economics was forced to isolate individuals from a common good to which all can agree or come to peace with. A post-Enlightenment economics is thus a power-scheme and a game of manipulation, in which the poor almost always lose, because their self-interests are always trumped by the eminent domain claims of those with greater choices, more "freedom," and more power to write the rules and codes of economic behavior in our society.

In his time, Francis of Assisi upended the codes of access for his brothers and sisters. Growing up as he did with a view of a majestic and apocalyptic God of judgment, it was no wonder that, for the first twenty years of his life, he never questioned how men gained access in his hometown of Assisi. The codes of access were hierarchically drawn and they favored the rich and powerful. As a young man, Francis wanted status and access to the good things of life, which were enjoyed by the *majores* of his day.

Trouble was that Francis was not born into the wealth that would have assured him such access. His pedestrian upbringing, even as the son of a wealthy cloth merchant, destined him to be forever part of the *minores*, fated by God to serve the high and mighty.

Francis' first break with this code came when he sided with his father on a plan to force entry into the upper class by fighting for it in the wars between Assisi and Perugia. We know how disastrously

Francis' military campaign turned out. It left him deeply shaken and profoundly traumatized but with a deep moral injury, one that would question his society's view of God and the purpose of life itself.

Francis turned away from a God of majesty and turned to a God of minority, a God who bent low and lifted up the poor because of His great mercy. This God of the incarnation was anything but a stingy God. In fact, this God was abundantly good to all. This God was merciful and generous.

Because of this, Francis created a new code of access. He created a fraternity of equal access that allowed anyone to join his community, with only one provision. The individual had to renounce all his possessions and give them to the poor. That is, the individual had to create an empty space within, which could only be filled by the care, compassion and support of one's brothers. There would be no false props in this fraternity of equals. Every friar restarted his life *sine proprio*, "with nothing of one's own." Every friar began again with nothing to protect and nothing to defend, except the very peace and security that this life with violence and greed afforded.

The goal of the fraternal economy as Francis envisioned it was not the acquisition of goods. It was geared towards a security of mind and heart that eluded his contemporaries, mired in the violence and greed of their times. Religious poverty is sorely misunderstood if it is designed as an emotional experience of insecurity. In Francis' mind, the world was insecure enough. Francis knew well the politics of his time and its failures.

Francis' fraternal economy made space for brothers of differing talents, cultural backgrounds, and class divisions. His brothers came from different walks of life and from the different strata of society. Some were literate; others were not. Some knew how to work; others did not. Some knew privilege coming from the ranks of the *majores*; others had suffered the indignities and poverty of being among the crowd of *minores* who were destined to serve the rich and wealthy for the rest of their lives.

Francis' new code of access opened a new space across the divides, not simply to meet one another, but to become (and not want anything but to become) brothers to one another. Francis' fraternal economy with its new code of equal access was a grand

experiment in his day. It opened the minds and hearts of his contemporaries. Eventually, it would usher in the Renaissance, allow-
ing philosophers, poets, artists and scientists to explore and accept
all aspects of the "human." Indeed, it would take centuries for
this code of equal access to change the minds and hearts of those
who protected the social exclusion of women, the segregation and
apartheid of blacks, and the discrimination against gay men and
women.

The fraternal economy that Francis initiated is not primarily
about what we do with money. Francis was phobic about the power of coins and for good reason. Money has a way of quantifying
and thus delimiting the human spirit. And Francis wanted none of
that. Francis wanted his brothers and sisters to find out what they
were supposed to do, under the inspiration of God, and set about
doing it, as long as it was not against the rule of love (the Gospel).

Francis' fraternal economy is not primarily about dollars and
cents, market shares or stock derivatives. It is about the destiny of
men and women in the real world and how they come about a new
security and peace in God. By the time his captivity as a prisoner
of war had come to an end, Francis had given up on the violence
and greed that fed the frenzy of Assisi. He found his peace in
mercy – in the mercy that God had for him and in the mercy that
he could show to those who were poor and suffering. Francis gave
away everything he had and felt the first taste of freedom in his
whole life. He had given up the need to climb and be right. He had
let go of the desire to imitate majesty and control the world. He
would never again have to go to war, because there was nothing
that anyone else had that he wanted. There was nothing he had
that he would not forfeit. He had Christ and Christ had him and
that was enough for Francis to feel the "peace that passes all understanding."

We have said that Francis' defining moment came not when he
stood naked in the square and rejected his father's economic world.
It was not when he met the leper at the crossroad and kissed him.
The real turning point in his life came, he said, when the Lord gave
him brothers. It was at that moment that Francis began to shape
his "fraternal economy." It was then that Francis could create a
world "on earth as it is in heaven," where brothers and then sisters
could love and share with one another without discrimination or

segregation. They could live as the Trinity did – "as a free communion of persons without domination or deprivation."

Francis' fraternal economy is indeed an economy of communion that begins with an ontology of abundance and generosity, the belief that God is all good and supremely good, a *fons plenitudo* of graciousness and creativity. It is an economy, thereby, that holds to the inviolable dignity of each and every human person, regardless of origin, race, color, creed, orientation, tribe, class, caste or religion. Francis' fraternal economy operates from the fundamental principle that communion is possible and peace is achievable, with God's generous grace. Thus derives Francis' insistence that the brothers not own anything of their own and they merely "use" the good things of this world.

Francis argued that ownership demanded protection, oftentimes violent protection. Francis didn't want to own the world. He thought striving after ownership was a fool's run. The world belonged to God and God was willing to share it abundantly and generously, if we but open the ethical space within not to control, dominate or deprive one another in our quest for happiness. Francis demonstrated that truth in his most exciting experiment: a life with nothing of his own. Francis believed with all his heart that God was generous and kind. His soul convinced him of the lush fullness that flowed from the heart of God, if we be but open to it.

And so, Francis created an experiment that has become our spirituality to this day. He would take the lowest place, the most vulnerable spot, the humblest of human venues, across the wide spectrum of human experiences, to see if the fullness of God reached him even there. Remember that his contemporaries strove after majesty and power. Francis reversed the game. He would test God's generosity not at the points of majesty, but he would wait for it at the points of life's minority, where we are down and out, exhausted and expended. Would God be as faithful to those at the end of the line, as God is to those at the front?

After a lifetime of experimenting, Francis came to the conclusion that God never faltered. Yahweh was indeed a God of mercy "to the thousandth generation." God's love and kindness were full even at the points of emptiness and exhaustion. God's abundance reaches us undiminished even at the points of our deepest poverty, if we but open our broken hearts ever wider and keep the faith.

Index

A

abundance xxi, 10, 11, 15, 24, 254
accountability 44, 174, 175, 184, 185, 248
AIDS 159, 174, 206, 207, 208, 227
applied Franciscan study xxii, xxiv
attitudes 121, 123, 217
Augustine 32, 61, 62, 142, 160, 177, 212
austerity 24, 248, 249

B

Bales, Kevin 37
bankruptcy 6, 175, 243
banks xxiv, 5, 6, 7
Battle of Collestrada xx, 58, 79
Boomers xvi, 48
brand symbolism 53, 54
Brueggemann, Walter ix, x, 10, 138

C

Capuchin-Franciscans 70, 159, 232
Chinnici, Joseph 103, 174
civilization of love 25
class xvi-xxix, 4-7, 22, 44, 52, 70, 93, 94, 105, 164, 165, 177, 178, 187, 197, 204, 209-219, 224, 231, 237, 240, 250-254
cluttering the soul 62
commercial desires 23, 62
Common Security Clubs 13
competition x, xii, xxi, xxix, 11, 18, 24, 25, 31, 32, 41, 64, 65, 70, 74, 92, 95, 96, 107, 129, 138, 141, 146, 153, 160-162, 166, 224, 236, 250, 251
Conference on Pastoral Planning xiv
consumer xxvi, 8, 23, 27, 29, 32, 34, 40, 45, 50, 52, 53, 56, 59, 62-64, 111, 141
Consumer Culture 28, 49, 54, 112
consumerism xxvii, 14, 28-35, 39, 40, 41, 43, 45, 47, 49, 53-58, 61, 62, 64, 66, 224
Corporate Imagination vii, 67, 171

G

Globalization xxv, 94, 95, 139, 140, 141, 233
Gospel Brotherhood vii, 78, 109, 158
Great Recession vii, xxiii, xxiv, xxv, 1, 3, 4, 17, 19, 20, 49
greed ix, xix, xx, xxi, 5, 8, 10, 12, 15, 18, 23, 28, 30, 40, 53, 54, 58, 60, 64, 65,
        70, 73, 79, 82, 91, 93, 95, 96, 107, 146, 161, 166, 244, 252, 253
Gross Domestic Product 5, 9

H

Hobbes, Thomas 56, 250
Human Trafficking 35, 36, 37, 38, 39, 47, 51, 57
Hume, David 18, 73
humility 82, 91, 93, 100, 101, 104, 106, 113, 159, 160, 163, 235, 236

I

Imoda, Franco 113, 114, 115, 116, 117, 118, 119, 127
income inequality ix, xii, xix, xxiv, xxvii, 49, 69, 250
inconsistencies 126, 127, 128, 129, 131, 132, 168, 198, 238, 240
Institute for Policy Studies xxiii, 10, 13
institutions of multiple interests 178
International Compassion vii, 67, 164, 201, 209, 212, 213
invisible hand 70, 73, 250
itinerancy 84, 90, 101, 137, 204, 235, 236, 237, 239

J

John Paul II 18, 29, 30, 40, 41, 42, 47, 77, 83, 84, 92, 175, 180
Justice 47, 109, 152, 155, 158

K

Kavanaugh, John 30

L

Laborem Exercens 18, 41, 180
leper 15, 45, 59, 80, 81, 105, 253
Liberation theology 109
Lonergan, Bernard 112, 117, 118

M

majores xx, 45, 96, 164, 204, 212, 237, 251, 252
mal-employment xxv, 17, 250
Manent, Pierre x
Massingale, Bryan 55, 109, 174, 234, 235